MW01069462

THE
FAIRBANKS
FOUR

MURDER, INJUSTICE, AND
THE BIRTH OF A MOVEMENT

BRIAN PATRICK O'DONOGHUE

Published by Sourcebooks
P.O. Box 4410, Naperville, Illinois 60567–4410
(630) 961-3900
sourcebooks.com

Cataloging-in-Publication Data is on file with the Library of Congress.

Printed and bound in the United States of America.
MA 10 9 8 7 6 5 4 3 2 1

This book is dedicated to Curtis S., the villager raising questions,
Shirley D., the irrepressible Athabascan championing those boys,
Gary M., first among many unstoppable University of Alaska
Fairbanks sleuths, and most of all to my wife, Kate Ripley, partner
in many fine adventures amid these courthouse storms.

AUTHOR'S NOTE ABOUT SOURCING

Events covered in this book are uncomfortably true, documented in Fairbanks police files and Alaska State Trooper reports, news clips, transcripts of three 1999 murder trials, and numerous appeals. Most quotes come from my own published stories and recorded interviews. I have taken liberties in reconstructing memorable face-to-face conversations and class discussions. For reasons that will become clear, 2015 courtroom video and tweet coverage by my students proved invaluable down the stretch. Readers interested in digging deeper will find source notes in the back pages.

—Brian Patrick O'Donoghue
University of Alaska Fairbanks, professor emeritus

CHAPTER 1

"LOOK, LOOK, THERE'S A LITTLE BOY!"

RESCUE MISSION, FAIRBANKS, ALASKA, SATURDAY, OCTOBER 11, 1997
Melanie Durham put her book down and headed for the shelter's common room. Flipping on the TV, she settled in watching Conan O'Brien's *Late Night*. An animal trainer's act kept her occupied until the host announced David Bowie as his next guest, following commercials. Being no fan of the glam rocker, Melanie took that as her cue to seek fresh air.

Slipping on a heavy sweater, Melanie stepped out onto the shelter's second-floor balcony, an airy structure screened by a wood-plank lattice. Traffic seemed light tonight, even down the block near Barnette. Though chilly out, it wasn't biting; northern lights cold, that's what she called nights like this one. She smoked a cigarette, then continued up the outdoor staircase, bound for the top balcony, which offered a better vantage should the aurora dance tonight.

Leaning on the upper railing, Melanie heard what she took to be a smackdown underway on the streets nearby. She couldn't locate the source; trees and other buildings blocked views in that direction. Then came another punch, followed by faint cries for help.

Three, maybe four more hard punches followed. An angry guy with a guttural voice was involved. Melanie couldn't make out the words, but he

sounded older, very intoxicated, "and had a Native accent." Punches continued in what struck her as a measured pace, as if the assailant carefully aimed
the blows.

Melanie raced down the staircase, making straight for the office.
"Somebody is taking a beating out there," she told the night attendant. "I
can hear it connecting. It's really, really bad."

The pair opened the front door. All seemed quiet on Ninth Avenue.
Melanie wanted to call the police. The staffer balked. "Do that yourself if
you feel so strongly," the woman told her.

Melanie hesitated. She'd dealt with police at her doorstep, responding
to domestic violence calls. Just that summer, she ended up being the one
charged.

Despite her deep concern, Melanie followed the attendant back inside.
Returning to that balcony, she smoked another cigarette. Nothing sounded
out of order. Traffic seemed about right for a weekend downtown. If a person
needed help nearby, surely somebody would notice.

THE PRICE OF FREE MONEY

Fairbanks, the state's second-largest community, had a city population of
roughly thirty thousand, nestled within a broader urban community of
some ninety thousand residents. While tame compared to the 1970s, an era
defined by the construction of the Trans-Alaska Pipeline, downtown night-
life still catered to blue-collar spirits, particularly on weekends, when bars
remained open until 3:30 a.m. Saturday and Sunday.

That second weekend of October 1997, most Alaskans were feeling
flush; checks worth $1,296 apiece were hitting the mailboxes of 550,000
eligible recipients: basically, anyone with proof of one year of residency in
the forty-ninth state. The annual windfall came from the earnings of the
Alaska Permanent Fund, the state's oil-revenue savings account. To put the

largesse in perspective, not only were those 1997 dividends the biggest ever, but the $720 million distribution marked the largest payout since checks were first issued in 1982.

Dividend dollars, as they were known, spurred sales of cars, big-ticket appliances, vacation flights to warmer places, and shopping orders from rural villagers and others living outside the highway system.

For many, the extra cash answered prayers. Others, feeling that bulge in their pocket, splurged, often to excess, resulting in a brief, predictable surge in amiable drunks, escalating quarrels, traffic accidents, and general mayhem.

In urban areas, some looked forward to darker opportunities unleashed by chaos downtown. As Chris Stone, who turned fourteen that fall, later explained under oath, "Rollers call it the dividend season."

Though authorities braced for what was coming, Fairbanks's thin blue line only stretched so far.

Late that Friday night, a passerby happened on a fellow Native man sprawled face down on the sidewalk as three Black teens sprinted away. The group fled in what the observer described as a grayish car, about the size of an older four-door Ford. The mugging victim got up on his own and didn't appear seriously injured according to the Good Samaritan, who followed him into the Pastime Card Room just to be sure.

Minutes into the new day came reports of another downtown assault, a robbery, and an ongoing domestic row over on Noble Street. "Now the neighbor, a white male, is out in the parking lot in his underwear," Dispatch advised the responding patrol car. Soon after, officers dealing with that domestic squabble requested backup along with an ambulance for a pistol-whipped victim. The neighbor in his skivvies was believed to be hiding in an apartment building. "He's extremely intoxicated," reported an officer on the scene, "running around chasing a female with a firearm as well."

"You guys use caution there," a dispatcher warned the tactical team of the Fairbanks Police Department (FPD). "If we've got the right person, he's got an extensive criminal history, including weapons offenses and a couple felonies."

FRATERNAL ORDER OF EAGLES HALL, 2 A.M.

The Cotter-Jones wedding at Eagles Hall was timed around dividend weekend's predictable influx of friends and family from outside town. Like the newlyweds and many of the guests, Calvin Moses was a villager, born in Tanana, an Athabascan community of about three hundred named for the river flowing past, valued for its longstanding regional hospital. Moses grew up in Allakaket, a smaller village located on another winding Yukon tributary farther north.

The reception remained in high gear as Moses exited the steamy old hall at about 2 a.m. Threading his way past smokers and others cooling off under the outside canopy, Moses continued down the hall's front steps, heading for his car.

Streetlights and a dusting of snow added sparkle to the pavement. The temperature remained inviting, well above zero, not bad for mid-October in Fairbanks, Alaska.

Firing up his white Cutlass Ciera, Moses cruised to Arctic Bar. He wasn't looking for a drink; he'd been a teetotaler for a decade. Two sisters from out of town were counting on him for a lift to a motel-hotel complex over on Tenth Avenue.

He found Louise and her sister ready to go. Riding in the front passenger seat on Ninth at about 2:45 a.m., Louise suddenly cried, "Look right there," nodding toward the roadside. "Look, look, there's a little boy." He lay sprawled in the shadows, head and torso angled toward the approaching car, legs askew farther back. Moses slowed to a crawl, pausing as the headlights illuminated puffs of breath rising in the cold night air. Was that blood on the kid's face? He couldn't tell.

No one in the car had a cell phone that night in 1997. Louise wanted to get out and help the poor kid. Moses and her sister talked her out of it. Whoever did this might still be around!

Pulling away, Louise stared back. Were that poor child's pants down around his knees? She couldn't say for sure, but it looked like it.

2:50 A.M.

"Man down," radioed Dispatch Center.

Odds were this call involved a drunk, judged Mike Gho, a veteran city fireman and paramedic in training. He and two other first responders piled into the ambulance. The crew rolled out the station's big bay door onto Seventh Avenue, hung a hard left at the corner, and reached Ninth Avenue within seconds.

So where was the guy? Trees and thick hedges filtered the overhead lighting, casting broad shadows. The crew cruised the whole block without seeing anyone at all. On the second pass, they spotted him.

This young man didn't react to questions and shouts, not the way someone sleeping off a bender often will. It was eight degrees out. Hypothermia might account for his quiescent state. But look at those head bruises and indentations. What about that patch of blood, approximately 20 cc, coloring snow beneath that ear? And why were the kid's pants down around his knees?

Was he hit by a car? Beaten? Whatever the cause, the way Gho read it, "some kind of trauma took place."

Concern grew as the patient straightened his arms and curled; movements associated with possible brain damage. Neither pupil reacted to a flashlight, another sign of cerebral distress. Working swiftly, the first responders cut open his coat and other gear and examined him for injuries. Nothing leaped out, yet this patient's overall condition appeared grave, very grave. The crew prepped him for rush transport using a backboard and neck collar.

3:04 A.M.

"Ambulance crew states he's a critical trauma patient," a dispatcher advised police. "They don't know if it's a hit-and-run or an assault or what. They're going to have to transport." Within two minutes of that call, the ambulance pulled into Fairbanks Memorial Hospital's emergency entrance. On a night marked by sirens, mayhem, and arrests throughout downtown, this last-ditch sprint for life would echo for years.

THE PIECES COME TOGETHER

"I need someone to come to the house and get my son," pleaded the woman on the phone.

"What?" asked the guy fielding the 911 call.

"I need someone to come to the house and get my son," Carol Pease repeated, sounding breathless. Her son Kevin was "freaking out," she said, adding that he'd "been drinking" and hit her.

Just shy of six feet tall, built like a two-hundred-pound boxer, and crowned by long, light brown locks, Kevin Pease's reputation commanded attention. Only weeks before, the high school senior's failure to heed a stop sign escalated into a memorable arrest. Kevin told the officer up front that his driving license had already been suspended. Candor notwithstanding, the burly teen was cuffed and arrested on the spot. Also noted in the write-up: Pease started kicking the driver's side rear door, breaking the interior padding.

Tonight, word swiftly spread he was at it again. "Kevin Pease, nineteen years of age, has assaulted his mother, Carol Pease," Dispatch alerted officers in the field. "He's supposed to be tearing up the downstairs apartment at this time. There are several warrants for his arrest."

With everything going on, dispatchers were begging off-duty staff to come in. "Please, please, please, we're shorthanded," coaxed one in a recorded call.

A beleaguered supervisor questioned whether that man-down situation on Ninth Avenue warranted active follow-up. "Possible 10–79," responded an on-scene officer, signaling them to notify the coroner.

ALASKAN MOTOR INN

Night manager Mike Baca sought help dealing with a raging party. "And they're all minors, dude," he told the dispatcher.

"We'll be over," the guy assured him.

"And do you know how long that will be?" Baca inquired.

That drew a hearty chuckle, followed by, "We've got a lot of things going on right now, but we'll be over as soon as we can."

Hanging up the phone, Baca, a stocky twenty-seven-year-old sporting a worn hunting hat and lumberjack shirt, paced back and forth beneath the motel lobby's surveillance camera, repeatedly pausing by the front window and gazing out. He did this several times, then bolted out of view.

On his return, the night manager made straight for the phone. "Cancel that," he said, explaining that police assistance was no longer required. Regardless, a uniformed patrol officer soon showed up to make sure all was in order. Baca assured him he'd handled it. "Pepper spray set them all running! It sure did," he bragged. "Even the one who pulled a gun!"

On his way back to the station, that same officer spotted a tall, slim Native youth wobbling north on Fifth Avenue. Flipping on the car's rotating lights, the cop pulled over, swiftly confirmed the kid was drunk, and collared him. Another patrol car fetched Baca, who identified the youth as one of the troublemakers he'd run off. Back at the station, seventeen-year-old Eugene Vent was ticketed for his third alcohol-related offense within two weeks.

Though the youth wasn't packing a weapon, Paul Keller, FPD's balding, mustached, chief detective, had a hunch this punk's criminal bent went further. Vent was detained for questioning, and Keller reached for his long coat.

Night manager Baca welcomed the new listener; he was just getting going when Keller interrupted. "Did you happen to see a guy earlier in brown camos?" the chief detective inquired, mindful of the gear worn by the young victim clinging to life at Fairbanks Memorial.

"Yes, there was!"

"And do you know what happened to that guy?"

"No, I went into the room, and I told them, 'I've already called police. You need to get out of there.'"

"And what time was that?" the detective pressed.

Baca missed the question, again reliving how he broke that party up. "They all took off running. None of them walking. They were running! And none of them were eighteen."

Keller pulled out Eugene Vent's mug shot. "Is that the guy?"

"That's the guy!" Baca confirmed.

"Write that you drove over. Saw a guy and picked him out," Keller advised.

"That's the guy," Baca repeated, circling the lobby under that surveillance camera with both hands jammed in his long overcoat pockets. "One of the guys anyway."

Sometime after 5:00 a.m., in the basement of an old building shared by the FPD and firefighters, Detective Aaron Ring and another officer began interrogating the young suspect, likely still buzzed, with no adult present.

Events lined up. Eugene Vent attended Howard Luke Academy, a small public high school named for a Native elder. Flipping through a recent yearbook, Ring found Eugene pictured wearing a Hawks jersey, #41, grinning alongside the basketball team's coach. Seated to the left in that same photo, dwarfing teammates on either side, filling jersey #31, stood Kevin Pease.

Within a few hours, Eugene not only accepted responsibility for assaulting the kid clinging to life at the hospital, but he'd conceded that Kevin and basketball team captain Marvin Roberts took part as well.

That afternoon, George Frese, twenty, limped into Fairbanks Memorial's emergency room leaning on his girlfriend. "Foot pain," noted the lanky Athabascan's triage assessment. "Got in a fight last night, doesn't know how it happened. He was drunk. Has a bruise… Kicked someone last night but doesn't remember anything else. States awoke this AM @ home foot hurting."

A nurse aware of the teen in a coma with a bruised face alerted Detective Ring, who was still at the hospital following up.

George Frese was awaiting an X-ray of his bad foot when the detective asked him how he hurt it. George said he wasn't sure. They continued talking, and the detective's interest grew. A year or two older than the others, this young Native man had also attended Howard Luke, though he dropped out before graduation.

Detective Ring informed George and his girlfriend about the kid clinging to life over in Fairbanks Memorial's Intensive Care Unit. At this stage, the detective advised the couple the police were mainly sorting out who did the damage. "If you were there and you took off because you didn't like what was going on," he suggested, "which is what Eugene said he did, then we can talk. We can work with that."

Later that day, towering police sergeant Dave Kendrick stood alongside a tiny nurse in the ICU, holding one of George's boots alongside the victim's face. Both agreed; those facial bruises and that tread pattern matched up perfectly.

By sundown, detectives had signed confessions from Eugene Vent and George Frese.

One name still eluded the authorities.

BREAKING NEWS

University of Alaska basketball legend Darryl Lewis majored in journalism. Following graduation, he landed a job as a newscaster for KTVF, Fairbanks's top-rated TV news station. He was on his own when police showed up that Saturday, requesting help identifying the young victim lingering in a coma.

D-Lew, as the tall Black man was known, did everything with heart. He figured that poor kid likely had family close by. Had to. And if so, his people need to know!

For the first time in his career, he broke into regular programming with a bulletin urging viewers to contact authorities if they recognized the unidentified victim, then cut to a close-up of the dying teen's bruised face. "If anyone is missing their child," Lewis found himself saying, "call FPD."

Grim stuff, he knew. If the bosses had problems with what he'd done, so be it.

Glimpsing a squad car out front and police approaching his house, twenty-one-year-old Chris S. Kelly retreated upstairs and hid. The young dealer figured the law was coming after him for parole violations.

The patrolwoman accompanying the chief detective to the modest home knew better and dreaded every step. What stuck with Officer Peggy Sullivan afterward was the way the dying child's mother fainted in her arms.

Kelly heard her cry out and came racing downstairs. The news staggered him. Not only had he been tipped that his little brother might be in over his head partying at Noah's, a shady motel, likely this was payback from a dealer he'd recently ripped off. Kelly choked up. Either way, his little brother may have paid the price.

Within the hour, Evalyn Thomas, a hardscrabble single mother of four, identified the boy on the respirator at Fairbanks Memorial Hospital as her youngest child, John Gilbert Hartman. "JG" to friends and family. That Sunday evening, roughly thirty-six hours after he was found and barely a month past his fifteenth birthday, a handsome, popular boy known for his fondness of comic books and many girlfriends ceased breathing.

"Teen Dies in Hospital after Downtown Attack" headlined Monday's lead story in the *Fairbanks Daily News-Miner*, reporting on what was now a murder case. Four young suspects, identified as Marvin Roberts, Eugene Vent, George Frese, and Kevin Pease, were already in custody. Bail was set at $1 million apiece.

Police weren't looking for anyone else, Chief Detective Keller informed the press. He offered little detail beyond the crime's location, Roberts's role as the getaway driver, and the suspects' ties with Howard Luke Academy, Fairbanks's predominantly Native alternative school.

As for what happened and why, Deputy Police Chief Ken Steinnerd remained tight-lipped. "It's really premature to put in the paper what the motive is when we would just be guessing," he told reporters. Nor would he discuss the murder weapon.

By the following day, authorities linked the murder to a party at the Alaskan Motor Inn, attended by as many as twenty drinkers, most of them minors. Mike Baca reveled in the spotlight. "He came out with his gun," the night clerk said. "I kind of yelled a bunch of cuss words and he took off running."

Eugene Vent's arrest broke the case, Detective Keller confirmed. Not only did the youngest suspect confess, but he said all four took part in beating and stomping John Hartman. Another member of the group, George Frese, backed that up. That wasn't all, the chief detective told reporters. "After the physical assault, the victim was sexually assaulted."

He declined to go into further detail.

ALASKA: VAST YET SMALL

Over the days and weeks that followed, Hartman's murder dominated staff meetings at the *News-Miner*, where my wife, Kate, and I worked in the newsroom. I urged the cops and court reporters chasing the daily developments to answer a pair of questions: What was Hartman doing out and about at 3:00 a.m.? And how was it that his mother and older brothers didn't notice the kid was gone the better part of a day?

As often happens in Fairbanks, Kate and I knew John Hartman's mother. The connection came through Evalyn's work for the Yukon Quest International, a thousand-mile sled dog race founded by Leroy Shank, one of the newspaper's pressmen.

Barrel-chested, gregarious ol' Leroy was quite a guy: gold-rush history buff and disgruntled Iditarod musher. As he saw it, the so-called Last Great Race boiled down to sprints between cozy checkpoints. Being a former trapper, he also frowned on rules that allowed mushers to start with twenty or more dogs, free to drop slower pullers en route. In his opinion, that encouraged racers to treat sled dogs, those real athletes, as disposable.

After his second run to Nome, Leroy Shank launched the Yukon Quest, a rival thousand-mile race, offering what Leroy viewed as a better measure of sled dogs and their masters. Mushers couldn't take more than a dozen dogs in Leroy's mushing marathon, making top-notch care essential throughout. The Quest followed trails blazed in Jack London's day, testing bloodlines and survival skills on seldom-traveled portions of the lower Yukon River, wilder, lonelier country than the Iditarod Trail, as I can personally attest.

When Kate and I first met her, Hartman's mom ran the gift shop at Yukon Quest headquarters downtown. Evalyn Thomas was generally the first person any visitor encountered. She really liked Kate, the paper's lead Quest reporter. My coverage of the organization's fundraising troubles drew Evalyn's ire.

Though we hadn't run into her for several years, Evalyn's loss hit home. Anyone with kids—and we had a toddler—felt for her.

At that time, I was the only reporter in town chasing a wildlife-management debacle. The tale involved a fur trapper, state game officials, and a would-be do-gooder.

Assistant District Attorney Jeff O'Bryant, whom I'd never met, got right back to me. After a few jokes about our shared Irish heritage, he discussed the controversy with surprising candor. "It should be a total embarrassment for everybody. All of them, in a sense, came really close to getting charged."

The dustup concerned wolf snares set in a distant wildlife refuge. Placement of the trapline was legal. Trouble arrived when a caribou herd passed through well before the trapper's return, leaving half a dozen big-antlered reindeer entangled in those snares. Four died by the time he returned. By then, that caribou meat had spoiled; none was salvageable for distribution among needy families, the customary outlet for game taken illegally or inadvertently outside the rules.

With the tacit approval of local wildlife officials, the trapper *didn't move* his trapline or those carcasses, leaving snares set near rotting meat. That's illegal baiting.

Word about the situation reached an animal rights activist who flew out to the site and freed a two-year-old wolf caught in what now amounted to illegal snares. Controversy erupted over the activist's video post, showing that wolf limping off, apparently injured, dragging portions of a snare embedded in one paw. The activist urged game officials to mount a rescue. The trapper wanted the meddling fool who "stole his lawful pelt," as he put it, charged.

My new pal, the prosecutor, refused to take sides, handing me a stellar closing quote: "They should have left the wolf alone," Assistant DA O'Bryant said. "Mother Nature would have healed itself." That view spurred comments briefly rivaling ongoing discussion of the kid's murder and its social implications on *Problem Corner*, Fairbanks's long-running radio call-in show.

———————

Local coverage of the teen's killing was all but scripted to fan flames. A widely circulated portrait showed the young all-American victim clutching a football, proudly attired in his Redskins city league jersey. TV news coverage repeatedly featured the grieving mom sitting alongside her youngest son's father, fingering their boy's youth-league championship trophy.

Three of the four suspects—Marvin Roberts, Eugene Vent, and George Frese—were Athabascan Indians with family ties throughout interior villages up and down the Yukon River and its tributaries. That made the local murder a matter of regional interest.

The suspects' arraignment hearing turned into a spectacle. Cameras flashed, and videographers jostled for position as the four accused approached the courtroom single file, clad in orange jumpsuits. Each gripped portions of the long chain binding them together using hands cuffed to their waists. Most appeared startled if not shocked by the furor.

A defense attorney blasted those chains as grandstanding and prejudicial.

The measures reflected the high-risk persons involved, curbing violence and escape attempts, countered the officer leading the detail. The restraints stayed on for the duration.

Letters to the editor reflected shock and community divisions. "Anyone of us could have been the unlucky one," wrote Bob, explaining that he crossed the area where Hartman was found on his daily hike to and from work. "This murder could have easily ended up in the category of unsolved cases. This should send a very strong wake-up call to residents—our police department is undermanned."

From Karen, a local woman then living in upstate New York: "Fairbanks needs to take the tragic death of John Hartman as a wake-up call in the middle of a reoccurring nightmare," she wrote. "I've learned it wasn't the state or the size of the population contributing to this plague of violence; it is simply becoming the nature of society."

Some discerned a spiritual crisis. "The answer is Christ," wrote Dot, another local subscriber. "We have outlawed God in this country, so the outlaws have free reign."

"What happened to innocent until proven guilty?" asked Carla, a non-Native resident of Tanana, a small yet prominent Athabascan Native village 120 miles northeast of Fairbanks, the place suspect Marvin Roberts called home before his parents split up. From what Carla recalled watching the young scholar grow, she cautioned against making assumptions. "Such violence sickens everyone I know in this village," Carla wrote. "But none of us know what happened that night and won't know until evidence is presented at trial."

The week following Hartman's death, civic leaders convened an unprecedented town hall forum. "I'm not satisfied to live in a community where someone cannot walk down the street without getting assaulted or killed," borough mayor Jim Sampson declared, opening the session. He was joined by city mayors from both Fairbanks and North Pole, local police, state troopers, the school district president, union leaders, and many others.

Fairbanks city mayor Jim Hayes, a former prosecutor, reeled off sobering statistics: eight 1997 murders, three hundred assaults, even more domestic violence cases. Figures had climbed in every category, he warned, and the year wasn't over.

Police Lieutenant James Welch joined Hayes's call for a united community effort. "Everybody has eyes. Everybody can pick up the phone," he said. "I'm not asking for people to be vigilantes. I'm asking for people to get together."

He and other local officials caught an earful. "You're ruining the most beautiful place I've ever been to," declared Jada, a Southside Neighborhood Association member. "God help you people if something happens to my daughter in this town. You've done nothing!"

Athabascan community leader Shirley Demientieff struck a conciliatory note, inviting the public to join her in a candlelight vigil honoring John Hartman *and* other local victims of violence. She dubbed the planned route "a path of sorrow and remembrance," starting from the Eagles Hall, the site of the wedding reception now shadowed by association with the four murder suspects, proceeding from there to the intersection where John Hartman lay dying in the shadows.

COMMUNITY PRAYERS

NOVEMBER 8, 1997

Some fifty people answered Shirley's call. Walking single file and carrying flickering candles, young and old proceeded along sidewalks, rounding street corners, crossing bridges, pausing at locations associated with violent deaths. There, prayer circles formed, and Reverend Scott Fisher, the long-haired pastor of St. Matthew's Episcopal Church, offered blessings. "This ground is holy," he proclaimed, "because the community walks upon it."

The procession kept stretching and widening. By the time marchers reached the bus station where a forty-two-year-old Native man was shot to death several years before, Reverend Scott's swelling prayer circle spilled into the street.

Though difficult to bear, Hartman's mother took part. "I've been avoiding it," Evalyn Thomas told a reporter as the procession neared the corner where her own son was found. "I've been taking the other way around, though we live three blocks away." On this day, the grieving mother drew strength from the turnout. "All these caring people have to stop this from going on," she said. "That's why I'm here."

CHAPTER 2

HOWLS AND CONVICTIONS

Bail for the four suspects was set at $1 million apiece. With support from village friends and family, Marvin Roberts alone posted the required bond. Though the terms mandated home confinement, news that he'd been released from jail sparked outrage. "Well, Fairbanks, Alaska, looks like open season. We are truly savages now," commented Mary Carter in a letter to the editor. "We can roam the streets raping and beating men, women, girls, boys—doesn't matter, whichever you prefer is fair game." The writer, a resident of Healy, a coal mining town south of Fairbanks, closed by observing, "Too bad the victim couldn't have another 24 hours with his mom."

Letter writers who stood behind "those boys," as many now called them, generally knew the suspects or their families. "We aren't some Third World country where you can be locked up on a whim," wrote Adrienne Grimes, a former classmate. "Would you like to know what horrifies me? It's the judgmental way in which my fellow citizens are behaving."

A local man's call for capital punishment drew swift rebuke from one of Marvin's aunts living in Ruby, a small Yukon River town, 260 miles west of Fairbanks. "How can you wish death to someone that's innocent until proven guilty by court?" Lena McCarthy wrote. "In our native culture we never wish bad luck on anyone, under any circumstances, or it will turn back on us. Tell me, Mr. Bowen, if some member in your family was arrested and charged with a crime would you wish death upon them also? I think not, you should accept our Native culture."

An accusation that Marvin was seen moving around in violation of the terms of his release soon landed him back in court. "I haven't left the house at all," he assured the judge. "This is the first time I've ever laid eyes on her," he said of his accuser, denying he ever owned a red coat as described.

All true, swore his mom, Hazel Roberts.

Judge Niesje Steinkruger commended Hazel's avowed efforts enforcing the rules, then sent her son back to jail. "Reasonable doubt" wasn't enough, the judge said. "We are at a much lesser standard."

All but one of the suspects relied on public defenders. Marvin Roberts's grandmother, other relatives, and friends raised the $10,000 needed to retain Dick Madson, Alaska's most famous defense attorney.

What made Dick Madson so special?

Ask Joe Hazelwood, drunken skipper of the *Exxon Valdez*.

REWIND: PRINCE WILLIAM SOUND, MARCH 24, 1989

Hours before the first spill-response boats reached the scene, a photographer and I were circling above the *Exxon Valdez* aboard a *News-Miner* executive's plane. A tiny lone fishing boat towing a strip of floating boom appeared to be trying to corral the black pool spreading from the gutted supertanker.

In a matter of weeks, the devastation unleashed by Hazelwood's crew defied comprehension. Miles and miles of beaches were awash with oiled birds, dying crabs, and other poisoned species. Coastal Communities were stripped of fishing and tourism income, overrun by federal inspectors and rock scrubbers cashing in on the black tides.

When seating an unbiased jury in Valdez, Alaska, proved impossible, Hazelwood's arraignment hearing was relocated to Fairbanks, some 360 miles north. That November, as charges were pressed in the federal court-house, Hazelwood's defense team, led by Fairbanks attorney Dick Madson, boldly reframed his infamous client's role.

"He called the Coast Guard," the big lawyer declared. "He said, 'We're hard aground and we're leaking oil.' The point is *he helped the government*, and that help is being used against him."

Charles Mason, the paper's chief photographer, and I intercepted the captain fleeing the building, head bowed, avoiding eye contact, both hands jammed in his pockets. His escort, a tall, bearish, gray-bearded defender, paced alongside.

When all was said and done, Hazelwood got off with a $50,000 fine and a couple summer vacations collecting Alaska highway trash, little more than a parking ticket for the nation's largest oil spill. Credit Dick Madson for that.

DELAYS AND APOLOGIES

A full year passed before Judge Steinkruger began selecting a jury for the trial of George Frese, the first Hartman suspect facing judgment. Ninety-eight jurors were called, with more than forty excused by defenders or the state, most often citing the person's apparent familiarity with the case. After four days spent seating a jury of twelve and a single alternate, Judge Steinkruger still had qualms. Citing the possibility of hidden bias, she ordered Frese's trial moved to Anchorage, 350 miles south, a first for the town founded on a gold strike in 1903.

The prosecutor lamented the expense of transporting and housing witnesses and court personnel so far away. The move prompted a soul-searching editorial. "It was in part this paper's detailed coverage of the case that has made the judge uneasy. In other words, some say, 'If *News-Miner* editors don't like trials moved, they ought to think about that in advance and play down crime coverage.'"

The editorial writer challenged that: "Given the facts, it appears the climate making it impossible to seat a jury on this case was created in the courtroom, not the community."

No matter. Precedent was set, and in February 1999, George Frese was tried and soon convicted in Anchorage, where he appeared sullen and quiet as the verdict was read, noted the freelancer covering the distant trial, "muttering obscenities as he exited in handcuffs."

Though Hartman's mom attended every trial session and remained close by her motel phone, court staff failed to call as promised when the jury returned. "I'm very mad at the judge," Evalyn Thomas told reporters, prompting Judge Steinkruger's apology on behalf of the Alaska Court System.

The prosecutor focused on the outcome. "Hopefully, under the circumstances," Jeff O'Bryant said, "she was at least happy about the verdict."

———————

Eugene Vent, by then nineteen, elected to testify in his own defense when he faced Judge Benjamin Esch that summer. Though really scared, he sensed that jurors, some of them at least, were listening to his lawyer's final argument. They seemed to get that being so drunk left him in a highly suggestible state of mind. It gave him hope.

Then came O'Bryant's closing argument. The prosecutor began by placing a dummy on the courtroom floor, which he circled, repeatedly kicking for emphasis, describing the teenager's guilt. Watching jurors' faces, Eugene sensed attitudes hardening.

Marvin and Kevin were tried and convicted together that August. "They had to ignore every witness we put on," Dick Madson griped afterward. The old defender couldn't get over the jury's apparent disregard for a pair of mature women who swore they were watching Marvin dancing at the crucial hour and alibis from other friends riding in his car with him before and after. "I quit. I'm not going to do this anymore," he told reporters.

Though three of the young men convicted were Athabascan, regional Native councils and corporate offices remained noticeably silent. One lone tribal council in a small village located 120 miles northwest of Fairbanks stood apart:

TAKE A STAND FOR JUSTICE

WHEREAS: The Native Village of Tanana believes that the District Attorney's office, the Fairbanks area's policing, and judicial systems have failed to provide adequate investigation and protection under the law; and

WHEREAS: It is widely known within the Native communities that these agencies routinely treat Alaska Natives with a degree of prejudice that often leads to injustice and repeated violations of their Civil Rights; and

WHEREAS: Tribal leaders and tribal members in the Interior need to take a firm public stand in support of unbiased justice for these young men.

That March 1999 resolution from a tiny but influential traditional Yukon village urged Tanana Chiefs Conference, Interior Alaska's Native political voice, to create a "permanent task force to monitor judicial and legal systems in Fairbanks." That wasn't all. Resolution 99–33 called on "all Tribal leaders, members and organizations" to join in "demanding that the Justice Department investigate the actions of the police, prosecutors, and judges in the case of the three boys currently charged."

SENTENCING BEGINS

LATE JANUARY 2000

Those who spoke about George Frese's prospects for reform offered conflict-
ing portraits. His daughter's grandmother described him as kind to animals
and children. Hartman's stepfather all but cursed him. "Your act was so sick
it couldn't have been the act of a human," he told George. "It was the act of
a rabid dog."

Defending those four convictions, Prosecutor O'Bryant compared
Hartman's assailants to a predatory pack: "He's outnumbered. He's taken
down much like wolves take down a larger animal."

Nearly a year to the day after the first of the Hartman suspects faced
trial, the result commanded front-page attention: "Frese Gets 97 Years in
Hartman Killing."

Clutching his prepared statement with shackled hands, George
denounced the justice system as corrupt and accused the media of fabricat-
ing the truth. "I will be redeemed," he declared.

When their turns came, all three codefendants maintained their
innocence at sentencing. "I'm a scapegoat for officers of the law," Kevin
Pease declared that February when he, Marvin Roberts, and Eugene Vent
faced judgment together.

Judge Ben Esch, the tall, graying man who presided over their trials,
wasn't impressed. "It's a question of when the homicide was going to occur,"
he told Kevin. "Not if." Citing Kevin's extensive juvenile record, including
a conviction for armed robbery at sixteen, Esch sentenced him to seventy-
nine years.

Eugene drew thirty-eight years, nearly twice as long as he'd been alive.

As for the stellar student with nothing but traffic tickets tainting his
prior record? The man in the black robes gazing down sent Marvin Roberts
away for thirty-three years.

A VILLAGER'S QUESTIONS

"This letter is about the interrogations and convictions of the four young men charged in the beating death of John Hartman, October 11, 1997, hopefully opening up more questions and answers."

Marti, the *News-Miner*'s machine-gun-fast typesetter, checked her notebook. Sure enough, thirty days had passed since the writer's last published letter to the editor. She wasn't surprised; Curtis Sommer knew the rules, and the Tanana villager seldom missed his turn. She keyed the letter into the system and forwarded it to me. Fretting about libel was part of my new job as the Opinion page editor.

"In reading the transcripts of the interrogations," wrote Sommer, "my impression is the four men knew nothing about the murder. Two were drunk and questioned for an extensive period. All four denied, and to this day deny, any involvement. It reads as if they already had their minds made up the boys were guilty."

The villager blasted the judge's handling of a critical exhibit in the first murder trial and took a lot of shots at a trial witness named Arlo Olson, whose testimony about an earlier mugging the same night somehow figured in the convictions. That wasn't all: Sommer stated that John Hartman smoked crystal meth at a party the night he died. I didn't recall *that* coming up before. He also claimed that Hartman was found wearing someone else's pants.

I wasn't surprised the case commanded attention in Tanana. I recalled being impressed by the village council's leadership during a fly-in assignment covering an elders' conference. When was that? Five years ago? Likely more.

Still, even if the writer's assertions were true, I couldn't help but imagine how Kate and I'd feel if one of our boys died, as the writer seemed to imply, drugged up after swapping pants? I spiked Sommer's letter for fact-checking.

Vetting Sommer's claims required multiple courthouse visits. Skimming trial logs—all I had time for—turned up arguable support for his assertion that this Olson character, apparently a key witness, probably lied under oath. And I found testimony indicating Hartman indeed popped pills and collapsed at a party an hour or so before he was jumped.

Faxes flew between the newsroom and the village clinic where Curtis Sommer worked until I was satisfied his letter didn't invite a libel suit. His closing line stuck with me: "Too many people in positions of authority and law laugh at the phrase 'double standard of justice,' but Natives know how hard it is to have lived under it."

The villager's monthly critiques kept coming. I held up fewer and fewer as my grasp of the Hartman case expanded, vowing to dig deeper—if I ever got time.

WITHOUT EVIDENCE?

"Is there equal justice under the law? Does race play a factor in the length of sentences or denial of probation in Alaska?" As usual, local columnist Gary Moore challenged assumptions. This latest piece, "Racial Split in Alaska Justice?" weighed the Hartman judgments alongside a trio of young white offenders locked up for murdering a cab driver in August 1998.

Dale Depue and his stepbrother traded cocaine for a free ride by cab driver Maurice Lee Smith, then lured the poor bastard into the woods where they either jointly beat the guy to death or watched their friend, a twenty-eight-year-old martial arts instructor, cut the guy's throat.

Stories differed.

All three were arrested based on evidence recovered from the cab, found ditched in a river. The teens cut deals with the state, admitting they kicked the guy around, fingering their older partner as the actual killer. Both received lighter sentences for their testimony.

"In the Hartman case," the columnist pointed out, "the Native defendants never wavered from their declarations of innocence, yet they were sent to prison for an average of a half-century each. What was the significant difference among the facts in these two cases," Moore asked, "that warrant each of the Native defendants receiving average sentences of 30 years longer than the white defendants?"

He accepted that plea bargains figured in the disparity. In a sense, Dale and his brother were rewarded. That didn't mean Moore was satisfied. "Why didn't the third defendant receive a harsher sentence once jurors found him guilty? Suffice to say, I can only conclude there may be ample reason to look deeper into Alaska's justice system for cases of possible racial disparity."

A hell of a column, though I didn't entirely buy the emphasis on racial bias. The way I saw it, the cab driver was a willing participant in a drug deal that went south. What happened to John Hartman, barely fifteen, struck me as far more egregious: brutally head-stomped for no known reason, and according to police, raped or molested with a baseball bat or bottle. All that, I felt, warranted severe judgments.

INVESTIGATIVE REPORTING 444

Photojournalist Charles Mason now headed the journalism department at University of Alaska Fairbanks. In late August 2001, he unexpectedly reached out. "I seem to recall you have a graduate degree. Is that right?"

I did, a master's in broadcast journalism from New York University.

"Have you ever considered teaching?"

I hadn't.

Fall classes were starting soon, Mason said, and the department had an emergency opening. Was I interested?

Kate had already quit the *News-Miner*, setting career aspirations aside as a stay-at-home mother to our two young boys, Rory and Robin. We lived in a rustic log cabin, thirty miles from town, with sixteen sled dogs staked outside, hauling water as needed in a big plastic tank strapped to the bed of my old Dodge pickup.

Wendy, who'd covered campus for the paper, raved about UAF benefits.

No-brainer, declared Kate.

I took the university job.

A kid wearing a ball cap glanced at the lumberyard receipt and motioned for me to follow him. "What do you do for a living?" he asked as we loaded two-by-fours in my pickup for a late summer project.

"Just quit the *News-Miner* to teach journalism at UAF."

"I'll be in your class," declared Casey Grove, introducing himself. His family subscribed to the paper. He thought he recognized the name on the job ticket. And I realized that I'd published letters to the editor from his dad, a prolific contributor.

Mason threw a party before classes started that fall. The crowd reflected his career moves: a mix of faculty and students, local photo buffs, and hard-core journalists. A good group for testing my planned approach for teaching Investigative Reporting, the course I was most excited about.

So what do you think? I kept asking, sharing my ideas for a class project settling questions about John Hartman's murder. In this crowd, most were familiar with the case. A sensitive subject, several pointed out. Did I really want to dig that up again?

Won't be dull, I countered.

Was this a wise move? For a new instructor? That question came from a career academic and didn't concern me in the least. I viewed this university gig as a temporary detour.

No one offered cause to believe I couldn't involve students in such a project. I took that as permission.

A half dozen juniors and seniors showed up for the first session of

Investigative Reporting, the perfect size for what I had in mind. "I'll be running this class as I did special projects back at the *News-Miner*," I told them.

Michael Drew, a hefty journalism major who tended to stutter, nodded. He'd interned at the paper, working on a terminal close to mine. He'd seen what a team of reporters can pull off, pooling contacts and areas of expertise, contributing to a comprehensive story or, better yet, a series, my specialty as the paper's special projects editor.

When I finished going over the syllabus requirements, I had everyone pack up and follow me outside, across a courtyard, continuing into the university's main library, around and down several flights of steps, on into a lobby decorated with huge oil paintings of icebergs and historic sailing ships. ALASKA COLLECTION proclaimed the sign over the entrance to the room beyond.

Inside, we continued past low bookshelves toward a line of chest-high steel-gray cabinets. I yanked open a wide drawer, revealing several dozen four-by-two-inch boxes labeled *News-Miner*. Each contained a yearlong spool of microfilmed pages from the region's one-hundred-year-old paper of record.

"The good news," I announced, "is content from this era is well indexed. We have Mary Beth, the paper's reference librarian, to thank for that."

From there, we backtracked. "And this is our actual starting point," I said, standing by a tall bookshelf lined with the paper's bound index volumes, labeled year by year.

I put the class to work reviewing the 1997–2000 volumes, flipping through pages, collecting publication dates for keywords, such as *Hartman*, *murder*, *trial*, and *police*, targeting any microfilmed stories that seemed worth printing out.

As the clock wound down, students took turns summarizing what stuck out in terms of headlines and story angles.

And I assured them of this: We'd likely cast a wide net as we learned more.

Indeed, while those clips gave us details about the murder and police investigation, the coverage didn't begin to convey the furor I recalled in my previous role as Opinion page editor.

IR met once a week for three hours. We spent the following class scrutinizing letters to the editor. Right away, students came across demands for action that pivoted off the crime without mentioning the victim or the suspects by name. The author of a letter titled "Chronicle," for example, blasted "penny-pinching officials" and "tax dodgers," then took aim at the Hartman coverage. "Our hometown newspaper features photos of the accused four over another photo of a cute little white kid playing with guns, then follows up with another spread deploying the three Native defendants together, and a separate cut of the white defendant. Trying to start a race-war *News-Miner?* Well, as usual, you're too late: it started long ago."

Our expanded search yielded more than eighty microfilmed stories and letters referencing the teenager's murder, the investigation, the three separate trials in 1999, and early appeals, several of which had already reached the Alaska Supreme Court. I had students enlarge the clips for readability, then print out copies of everything.

When the class next met, I passed out stapled sets of those stories and letters along with highlighter pens. "Every name represents a potential source," I emphasized and put them to work.

EVIDENTIARY, MY DEAR WATSON

Coast Guard retiree Frank Shepherd drew on his military police training, combing those clips for any hint of physical evidence linking the group convicted to Hartman's murder. That's what any competent investigator would concentrate on, he told the group. Frank soon unearthed several nuggets buried under the headline "Police Push to Solidify Case in Hartman Killing." The story covered a pretrial hearing on defense complaints that Fairbanks police weren't keeping pace in sharing investigation reports and interview recordings. The presiding judge warned Detective Paul Keller that evidence could end up excluded.

Keller blamed staffing shortages. "We were supposed to hire a temporary person, but that fell through." The deputy chief backed him up, citing ongoing budget and staffing woes, which already posed problems in sharing documents from a kidnapping case. How was FPD supposed to "actually transcribe" eighty-three taped interviews from the Hartman case?

Buried on the jump page, more than a dozen paragraphs below the news lede, Keller referred to "70 pieces of physical evidence that must be submitted to the crime lab." Jim Hayes, the Fairbanks mayor at the time, flagged cost issues but remained committed. "I'll find the money somewhere to get this done," he said. "These cases are just too important to us."

Budget woes weren't surprising, I told the class. Arguably the most influential voice in local politics belonged to the Interior Taxpayers' Association, a group bent on starving local government. Funding for Fairbanks police, the local fire department, and other city-run services suffered as a result.

A bail hearing story, published three months after the murder, indicated that test results on the evidence weren't what police expected. "There's not much in the way of forensics to tie these individuals to the crime," prosecutor O'Bryant told the judge. "But that does not undermine the state's case."

Our former military cop was incredulous. "You can't beat someone to death without blood and tissue evidence," Frank Shepherd declared.

———————————

Catching wind of my project, our friend Wendy shared her "Student Achiever of the Week" profile from May 1996: "Marvin Roberts plans to make a couple of million dollars before he retires. And the senior at Howard Luke Alternative High School plans to work hard to get there. That's one reason Marvin's favorite book is *The Count of Monte Cristo* by Alexander Dumas. 'It shows that anybody in the "pits" can get to the top of the world,' he says."

Those profiles were a weekly *News-Miner* feature. Wendy drew on nominations from teachers choosing the honoree. "Enthusiastic in class and helpful," Marvin's teacher said, referring to him as a "serious student" motivated to "establish and maintain high standards."

Wendy also interviewed Marvin, of course. He identified business, math, accounting, and computers as his favorite classes. "By doing these," he said, "I figure I can get an edge in this area and be more successful."

That profile ended on an odd note: "The most interesting thing Marvin has learned lately is not to miss school. 'I've missed a lot of school and it showed on my grade report,' he says. 'I'm trying hard though, and it will also show.'"

What was that about? I stared at the clip, weighing the opposing perspectives. Marvin Roberts: honors student and basketball team captain, grinning for that profile piece, or Marvin the getaway-car driver, punching the accelerator, fleeing multiple robberies and that fatal assault.

GABE'S BOX

Undergrads proved surprisingly timid. Most shied from cold-calling strangers, let alone knocking on doors. Some acted as if talking to strangers was illegal.

Not Gabe Scott. The red-bearded senior went straight after answers. He'd been networking with the convicted men's families, their lawyers, and staff, copying everything and anything he came across related to the case. In late fall 2001, he marched into my office and laid a worn cardboard box on my desk.

A hodgepodge treasure trove, Gabe's box was stuffed with police interview transcripts, investigation reports, numbered tape recordings, and Hartman's autopsy report. Gabe had even found Eugene's ticket for underage drinking the night of his arrest.

Though full of gaps throughout, the upperclassman's score offered our first inside look at the police investigation, documented through reports, recordings, and data disks shared under pretrial discovery rules. Organizing what he'd found proved challenging. Depending on the defendant and trial, page numbering often differed on otherwise identical pages; sections of text were occasionally double underlined by hand. Some pages had little heart doodles alongside the suspects' names. The scrawled comment "How many times did he have to tell them?" appeared on a detective's typed statement describing Marvin Roberts's denial that he was involved.

Gabe traced the annotations to Marvin's older sister Sharon. It turned out that she'd hand-transcribed dozens of police interviews and other recordings as a cost-saving measure. While that made sense, it also raised flags. "We can't necessarily rely on what she's typed up," I warned the class.

The tape cassettes offered scattered portions of the interrogation sessions and conveyed the pressure several suspects faced. Gabe's box also yielded a federal report on the handgun found in Marvin's car. Hearing that, Frank stiffly informed me, "That's illegal for us to even possess."

I found that hard to believe, but old Frank was serious. The former Coast Guard policeman took possession of the report, announcing he intended to mail it someplace official.

REWIND: FAIRBANKS POLICE HEADQUARTERS, OCTOBER 11, 1997

Marvin Roberts, nineteen, faced questions from three sides. It was his first visit to the station, and Sergeant Dave Kendrick, a towering presence, Detective Aaron Ring, and Investigator Paul Geier took turns. They informed Marvin that a car with his license plate was observed near the crime scene; skid marks near the victim scientifically matched his tires. They informed him a school friend from Howard Luke Academy had already admitted his involvement. Come clean, they urged him. Then they played a portion of Eugene Vent's recorded confession.

"This is the first time I've heard about that," Marvin said incredulously. "Give me a lie detector test, man."

Instead, police showed him photos of the victim's swollen, bruised face.

"It's not going to tear me up," Marvin countered, "because I wasn't even there."

Though Marvin had smoked pot with Dan, a friend he was cruising with that night, judging from the transcript, there was nothing hazy about his memory. He described his encounter with George and a couple basketball teammates at Eagles Hall. He listed off friends he'd given rides to that night and described a brief encounter with Eugene, lounging on a bed at the time, during that party at the Alaskan Motor Inn.

What he hadn't done that night, Marvin insisted, was give George, Eugene, or Kevin a lift. "I'm innocent," Marvin repeated. "I wasn't even there."

Briefly conceding the little Dodge Shadow might have been stolen and returned before he noticed, Marvin declared, "If my car was there, it was there. But I didn't see nothing. I would've stopped it!"

So why are you acting scared? he was asked.

"I'm scared because I'm innocent!"

Gabe's score included an earlier shaky home video that opened on several rows of students wearing traditional black mortarboard caps and matching gowns. The camera rolled back time, capturing a young Athabascan sporting a gold sash for academic excellence, rising from a folding chair and quietly threading his way past fellow students. He straightened his shoulders as he reached the aisle. His smile widened as he neared the podium.

Class salutatorian Marvin Roberts began by teasing a classmate with long dark hair seated in a wheelchair in front, the girl who narrowly edged him out as valedictorian.

Mirth faded as the young scholar faced the crowd.

In a firm, practiced voice, he praised Howard Luke Academy's teachers for instilling the tools necessary for success. He thanked his mom, then solemnly spoke of the future, touching on hazards awaiting the Class of '96. "Every choice we make is important," Marvin said, "because it often determines what our future pathway will be."

Exiting the stage to applause, Marvin looked hugely relieved. By the time he neared his row, he was swaggering.

After a couple of false starts, we began charting chronological details on a ten-foot roll of unused newsprint set aside for me by a pressman. "Police Activity" served as our central reference line, showing the timing of relevant 911 calls and other events logged by local police, troopers, and other authorities. Our "Prosecution Timeline" was located near the newsprint's bottom edge, noting the official chronology supporting the state's case. In between, we had individual timelines for the men convicted, tracking their movements, observations from friends, and anything else that seemed relevant using sticky notes. We shifted those notes around as new information sharpened our grasp of the timing of related events: when cab rides began or ended, when the movie ended at the theater, when a TV commercial aired, and David Bowie's walk-on appearance on Conan O'Brien's late-night TV show.

Everything pivoted off the "Riding with Marvin" timeline. Our kid with the car apparently spent half the night giving lifts to or from that wedding party at Eagles Hall. Confirming where and when he drove his little Dodge Shadow along with who cruised with him proved difficult. Quite a few of his passengers were partying hard that night. Others simply paid no attention to time. Even couples and groups riding with Marvin sometimes disagreed about timing.

DEGREES OF GUILT

FAIRBANKS CORRECTIONAL CENTER, FALL 2001

I settled on the round steel seat facing the glass window separating visitors from prisoners at the Fairbanks Correctional Center (FCC). I'd sent word through Hazel Roberts that I was coming. We'd never met, but as soon as guards brought him in, I recognized the short Athabascan with the trim mustache and waved.

Marvin Roberts took a seat across from mine and hardly said a word as I quickly described my background, how Curtis Sommer's letters got me involved, and our goal of settling questions about the case. If you're truly innocent, I emphasized, there's nothing to lose in talking to us.

The young inmate seemed appreciative but said the timing was bad; a decision on his latest appeal was due any day. In any event, he wasn't talking to anyone unless his lawyer cleared it first.

One-of-a-kind client, that was how Dick Madson referred to Marvin. When I asked what he meant by that, the old defender ticked off examples: there may be a dispute over who first picked up the knife, who recruited who for the heist, or who first voiced the idea of stealing from the company. In forty years, he declared, "Marvin's the only client I've ever had who didn't do it, had absolutely zero involvement, wasn't even there."

For a hired gun, he sounded like a true believer.

He urged me to track down an Athabascan woman who worked for the company that operated the Trans-Alaska Pipeline. As witnesses go, Madson said, not only did Eileen Newman exude credibility, but Roberts's strongest alibi rested on what she and another woman chatted about during the big wedding reception at Eagles Hall in the hours when so many lives changed.

That sounded interesting, and I promised we'd track her down. Meanwhile, I reminded the old defender of the day *News-Miner* photographer Charles Mason and I intercepted him fleeing the federal courthouse alongside Joe Hazelwood, capping an ecological and community disaster that at times seemed might never end.

"PARTY POOPERS' TABLE"

Eileen agreed to be interviewed right away. Given the importance Madson attached to her trial testimony, I wanted this one on camera, capturing emotion along with the words. Students were unpacking gear on the floor of Eileen's house when Gary Moore, my former columnist, came strolling down the staircase, wearing an old T-shirt and a wide smile. What the hell? He seemed at home. Were he and Eileen an item? Sure felt like it. And I didn't recall ever discussing his potential conflict of interest, writing about a case involving a woman he was seeing.

For the moment, I set it aside.

Eileen was from Rampart, a small Yukon village upriver from Tanana, where Marvin's biological father still lived. Though a few years older, she'd known Marvin his whole life. The night of that wedding reception at Eagles Hall, Eileen sat with several other expectant mothers. "We were joking it was the party poopers' table," she recalled.

Returning from the bathroom that night, Eileen's eyes skipped toward a man slouched in the hallway with a bloody brow. He seemed beaten up; she realized the woman on the nearby payphone was in the middle of reporting the assault.

That 1:35 a.m. 911 call, logged as "Robbery, 400 1st Avenue," places a time stamp on Eileen's testimony that right afterward, she and a pregnant friend watched Marvin Roberts dancing with the woman's niece. If true, that directly contradicted the prosecutor's claims about Marvin's involvement in a spree of violence culminating in Hartman's fatal assault.

Frankie Dayton, the guy Eileen noticed bleeding by the phone, hailed from Kaltag, a small Athabascan village located on the upper Yukon where the Iditarod Trail turns toward the coast. That night in 1997, Dayton split the reception and was walking toward another bar when several guys jumped him.

Eagles Hall was a half mile from where Hartman lay sprawled in the street. Could Marvin have been involved in that getaway, circled back, parked, and made it onto the dance floor by then? It didn't seem possible, but what if the assaults weren't connected?

Eileen insisted she called Fairbanks police soon after Marvin's arrest, but no one followed up. Eugene and George were both convicted before any judge or jury heard the sober "party pooper's" perspective. Jurors in the final trial were the first to hear the Athabascan woman's timely observations, which she thought ought to at least clear Marvin, arguably all four, since his access to a car was crucial to the state's whole case. "If they choose not to believe me," Eileen told us on camera, referring to those jurors, "all I can say is they don't know me."

OF EVIDENCE AND OPPORTUNITY

SEPTEMBER 27, 2002

"Greetings. Greetings. Greetings!" declared assistant district attorney Jeff O'Bryant.

"How you are doing!" I shot back.

"Still short, bald, and ugly," the prosecutor deadpanned.

"What?"

"Still short, fat, and bald," he repeated, "but we're hanging in there."

Clearly, I'd caught the prosecutor in a good mood. I seized the moment, requesting his help gaining access to the Hartman case evidence, full copies of Ring's interrogation tapes, and other evidence court clerks were holding back. "What I've received are things that trickled through the families. Even the defense is saying bar rules leave them wary."

"Yeah," O'Bryant said. "The bar rules put me in a bind." Get a copy of Alaska's criminal rules, he said. Sections C or D addressing the exclusive possession of documents covered it.

With appeals still pending, he claimed to be duty bound from letting us anywhere near evidence. it. "I mean, it's secured. It's evidence!"

"Shouldn't there be full copies available in the public record?" I argued. For example, the pictures that supposedly showed Frese's boot tread matched Hartman's bruised face? Couldn't we at least photograph that?

"Then we've got tainted evidence," O'Bryant said firmly. "I'm not going there."

That directly conflicted with the advice I got discussing the case with big name journalists at the Investigative Reporters and Editor's national conference in San Fransisco. "Most were thrown by the idea we can't view or copy evidence presented in trial."

"I don't know what to tell you," O'Bryant said wearily. "The court system, upon completion of the trials, told me come and get my exhibits. And I did. And the Fairbanks Police Department has them locked away in evidence. Safe and secure."

I couldn't resist: "Aren't you worried about that? I'm kidding," I added quickly.

"I know. It's not $10,000. It's *just evidence of murder*," the lawman shot back. "How's that for a response?"

Brilliant, actually.

We both cracked up.

REWIND: FEBRUARY 25, 1996

I'd been away for months covering the legislature in Juneau, followed by the marathon journey home, requiring an overnight ferry out of Alaska's landlocked capital, followed by seven-hundred-plus wintery miles up the Al-Can highway.

Today's sudden assignment sounded curious. Mayor Jim Hayes had something to get off his chest. That was all I knew hustling over to city hall. Could Alaska's first Black mayor be eyeing higher office?

"I just got this Wednesday," the mayor began, signaling he'd been sitting on whatever was brewing for several days. An unidentified tipster had flagged a $1,700 discrepancy in the police department's cash pots, he said. The discrepancy was the focus of a closed-door staff meeting this morning. Hence my sudden assignment.

"I called for an investigation, and that is continuing," he now declared. "I am on top of it," he added, sounding anything but.

Attendees at that meeting included Public Safety Director Mike Pulice, Chief Detective Paul Keller, and another pair of Fairbanks police officials, Hayes said for the record. He declined to get into the details, other than a surprise audit was already underway. He aimed to share the results at the Golden Heart City's next council meeting. "That's your story," Hayes emphasized.

"Is there a price tag on that audit?" I pressed.

The beleaguered minister turned politician didn't have any figures. Cost didn't factor. "I'll find it someplace," Mayor Hayes assured me. "It's important enough for me to have this done. I'll find it in somebody's budget."

In a matter of days, the audit turned up whopping discrepancies throughout the department's accounts. From petty cash used to pay for office snacks to money seized as evidence, nothing in that secure locker, receipts, or ledgers added up.

"Police Audit Finds $10,000 May Be Missing," headlined the *News-Miner* on March 5, 1997. By then, Mayor Hayes had called in Alaska State Troopers to investigate the hometown officers in blue.

Sergeant Jim McCann, a renowned detective heading the local troopers detachment, referred the case to the agency's better-staffed Anchorage counterparts. "There's three of us and a million cases," he quipped. Community relationships within the Fairbanks smaller law-enforcement community also factored. "It puts us in a bad position to do this locally," McCann told Douglas Fischer, a hustling young reporter chasing daily developments.

Over the months that followed, publicity surrounding what became known as the "evidence locker scandal" grew and grew. Mike Pulice, who supervised both local police and firefighters as Fairbanks's public safety director, soon emerged as a leading suspect, in the public eye anyway. Why? He refused to take the polygraph test required of other staff with access to that evidence room and other critical storage areas.

Nine months after the scandal first broke, troopers and the federal prosecutor overseeing the investigation essentially admitted defeat.

MISSING EVIDENCE CASH REMAINS A MYSTERY

SUNDAY, NOVEMBER 24, 1996

Douglas's wide-ranging recap of the failed investigation made for a great read, full of rich characters and deep divides among police personnel, leaving readers chewing over the whodunit!

The trooper investigator's summary read like a naughty child's report card. "Pulice could not have taken the money from an area controlled by Ann Stepp, an employee who disliked him so much unless he could be sure he could cover up the loss."

Assuming Chief Pulice somehow managed to pull off that heist, he would have had to alter the logbook handwritten by yet another FPD employee. The lead investigator fingered Stepp, the woman with a grudge, as a more likely suspect, citing her forced $3,000 pay cut, which coincided with a $3,000 raise for the chief's girlfriend. His final report noted: "Stepp is the only person who had both unrestricted access and no controls." And no way to hold anyone accountable, Alaska State Troopers concluded, because too many people had access to that police evidence locker.

Lawsuits by a disgruntled employee kept the story alive well through New Year's 1997. By then, the Fairbanks Police Department's reputation amounted to a late-night TV punchline.

CHAPTER 3

"YOU CAUGHT THAT!"

Inmate Marvin Roberts called as I was packing up for the day. The judge rejected his motion for a new trial, he blurted out, sounding low.

I was anxious to hit the road home, a thirty- to forty-minute drive from campus on a good day, which this wasn't. "What about that interview?" I snapped. "I'll bring in a video crew. It'd be your chance to tell your story."

"Maybe if you give me a list of questions."

"Can't do that."

Marvin eventually agreed to a formal sit-down interview with a UAF student crew. I worked out the details with corrections officials and submitted the required paperwork. All but one of my Investigative Reporting students signed up to go. The exception was Karl, a member of UAF's nationally ranked rifle team. My field trip conflicted with practice. Though I pointed out he could legitimately tell the coach he'd been in jail, Karl didn't go for it.

FAIRBANKS CORRECTIONS CENTER, NOVEMBER 1, 2002

A prison guard patted the five of us down, inspected everyone's shoes, then went through the camera kit and other gear bags. Another guard escorted us to a big room largely empty save for a few chairs. Light streaming in through barred windows gave the place a surreal feel. So did a wall map of Alaska tribal lands, surrounded by odd certificates.

Frank Shepherd began unpacking the big camera and tripod. Others scurried setting up our portable lights and running power cords. I'd chosen Russ, a tall, bespectacled poli-sci major from Boston, as our interviewer. He grabbed a pair of rigid plastic seat chairs and set them up facing each other, spaced roughly four feet apart, then stood back looking over the setup. Russ was my ringer. Casual blue jeans and the faded denim shirt belied the former soldier's training and experience, being one of General Norman Schwarzkopf's boys during Operation Desert Storm.

The young man we were here to see entered through a separate door under armed escort, shoulders squared. Catching my eyes, Marvin Roberts briefly smiled, lifting that pencil mustache. Taking a big breath, he studied our preparations. His eyes skipped from face to face as I introduced the crew.

Seated across from Russ, Marvin's toes barely touched the floor; he was shorter than I realized from visitor booth interviews. He and Russ made small talk as Frank fiddled with the video camera, adjusting audio levels from both subjects, along with our backup shotgun mic. When he got that just right, Frank stood behind the camera, squinting over the eyepiece, fingering the zoom lens with his free hand. Then he looked up, signaling all was ready.

Boston accent thick as ever, Russ began by asking Marvin Roberts about his latest failed appeal.

"Naturally, I was kind of floored by it," said Marvin, lifting his head and meeting the interviewer's eyes, "because I always have hope and faith that something will happen. But I should have expected it," he added. "I've been toyed with and stung by the state throughout this whole ordeal. So, I should have expected it. Still, it hurt. It hurt."

Did he run into the other suspects that night?

Marvin saw them all at that wedding reception but never together. "Just said, 'hi, goodbye,' you know."

What about Frankie Dayton, the guy mugged down the block from Eagles Hall?

"I went to use the bathroom and saw him coming down the stairs," recalled Marvin, referring to Eagles Hall. "So I figure I was inside when that happened." He added that he didn't really know the villager, not then. What caught his attention was the cut over Frankie's eye. "Ah, I wonder what happened to him," he recalled thinking.

Big Michael Drew leaned on a side wall as he listened, lips set, arms folded and resting on his belly. Gabe tugged on his beard, watching from a chair.

Too antsy to sit, I stood behind our tall portable light, gazing over Russ's shoulder, studying Marvin's reactions.

"Would you describe it as a wild night?" Russ asked.

Marvin didn't remember it that way. Eagles Hall was crowded, sure, but the whole scene felt joyous. "I don't think I sensed anything bad happening that night."

Moving on, Russ asked when the police got involved.

"Oh, man, it's like a bad nightmare," groaned Marvin, recalling the squad car's sudden appearance at his mother's house that Saturday night. He joined them outside, fielding questions about where he went after the reception. "I guess something I said seemed suspicious," he recalled, eyes widening, "because they asked me if I would come downtown. I have nothing to hide, so I said sure."

Back at the station, police ratcheted up the pressure. "They put me in a little room. Then, I don't know, maybe three or four officers, not at one time, they'd go after or interview me. Then they'd switch officers, I think, and try to do the good cop–bad cop routine. And they just kept grilling me. Kept grilling me," Marvin told Russ. "And I just kept saying, 'I'm innocent. I don't know what you're talking about.' It dawned on me I'm a suspect in something I didn't even do," he added, glancing up, looking earnest, then shaking his head.

The ride home included a rolling tour of the scene and the detective's escalating pressure.

Russ followed up on both. "So he was sitting in the back seat?" he asked, referring to Detective Aaron Ring.

"Yeah."

"And you were sitting in the front of the cruiser?"

"Yeah." Marvin nodded. "He said, 'This is where it happened. Just say you did it! Say you did it!' Stuff like that."

DEBRIEFING SESSION

Following the interview, we headed straight for the northern-most Denny's in the world, as certified by the local landmark's tall yellow sign. My treat. After placing orders, we shared impressions. Russ's handling of the interview drew raves all around. Marvin Roberts came across as bright, thoughtful, and remarkably calm. Maybe too calm? Frank reported that he'd closely watched Marvin's eyes, and nothing fit what he knew about blinking patterns associated with lies. "Perhaps it's because he's Native?" All of us were white and clueless.

Other takeaways from that celebratory brunch: Marvin Roberts had a scorpion tattoo; was that a prison gang symbol? None of us knew. He claimed to have read seven hundred to one thousand books over the four years since his arrest. Was that possible? Did our local prison even have a library?

More on point, Marvin confirmed what we'd heard; the DA floated a deal that would have resulted in his immediate release for time served—if he testified against the others.

He turned it down.

"He sh-sh-sure did not want to discuss where he drove that night," stuttered Big Michael Drew, our class skeptic.

Russ grinned. "You caught that!"

Our video of the interview backed up Big Michael's observation:

whenever Russ inquired about his specific movements, Marvin became evasive. "We drove out for a little bit," he said, responding to a question about an early passenger's ride that night. "Just running some time off the clock before we got down to the reception hall. We got down there, and I was there most of the night. I think periodically I might have left, but this was probably later on that night." At another point, he said, "I don't know if I should go into times. I was mostly at the reception hall. I don't think I should go into that," he added. "Not at this time."

"So," Russ softly pressed, "afterward? You went straight home?"

"I think I did," said Marvin, adding, "I don't think I should go into it at this time. I don't think I should go into that either. It might come back to hurt me if I go back to get a new trial."

Most disturbing, we all agreed: the kid with the car left open the possibility his little Dodge Shadow *may have been observed* cruising Ninth Avenue that night, near where Hartman lay dying.

"Yeah, they kept saying something to that effect," Marvin said with the camera rolling. "I don't know if I should go into it," he added, followed by a pause. "They said something to the effect, 'We know your car was there,' something like that." Sounding low, he explained, "I was like, 'Okay, my car was there, but I wasn't there!' I was thinking at that time maybe somebody stole my car or something when I was at the reception. And then brought it back." A big if, he acknowledged, "but that's what I thought."

A few days after the interview, Marvin Roberts called for the second time, suggesting a bunch of people we ought to consider interviewing. Out of the blue, he added, "I know I'm innocent. I think the other guys are too. *But I know I'm innocent.*"

"LIKE A FREIGHT TRAIN"

Calls from inmates were hit or miss, because the phone service required recipients to accept the jailbird's call. If I wasn't in my office, inmates couldn't leave messages, nor was there any indication someone tried to get in touch.

Anyone participating in a phone conversation can legally record it in Alaska without notifying others on the line. With my background in newsrooms, I generally recorded any calls or interviews I thought might prove important. Such as the day Marvin Roberts and I discussed his rejection of the prosecutor's deal.

"I was out on bail," he recalled. "My lawyer called up my mom's house. So I drove down there to his office."

Dick Madson floated a plea offer under discussion: five years for manslaughter.

"Wow, they're offering me a deal?" Marvin recalled thinking. "Because, like, they came at me like a freight train from day one." There was more to it, of course. "I couldn't say 'I did it' because I didn't!" he declared. "So I told my lawyer, no, no deal."

Any regrets?

"No, never!" the young inmate said. "I never question that decision. I know I'm innocent. I'm going to live with that till the day I die. God knows I'm innocent. I just wish the justice system did."

———————

FPD Investigator Paul Geier's October 1997 supplemental report linked John Hartman's fatal assault to an earlier mugging that same night.

Frankie Dayton was walking downtown, heard a car pull over, then was tripped or shoved down soon after. "DAYTON said that he fell to the ground, striking his right knee, right elbow, and his head against the sidewalk," Geier's report states. "He attempted to push himself up, but one of the subjects stepped on his right hand. DAYTON was then kicked on the right side of his back. One of the subjects reached into his right front pocket and took $15 from him."

Dayton passed out. He wasn't sure just how long, then got up and made his way back to Eagles Hall. Geier tracked down a pair of sisters who asked Dayton what happened. "He did not say a lot about it except that he was jumped by four boys, and they beat him up really badly," one of the women told the officer. Her sister's account raised the stakes: "DAYTON told her that four guys jumped out of car; pulled a gun on him and told him that they wanted his money, and that he was not the only one they were going to hurt. He also advised her that one of the guys was a big guy, that had thrown him down."

Geier flagged discrepancies: "DAYTON was asked if he remembered seeing or hearing any reference to a gun and he first answered no. DAYTON then advised that he was told not to look back and that at some time reference was made to a gun."

Five years later, Sergeant Paul Geier took my call and fielded questions without apparent offense, assuring me the case against the group convicted was solid. "Get the full interview transcripts," he said. "That will settle any doubts."

SEAFARING CONNECTIONS

My dad, like his dad before him, was a labor lawyer. Like him, when my younger brothers and I were old enough, summer vacations meant entry-level jobs in various trades. I hauled tools and parts up countless steps as an elevator constructor's helper. Another summer found this steamfitter's apprentice masked, shedding rivers of sweat, brushing soot inside industrial boilers. Though paychecks were good, dorms and textbooks looked sweeter by the day.

After our dad's death at the age of forty-nine, one of his union friends reached out to our mom. "Some of those boys must be seafaring age," he said.

The taxi dropped me on a Brooklyn dock alongside the SS *Sam Houston*, the largest ship I'd ever seen. A deckhand showed me where to stow my seabag, then guided me to a steel ladder descending farther than I could see. "Ask for the First," he said, pointing down. By the time I reached the engine room, I dripped sweat like rain.

"You might as well say goodbye to the lady," said my new boss, the first engineer, then sent me back up that long ladder.

A blast of ocean breeze greeted me on deck. The Statue of Liberty was already slipping behind SS *Sam*'s wake. Like standing on a continent breaking apart, I hadn't noticed we were underway. Over the following months, I embraced life as "the wiper," low mate of the engine room, chipping rust and mopping up whatever dripped from New York to Calcutta and back.

Years later, "Shipbreakers," a Pulitzer Prize–winning series examining the fate of old cargo vessels, brought those days back. When I heard that Gary Cohn, one of the lead reporters, was a visiting professor at our university's Anchorage campus, I reached out. Pretty soon, I was consulting Cohn on every step and student discovery.

That spring, Cohn was again a Pulitzer finalist. It didn't go his way, which left time for a late-season run to a state cabin north of town.

The trail took off from an old quarry. Howls gave way to frantic barking as I began hitching dogs in place. I set Cohn up with a team of four strong pullers hauling a small sled loaded with just enough gear for balance. I took eight dogs pulling a longer freight sled. Rory, six, climbed in the bag and seated himself on sleeping bags and other gear. By then, the dogs were leaping in place, madly barking. Signaling for Cohn to follow me out, I pulled the snow hook and rocketed off.

Cohn had a rough ride, rolling the little sled, occasionally riding on his belly, but he showed good survival skills, grabbing some part of the sled on the way down and hanging on.

That night, warmed by a crackling woodstove in a tight little cabin beyond cellular service, Cohn and I discussed the Hartman case at length. "See if they'll agree to take lie detector tests," he advised, referring to Marvin and the others. He'd suggested this before, and I'd looked into it: we'd need an examiner with no ties to local authorities. That meant bringing up someone from out of state. Cost estimates for that topped $1,000 when Marvin Roberts was jailed in town. Likely more now that he was incarcerated down in Seward, Alaska, miles and miles from Alaska's urban centers. Besides, lie detector results weren't even accepted as evidence in Alaska courts.

Admissibility wasn't the issue, Cohn countered. Readers would be interested, and the results *could* add weight to the innocence claims. Assuming, that is, Marvin and the others agreed to take exams—and passed them.

"I think you would want to know," Cohn said gently, adding that it would give him some confidence in his reporting.

I had big plans for the second Investigative Reporting class. But only three students signed up, leaving me bummed. I assumed the class would be canceled. Don't worry, our department chair assured me; the first group praised my approach, and public service aspects reflected well on the whole College of Liberal Arts.

Tom Delaune was arguably the best reporter at the *Sun Star*, UAF's student newspaper, which I critiqued weekly as faculty advisor. Sharice Walker's sharp questions in the News Writing class kept me on task my first semester teaching. She'd mastered the *AP Stylebook* overnight and struck just the right note in a feature story mocking Coca-Cola's varying price around campus. By then, I'd become aware the tall brunette was a single mom, raising two little girls. Our boys, about the same age, made life, work, and school a daily scramble, though Kate was now a full-time mom, shouldering more of the load. Somehow, Sharice calmly pulled it off solo.

Likewise, I expected a lot from a nontraditional student lobbying for permission to enroll. "If you only want journalism majors," emailed former columnist Moore, "I'll understand. But if you let me stay, I promise to work my ass off for you."

First we needed to discuss his serious conflict of interest: being married to Marvin Roberts's main alibi witness. Face-to-face in my office, Moore confided that with all the people coming and going at Eagles Hall that night, he questioned whether his wife had the timing straight. He'd ducked that big reception himself because he knew there'd be a lot of drinking, and he'd given that up.

While he wasn't sold on the innocence claims, Gary Moore vowed to be objective. Assuming I agreed, he planned to focus on the state's evidence, and he pointed out that my class satisfied an elective credit toward his business degree.

Truth is I valued Gary Moore's hustle and was never going to turn him away.

News clips compiled by the previous class laid the foundation for this second effort clearing up questions about Hartman's murder. When Laurel Ford, a late enrollee, and everybody else had the background down, I showed the video of Marvin's prison interview, pointing out places he seemed evasive. We spent another class discussing timelines mapped on the newsprint roll, tracking individual movements using sticky notes, and shifting them around as we discovered more about time-certain events. "You see how fact-checking sharpens our timeline?"

Eugene Vent's citation for minor consuming became a lesson in itself: the tall, skinny Athabascan youth was walking home when police stopped him. A quick breath test pegged his blood-alcohol content at 0.158, nearly double Alaska's drunk-driving threshold. Of course, this bust had nothing to do with drinking or driving; police were following up on the motel manager's complaint, alleging the punk pulled a gun on him and fled.

Was that even true? Eugene wasn't packing a weapon of any kind when he was picked up. If he'd carried even a pocketknife, I assured the class, he would have been charged for it. What struck me, I emphasized, was the seventeen-year-old's reported extreme state of intoxication. That and the timing of his statements. We needed to drill down on those.

SELF-ASSIGNMENTS

Students had the background. It was time to put it to use. "Give me written proposals," I emailed IR students, "for what you think is worth investigating about the Hartman case this semester."

We spent the following class hashing over ideas. Sharice Walker wanted to compare the sentences with other Alaska murder cases. "I propose limiting my search to murders committed in the greater Fairbanks area," she began.

Listening to her pitch, Gary Moore folded his arms and leaned back, faintly smiling. Catching my eyes, he shook his head. I jumped in, outlining his column covering similar ground. Gary took it from there, describing his efforts weighing sentencing considerations in that cab driver's murder alongside judgments in the Hartman case. Not only did racial bias in plea bargaining prove hard to assess, but Fairbanks's annual body count, averaging eight or fewer murders, apparently wasn't enough for meaningful statistical analysis.

He wished Sharice luck.

For his part, Gary aimed to nail down what Frank Shepherd previously identified as critical. Working title: "John Hartman Murder: Focus on Physical Evidence or Lack of It."

I passed out copies of Gary's two-page outline. Step 1: Need to examine photo of boot and mark on Hartman's face… On and on it went. Younger classmates looked concerned silently digesting it.

Laurel Ford's questions reminded me of birch leaves falling this time of year: random colors, dancing in the wind, and hard to catch.

Why was the electricity turned off in Frese's apartment?

What prompted Dale Depue to assault Hartman's friend?

Who came up with the idea of relocating the trials to Anchorage?

The thin sophomore with long blond locks was a photojournalism major, which made sense considering the eye for detail reflected in her story memo.

"The blood issue on Hartman's head confuses me," Laurel noted, citing comments by the driver who came upon Hartman sprawled in the street. "Moses states there was a lot of blood on his face while we are told there was only a dime-size pool on the ground when Hartman was found."

"Did he say that during trial?" I asked, addressing the class. "That would have been two years after the fact. What did he tell the police initially? What did others in the car say at the time? We need to check that."

Turning back to Laurel, I urged her to talk to the detectives about the confessions. "Do that in person," I added, aware I was being sexist; in my experience, pretty women have the edge getting macho cops to open up.

Tom Delaune hadn't turned in anything. As his turn neared, he looked furtive. I wasn't surprised when he began apologizing.

I cut him off. "You've got jurors."

Given all the publicity, I reminded the class, some if not all the jurors in the first two trials likely knew that Eugene Vent and George Frese incriminated themselves, though portions of their statements were suppressed. But what tipped the scales in that final trial? Marvin Roberts claimed to have had several alibis, I reminded them. Kevin Pease's movements, though harder to track, cast further doubt on the police scenario. Both never wavered in proclaiming their innocence. Indeed, Dick Madson, the legendary defense attorney, swore he was surprised by the verdicts, and I didn't think he was bullshitting.

"Track down jurors from that third trial and interview them," I told Tom. "With a dozen people involved," I assured the class, "someone will talk."

Before we broke for the day, I announced that I was taking on Arlo Olson as my own self-assignment, citing the prosecutor's closing argument, which we'd listened to on tape. "Simply put," O'Bryant told jurors weighing murder charges against Marvin and Kevin in the final trial, "if Arlo didn't see what he saw, and you throw out some of the state's evidence, the state doesn't have a case. No doubt about it."

Yet Curtis Sommer, that village letter writer who got me involved, and several others I considered credible insisted that Arlo Olson lied throughout those trials. If so, why?

LESSONS ABOUT LIARS

Any half-decent reporter fears liars. If not yet, I often warned students, *someday you will.* Possibly with deep regret and lasting appreciation for fact-checking.

World Plus made me a believer. When Raejean Bonham declared bankruptcy in December 1995, the sheer scope of her long-running fraud left those she'd fleeced in denial. By the time I joined other reporters covering the scam's collapse, the well-known Fairbanks travel agent faced $60 million in claims from more than twelve hundred investors spread across the country. Her sideline, peddling wildly profitable "mileage club" contracts, turned out to be a long-running Ponzi scheme.

Hints of trouble first surfaced three years earlier when Alaska securities examiners questioned whether World Plus had more than twenty-five investors, or capital valuation, mandating state oversight. Bonham fended off the inquiries with testimonial letters from business leaders and others whose participation signaled all was legit. "To date I have never had any problems concerning my investment return," wrote Palmer's district attorney. A federal attorney's wife went further: "As a white-collar prosecutor for the U.S. Attorney's Office in Anchorage, Ken is well acquainted with scam artists and Ponzi schemes. We believe Raejean Bonham is operating a bona fide business." Another state prosecutor vouched for her, as did several

Fairbanks police officers. So did a local credit union's executive officer, a prominent real estate broker, a local church pastor, and the general manager of Tip Top Chevrolet, one of Fairbanks's biggest car dealerships.

Sexy, stylish Raejean clearly courted those high-profile backers, secured their loyalty through generous returns on "air mileage trading," then used those testimonials as a shield. Alaska Superior Court Judge Richard Savell and his wife were among the patsies. Though his wife's name was on the letter, he returned my call for comment. "That makes me responsible as well," the judge acknowledged for the record, earning my respect.

Ponzi schemes typically fail in a matter of weeks or months. World Plus remained aloft longer than seemed possible through Bonham's sheer salesmanship, persuading investors to let their paper profits ride. As the inevitable collapse loomed, the wily embezzler chased new investors more and more recklessly, guaranteeing returns as high as 50 percent in a few weeks. Even after the crash, some clients remained in denial, blaming the court-appointed bankruptcy trustee's efforts to claw back profits from early investors. A Wasilla attorney I knew pretty well was among those who kept the faith. Defending Raejean at a special legislative hearing, he essentially begged the committee chair, legislators, fellow creditors, reporters—anybody who'd listen: Have faith! Nothing's wrong! The money's there!

It. Just. Had. To. Be.

Others who knew better ducked for cover. "That's not my signature," a local attorney told me, glancing up from the copy of a contract I unearthed reviewing the case files. He pointed out a blank spot on the page where he said his secretary's initials go on official correspondence.

"What about your own signature?" I asked, pointing to it. "Is that a forgery?"

"It sounds like something I might write," said the lawyer, staring at it. "I'm not saying it's a falsification," he said after a long pause. "But it might be."

When I learned that Marvin turned down a deal for a reduced sentence in return for testifying against the others, it gave me pause. So did Detective Keller's repeated assurances that Fairbanks Police bagged the right guys for Hartman's murder. No question about it; case closed!

Considering the source, I reviewed my old World Plus notes and folders. Though pretty sure, this warranted confirmation. It took a while, but I found it. "Prior to investing," Detective Paul Keller wrote to state examiners in 1992, "I personally looked into whether or not World Plus Travel was involved in a scheme to defraud residents of Fairbanks." Nothing appeared amiss, he assured regulators, and that wasn't all. "I have heard that World Plus was possibly involved in a Ponzi scheme. However, there is no indication by any members of this community that this is so."

How was it the old grump still carried that shield?

"ALL MY FAULT"

Carol Pease's directions were easy to follow. She lived in the last house on Fifth Avenue, a dead-end circle lined with old cars and trucks. My video crew, a pair of grad students, grabbed the department camera and lighting kit and followed me up the steps.

Kevin's mom seemed shy at first, then opened up. "He was mad because he didn't get to see his girlfriend," Carol Pease said, discussing the blowup that set everything in motion. "I was mad because he woke me up." The row escalated from overturned plants to making good on an old threat. "I've been meaning to call 911 on you for a long time!" That call, she believed, was what placed Kevin's name in the mix as a potential suspect. "It's just so stupid," she said tearfully. "And it's all my fault."

Editing the footage wasn't a priority. When I got around to it, audio levels were fine, but Carol and I showed up as blown-out ghosts.

Lesson for the professor: make sure students at least know the auto setting!

––––––––––

Our department chair encouraged me to attend a conference on the university's dime. I chose Investigative Reporters and Editors 2002 sessions in San Francisco. The organization specialized in deep-dive project reporting, which I'd always valued.

Criminal justice issues turned out to be a hot topic, driven by recent convictions overturned through DNA evidence. When I got back, I drew on the experience and updated my course plans for the fall semester, adding weekly story memos for IR and other advanced reporting classes. Sharing those keeps everyone up to speed, reporters from Chicago and Seattle assured me. Another helpful tip: no more sticky notes! By plugging contact info, interview notes, keywords, and dates into spreadsheets, we'd soon have a searchable database on the Hartman case.

As with many news assignments, I'd paid my own way, turning in receipts when I got back. The college's reimbursement check was cut for $750, less than half of what I'd shelled out, and I'd even split the room with Bob, a quarrelsome freelancer I'd known for years. The assistant dean who signed off on my travel authorization listened patiently, then pointed to one figure among many in the paperwork. That was the college's commitment, he explained. Faculty who *intend to spend more*, as he put it, pursue additional funding. Wasn't that obvious?

Hell, no! Even at the *Villager*, where paychecks often bounced, the boss eventually made good. It was the first time I'd ever been stiffed by an employer.

CHAPTER 4

QUESTIONS STACK UP

Laurel Ford returned from the police station with notes on Detective Ring's interrogation training. Great, I said. "Now call him back and get that on tape."

Tom Delaune still hadn't found the jury list. Story memos from the *Sun Star*'s ace reporter were full of excuses. Case records were poorly kept, one defense attorney had confided. He blamed that on schlepping files back and forth after the trials were relocated to Anchorage.

A police report noting two Salem cigarette butts collected at the crime scene caught Gary Moore's attention. Were those ever tested for DNA? Not necessarily, a crime lab tech told him, but the FPD detectives ought to know for sure.

Laurel ran that question by Ring. There wasn't enough DNA, he told her, adding that he hadn't put much hope in those butts, commonly found on every street corner.

The defense team's private investigator was startled to hear that. Not only had this never come up, Thomas Bole assured Gary Moore, violent offenders were now required to give DNA samples, so those old butts might yet reveal a match. This was one of the few stones that hadn't been turned in this case, the investigator said.

Following up, Gary unearthed a trove of files in the Anchorage court-house we'd never come across before, fifteen hundred copier pages' worth. The records haul included defense and prosecution score sheets on jury selection for the final Hartman trial; those alone yielded sixty names for Tom Delaune's juror hunt.

Eugene Vent's interrogation transcript read like a foreign movie script: intense, dramatic, yet open to interpretation. One could argue that Detective Ring simply kept the drunken youth talking, and damning details piled up. Certainly, he'd taken advantage of the kid's addled drunken state. "I might have given him gum," Eugene conceded at one point, discussing whether his fingerprints might turn up on items collected at the crime scene.

"I hadn't said anything about gum at that point," Ring testified at a pretrial hearing. "We had found gum at the scene. And so that kind of clued me in, maybe this guy was there. Maybe he knows what he's talking about." The detective explained that he'd sketched the crime scene, making a big deal about Eugene's familiarity with it. "Let me draw you a picture and ask you to show me one thing," he'd said. "And at that point," the official transcript noted, "he [Eugene] indicated the, uh, southwest corner of the intersection just off the sidewalk, and he put a little dot there for me."

We'd found a copy of that sketch, complete with "location of victim per [Eugene] Vent," handwritten by that big X.

Yet when we compared the written transcript with the corresponding audio recording Gabe unearthed, Eugene never mentioned John Hartman's location.

Laurel followed up by phone. "It's not that the tape recorder was turned off. It just ran out of tape," Ring assured the student, who captured every word with her little Sony recorder's suction-cup pickup.

DOWN THE STEPS

Marvin's reference to the stressful atmosphere of that old police station jogged my memory. Prior to the 1998 bond election that financed construction of Fairbanks's new public safety building, I took part in a media tour of the old downtown station. The assignment yielded a pair of stories about the woeful conditions in FPD's old HQ.

> The city reportedly isn't happy about the Fairbanks Police Department's preference for drying bloody clothes in bags strung up in a basement utility room, but it's a significant improvement over the method once used. "We used to let the blood drip right on the floor," recalled Assistant Chief James Welch.

That was "Scooter" Welch, and he was still on the job, I told my IR students. "He knew how to feed reporters."

> One of the rooms in the basement served as the town jail, according to our official guide, until a judge ruled that it "possessed conditions shocking to the conscience." That same dark quarters now serve as the male officers' locker room. "You've got one shower, one sink and one toilet for 34 officers," Welch said, standing under support beams added after a portion of the ceiling once gave way.

The takeaway for us, I said, is that the tour offers possible insight on Eugene Vent's state of mind in the hours after his arrest. From what I'd heard, interrogations were conducted in the basement of that old police station, likely in the little rooms located at the bottom of the narrow staircase. The place creeped me out, and I was free to come and go.

LOOKING FOR ARLO

Arlo Olson, twenty years old the year of the murder, had more than a dozen arrests by the time I picked up the chase. Most involved assaults or alcohol-related offenses, often both, according to the Alaska Court System's database. Some were recent, and that was promising. Another search, using VINELink.com, a national inmate locator site, showed Olson currently resided at FCC. Bingo! Visitation opened within the hour. I blasted right over.

The front-counter attendant held my ID, studying the list, then shook her head and handed it back. Olson had just been transferred to Northstar Center, a local halfway house.

The next opening for walk-in visitors there was between 8:00 and 9:00 a.m. Saturday.

The halfway house was on the west side of town. Our place was the opposite direction in Two Rivers, halfway to Chena Hot Springs; that round trip would eat up sixty miles at least. With cooler weather forecast, I'd planned to take the dogs out, pulling our four-wheeler. The route crossed a local farmer's fields continuing through woods to the Yukon Quest trail, likely muddy and rutted this time of year, perfect training conditions! Barring problems, I'd squeeze in long runs Saturday and Sunday, back in time to keep Kate happy through visible progress on the cabin's interior trim. Arlo Olson could wait.

Monday delivered a lesson; he'd just been cut loose.

––––––––––––

When my buddy Jake, an independent mechanic, needs to raise funds, he "shakes the tree," as he puts it, cold-calling regular customers, offering discounted tune-ups and other specials. Riffing off that, I called every Olson listed in Interior Alaska's regional phonebook, old girlfriends named in court documents, anyone likely to be in touch.

Students were seated by the time I backed through the door, juggling a cassette player and new sets of background material. "We have developments," I announced, dumping everything on the classroom's front table. "Just pull up chairs."

They scooted closer, and I hit the Play button.

"This is Arlo Olson," croaked a tired voice, drawing out the syllables. "Who are you? What are all these calls about? You called my mother? My grandfather? What do you want?"

I paused the tape. "Okay," I said. "You all know why we're interested in Arlo. What's this mean?"

"You've found him?" asked Laurel.

"It's better than that."

"Are you sure?" Tom wondered. "He sounds kind of pissed off."

"Don't worry about that," I said, scanning faces. "C'mon, think about it. What does this mean?"

Students shrugged and fidgeted. Even Gary Moore looked unsure.

"What this means," I said, "*is Arlo's going to talk to us!* He opened the conversation. That's a choice."

Weeks passed. Birch leaves danced with every gust of wind till they yellowed, browned, and dropped. Snow again blanketed the wily farmer's moose-bait seeded fields. Our four-wheeler was parked for the season, and I was running dogs hitched to a sled, clearing the mind, leaving engines behind.

Whipping through black spruce, mitts gripping that handlebar, riding those runners in bunny boots, watching dogs bounding ahead, such days are magic. Yet I couldn't outrun a sense of loss: Arlo Olson hadn't called back. And I'd been so sure.

"Ex-boyfriend Faces Charges in Kidnapping," headlined the paper, the second Monday in November. I skimmed the lead; domestic strife was just so common. Then I just about spilled my coffee. "Arlo Olson, 25, broke into his ex-girlfriend's Glasgow Drive apartment, hid and waited for the 24-year-old woman."

He apparently knocked down his ex in front their kids, put a knife to her throat, then took her on a meandering walk along several busy streets in University Park, southwest of campus. The spectacle prompted 911 calls and a tense standoff on a bridge, ending with Olson's surrender.

FAIRBANKS CORRECTIONAL CENTER, MID-NOVEMBER 2002

"You are a big part of this story," I told the unshaven, heavy-lidded Native man seated on the other side of the security glass. "I just want your perspective."

He listened on a handset, hardly uttering a word. I couldn't tell if Arlo Olson was stoned, sedated, or merely wary.

"Well, you think about it," I said finally, promising I'd be back.

On my return, Olson seemed a new man, welcoming questions about those Hartman trials, bragging how hard he prepped for them. "They tried to trip me up," he said at one point. "But I had it down. It was like taking a test," he said, grinning through the visitor's room glass.

After that, I dropped by FCC as often as I could for walk-in visits rather than formal interviews. Seated face-to-face, separated by glass, chatting on phones alongside other cons and visitors, I'd gripe about the rules that prevented me from bringing a pen. "Call my office," I'd urge Arlo Olson on my way out, "so I can take notes."

"To refuse this call, press zero," announced the prison notification system.

"Hey," I said. "It worked for once."

Olson chuckled. He frequently called these days, but unless I was available to hit that button, the prison service blocked him from leaving messages.

The inmate fell silent as I recapped my brief conversation with Franklene, the love of his life and mother of his children.

Kind of wild, but I soon realized I knew her dad, Franklin Madros Sr., through past assignments covering the Iditarod. For years, the tall, merry old Native with the big beaver hat served as the top race official in Kaltag, a key checkpoint. The village offered tall spruce stands for resting dogs and warm cabins for weary mushers, a perfect place to regroup before tackling the windy Bering Sea coast. Over the years, I'd often warmed my hands by the woodstove in Madros's cabin overflowing with kids. Franklene, named for her dad, was the youngest.

"Your clothes were in a bag," I informed Olson, "and Franklene told me she got rid of it. I don't know if that's true or not," I quickly added, sensing his disappointment. "You know? Maybe she's holding them or something. But she sounded cold."

"She didn't say where she chucked them?"

"She said she threw it out," I said. "Maybe it's true. Or she just didn't want to be troubled."

"Did you ask about the watch?" Olson asked, sounding low. We'd discussed that before; it was his grandfather's and apparently meant a lot.

No sugarcoating it. "She said she threw that out too."

Olson knew I intended to write about the case. I'd warned him that unless he expressly told me otherwise, everything we discussed was on the record; I didn't feel compelled to tell him I was taping every word.

There was no telling when Olson might call. When I wasn't set up for taping, I'd quietly hang up as soon as I heard that "inmate calling" notification, giving him incentive to call me back.

Our conversations inevitably circled back to family issues growing up. Olson was the oldest of three. His mother was Athabascan Indian. She and his white father weren't married when he was born at the Tanana hospital. That he even brought this up caught my attention; clearly, he had issues with his dad.

Olson rattled off village schools he'd attended like an old soldier discussing deployments: first grade in Kaltag, four years in Hughes, longer in Nulato. The moves reflected his father's career ascent from rural school-teacher to superintendent of the whole sprawling Yukon-Koyukuk School District.

Named for the pair of big rivers winding through the region, Y-K schools were a world apart from urban educational institutions. Most had a couple dozen students, staffed by a handful of teachers juggling K-12 curriculum. Though few had more than an office or two and a couple classrooms, many had nice gyms where visiting reporters and mushers were generally welcome to use the showers and crash on sleeping bags in the handful of schools located along the Iditarod Trail.

The district's 1994–95 yearbook photo offered a glimpse of what might have been: clean-shaven, bright-eyed young Arlo Olson, wearing a dark suit and tie, leaning forward with his chin resting on his fist, curly hair parted in the middle, flanked by other members of the district's academic decathlon team. What happened to that guy?

It wasn't the escalating family fights, he assured me. His grandma saved him from that. When it really got bad, she arranged for his plane ticket back to Kaltag, where he stayed with her until she died from swift-progressing cancer. After that, everything fell apart.

Our phone conversations followed a pattern: we'd bullshit a while, then I'd circle back to his role in the Hartman case. Take the day after John Hartman's assault: Arlo Olson and his friends were walking near a fast-food outlet when police stopped him. "Hey, are you Conan?" Detective Ring asked, mistaking him for one of Marvin's close friends.

Olson denied it and handed over his ID.

The detective examined it, then said, "We're looking for you too."

"And why were they?" I asked him. Olson said he didn't have the slightest idea.

His heart was really beating, he recalled, referring to another case he had pending at the time: assault charges involving him and his girlfriend, Franklene, then about nineteen, and pregnant with their first child.

We'd heard about it. Gary Moore was chasing down the details. Nothing was available online. The case files were kept in Galena, a village on the Iditarod trail, located 270 air-miles west, with the only courthouse on the Yukon River.

What prompted Detective Ring to approach Arlo Olson in the first place? That was what I wanted to know, and apparently, he did too.

"I was like, fuck," he recalled, "did I miss court? Am I going back to jail?"

"No, no, no," the detective assured him. "Just contact us."

Olson told me he promised he would, then ran and hid.

Police badgered his friends and repeatedly stopped by his grandfather's place, leaving messages. The old man got on him about it. Olson finally walked into the Fairbanks police station and gave a sworn statement identifying Marvin Roberts's little blue Dodge Shadow as the getaway car used by Frankie Dayton's assailants outside Eagles Hall. The same group of four, police soon concluded, attacked Hartman soon after, making Arlo Olson a crucial witness.

He had doubts and didn't want to testify, he assured me. Jeff O'Bryant and Ring knew that. "I told Jeff that I did not want to go on the stand. And that's when he would show me bits and pieces of Eugene's confession. Bits and pieces of George's confession to convince me I was doing the right thing. And it did!"

And Olson didn't mind the perks associated with those trials: they put him up at hotels and gave him pocket money for drinking. He beamed, recounting the day he'd missed a scheduled appearance on the witness stand because he was drunk.

LITERALLY TRUE

Playing sound bites of Olson's rambling claims in class. I reminded students, "We can't trust a word! By his own account, our guy is a born liar."

After the trials wound down, Arlo Olson found himself locked up for boozy scuffles. He told anyone who'd listen that he'd been pressured into testifying in the Hartman case. Word of his complaints reached defense investigator Thomas Bole and George Frese's lawyer, Bob Downes; each visited him in jail. Afterward, both said he confirmed that his testimony was coerced, yet he refused to provide a sworn statement about that. And Olson wouldn't let either visitor tape him.

What did Arlo Olson see gazing down the street from Eagles Hall? That was the big question. Whenever he called, I pressed for more details, recording his response. "I don't doubt you could see a fight, but could you really see—at that distance—the people involved?"

"No," he said, hesitating. "I don't know."

"Yeah?"

"I mean like the clothes," he said confidently. "And their hair and shit like that. But no, I couldn't make out, like, facial features."

"Right."

"And really, it's been so long. It's been, like, three or four years?"

"It's five years," I pointed out.

"I don't even remember a bunch of the assault myself."

"Right," I said, weighing the timing. "The grand jury happens about a week later though. And you were pretty certain about stuff, right?"

"Yeah."

"You have one minute left," blared the jail's automatic warning.

Olson quickly urged me to give Franklene another call.

I gave in, promising to check whether she came across anything she'd overlooked. "So it's not like I'm calling her a liar or anything like that."

"Yeah," agreed Olson, radiating positivity. "I'm pretty sure she just threw it out back."

––––––––––

Gary Moore labored over his final story, convinced it was a bust; he hadn't come across physical evidence placing those boys at the crime scene. Yet thirty-six jurors, weighing charges in three separate trials, all found them guilty. There had to be tangible proof of some kind: prints, blood traces in the getaway car. But all he'd come across were drunken confessions and jailbirds pointing fingers. What was he missing?

Gary wasn't done looking. It occurred to him that Olson may have been pressured into testifying. If so, how? And why?

Marvin Roberts and I stayed in touch through letters and calls. I'd been writing George Frese, Kevin Pease, and Eugene Vent as well, requesting details about their movements that night and the names of anyone they considered worth interviewing.

I closed each letter with a heads-up: "For what it's worth, Arlo Olson tells me he's heard there's a contract out on him. This could be sheer fantasy. But I think it's worth pointing out that you all have more to gain from his good health, leaving room for his memory to improve, than you would from his lasting silence."

Unconfirmed threats weren't something I'd write about for publication, I told students, figuring it was worth discussing. But what if Olson got stabbed or worse, and I hadn't lifted a finger? Not only did this put all four on notice, jailers likely read incoming letters to inmates, and this might prompt officials to better protect Olson themselves.

––––––––––

Students finally tracked down seven jurors from the final trial, the panel that convicted Marvin and Kevin. It seemed school friends left a damning impression.

"Every single person who came up to speak for the defense reeked of disbelief," juror Jamie Smykalski told Tom. He couldn't get over the way some of the kids testifying were grinning and flashing the defendants hand signs from the witness stand. "This Arlo guy," Smykalski added, "is either the world's best liar, in my opinion, or he saw what he saw. He was very convincing."

Another juror echoed that. "The key thing was the eyewitness," Gary Montini told Sharice. "I forget the guy's name, young guy that was out on the steps of the hall. He identified them while they were beating the crap out of some guy." He was talking about Olson, who he described as "courageous" for speaking out against fellow Natives.

He asked Sharice if she'd heard about their experiment. They were wrestling with the verdicts, he recalled, discussing the feasibility of identifying faces from as far away as the witness. They resolved it through a test.

That sounded unusual, but she wasn't clear about the circumstances when we discussed it in class. I urged her to keep asking questions.

"THEY DID WHAT?"

DECEMBER 2002

Climbing the steps to the public radio reporter's Christmas party, I had my fingers crossed, hoping our mutual friend would again attend. He and I'd discussed the Hartman case and my project at this same party a year ago. I badly needed his wisdom now.

Judge Richard Savell needed little persuasion. He and I broke away from the crowd, and I quickly described how Arlo Olson, the crucial witness, now admitted that he was never sure about what he saw that night. The prosecutor pressured him into testifying, in the final trial anyway, threatening him with perjury if he retracted. I had all this on tape. Did we have enough for a new trial?

Judge Savell wasn't sure. He couldn't recall perjury coming up in a similar context. Prosecutors have a lot of leeway, he observed. Honestly, he said, he couldn't offer any opinion.

Deeply disappointed, I plowed ahead, babbling about progress in other areas: our developing in-house case database, recent interviews, what Tom heard about the jury experiment.

Savell stopped me. "They did what?"

"Tested Arlo's vision, I guess," I said, explaining this apparently involved going outside.

"Was the trial judge aware of this? The attorneys? How many jurors were involved?"

I shrugged.

"I'd get my students looking into it," the judge said. "This may have traction."

The next IR class, I reassigned Sharice to work with Tom nailing this down. "Find the other jurors," I told them.

Sharice looked at me, incredulous. "You do know it's almost exam week?" she protested.

"Yeah, but *this matters*."

Savell faxed me a ruling overturning a verdict on similar grounds. That decision cited misconduct by a couple of jurors who looked into aspects of a case outside the courtroom. What my students heard about testing Olson's eyesight appeared far more egregious.

I could hardly sleep thinking about calls to be made and other things to check. We'd stumbled onto something with real-life consequences!

The final class of the semester, Tom and Sharice proudly announced that they'd found another juror who backed up what we'd heard about that little experiment. Jurors left the courthouse and compared their impressions down the street. They had the interview on tape.

That gave us, what? Two sources on the record from a panel of twelve?

"You're both getting an incomplete," I said, leaving them on the hook to work this over the holidays.

Their hunt stretched through January into February. Eventually, Tom Delaune and Sharice Walker tracked down seven of twelve jurors who voted to convict Marvin and Kevin in that last trial, along with the panel's alternate member. Three flat refused to discuss the case at all; the other four confirmed everything we'd heard and more. The experiment happened during deliberations; the entire panel left the courthouse for the express purpose of testing Arlo Olson's credibility.

FIVE Ws AND HOW

No one has the eyesight to make out facial details at two hundred feet away, let alone five hundred, swore Dr. Geoffrey Loftus, an identification researcher, who'd testified as an expert witness for the defense in that final Hartman murder trial. Some jurors had doubts. When Loftus's claim became a sticking point during deliberations, several members of the panel gathered by an Anchorage courthouse window, comparing impressions as they eyeballed people on the sidewalks several floors below. Somebody—we never confirmed who—suggested it might be better to do this down on the sidewalk.

The bailiff who let the panel out of the deliberation room that day assumed the jurors wanted a little fresh air or felt like finishing their lunches outside. "We got permission to go out with the court guard, and we paced off the distance," juror Edmund Habza told Tom Delaune. "Olson's testimony seemed more credible afterward."

Gary Montini, the juror who first mentioned the experiment to Sharice Walker, told her he found the demonstration persuasive though he wears glasses and couldn't really see that far himself. "More than half the people looked down there and said, 'Oh yeah, that's so-and-so.' That convinced me that the guy was telling the truth."

When jurors in that third and final Hartman trial began deliberations in August 1999, no one could predict how long that panel would be out. Judge Benjamin Esch, being from far-off Nome, arranged to handle requests from the jury telephonically. Even questions as simple as "Can we have lunch?" were to be made in writing and relayed to him for swift consideration. Figuring everything was in order, he jumped on a jet.

"What?" barked Judge Esch when I reached him by phone in late February, seeking comment for our breaking story. "That's the first I've heard of anything like that." If this indeed happened, he said, jurors ignored his instruction the opening day of the trial to not read back issues of the newspaper or consult maps.

A pair of former Alaska attorneys general sized up the stakes for readers.

"It's totally improper. I suspect it's grounds for a new trial," declared Charlie Cole, a Fairbanks attorney who'd served as the state's chief lawman under Governor Walter Hickel.

His successor, Bruce Botelho, agreed. "You've got jurors that on their own tried to reconstruct a situation that clearly could not approximate the setting."

The *News-Miner* tentatively agreed to publish the story under my byline, with an endnote explaining UAF Journalism's Hartman Justice Project and the students' investigative efforts. Leaving city editor Rod Boyce editing the piece, I sought comment from the last person I wanted to see.

BEHIND THE GIFT SHOP COUNTER

Evalyn Thomas still worked at Five Aces, the pull-tab parlor where she last saw her youngest son, full of life, angling for snack money along with his childhood friend Chris Stone. Entering the place, I braced for a cold shoulder or worse. Instead, Evalyn greeted me fondly, gushing about the day I proposed to Kate. How romantic! What a gutsy thing I'd done, popping the question on the floor of the capitol like that.

It had been years since that stunt; it touched me Hartman's mom remembered that at all. Voice softening, Evalyn asked whether Kate and I recalled seeing "JG," her little boy, playing behind the Yukon Quest gift shop counter. He used to come straight over from elementary school, she said, and pretty much entertained himself until she got off work.

I remembered that souvenir counter, full of Yukon Quest coffee mugs, bumper stickers, T-shirts, and such. But I didn't recall a kid playing there. Odds were good I walked right by him, a chilling thought.

I promised to ask Kate; she always noticed cute little kids.

Evalyn's expression hardened as I described the jurors' experiment and how our discovery might free Marvin Roberts and Kevin Pease.

After a long pause, she said, "The worst thing about these trials is reliving my son's death. Each time, I go through everything all over again. Do you know what that's like?"

I shook my head.

Gathering herself, she thanked me for the heads-up.

As we continued talking, Evalyn confided that she had her own doubts. She couldn't shake the feeling that her son's friend Chris Stone knew more than he was saying.

I promised to keep her in the loop moving forward.

CHAPTER 5

BREAKING NEWS

EXPERTS: JURORS ERRED IN MURDER CASE

TWO OF FOUR CONVICTED IN TEEN'S BEATING COULD SEEK RETRIAL OVER JURY'S "TEST"

The jurors' experiment, uncovered by an 18-month probe by students at the University of Alaska Fairbanks, goes against longstanding traditions. While such incidents are reviewed on a case-by-case basis, there is a large body of judicial rulings overturning verdicts influenced by research outside the courtroom.

"Bulletproof," declared my Investigative Reporters and Editors friend Gary Cohn, still teaching at the university's Anchorage campus. He compared UAF's jury scoop to one of his big stories in Philly. "Charges were dropped in a week," he recalled, predicting our discovery could have similar impact.

Letter writer Curtis Sommer wasn't so sure. "Ring is investigating the botched investigation! Hmm, isn't that like having the fox investigate a henhouse break-in?" Again, he urged anyone holding back information to come forward. "I do know that Native people in the villages would be grateful," he added. "You know, the same ones the DA told the all-white juries not to trust."

GOLDEN HEART PLAZA, MARCH 18, 2004

Despite a bone-chilling breeze whipping light snow coming down, turnout for the Native community's spring protest looked bigger than ever. Our discovery that Arlo Olson's bullshit influenced jurors had everyone riled up.

Shirley Demientieff led the way. ALASKA NATIVES STANDING UP FOR JUSTICE, proclaimed the tall placard in her right hand. Walking stiffly, she kept her other hand jammed in a pocket of her big loose parka. Heavy coats were today's uniform, zipped up or buttoned tight. The kid proudly keeping pace alongside Shirley was one of the few who didn't bother sealing up. MY BROTHER MARVIN IS INNOCENT, read the sign carried by Little Marv, the inmate's nephew.

After the march, I introduced Marvin's grandmother to my new batch of IR students. The old woman thanked them all for their work and offered to measure me for a pair of skin boots. I thanked her but declined, explaining it wouldn't be appropriate.

TV reporter Darryl Lewis, running solo as usual, hastily positioned his big TV camera on a tripod, hit the Record button, stepped back, and addressed viewers as ranks of protesters advanced behind him. "They say they'll continue to march, lobby, do whatever's necessary until the four men are free," declared D-Lew, T-shirt showing above the zipper of his big black parka, gripping a metal mic bare-handed, ignoring that biting wind.

The full package, aired that night, included an interview with Marvin's white-haired granny. "They offered him a plea bargain, and he wouldn't take it," she declared, frustration apparent yet sweetened by her village lilt. "'Because why should I admit to something,' he'd told her, 'I did not do?'"

Gary Moore and Sean Bledsoe, a gifted videographer, were now collecting credits for their investigative efforts through independent study. The paperwork I filed with the registrar specified "Hartman Justice Project" as the subject area, keeping everybody mindful of the original victim.

Gary called from the Alaska Court of Appeals in Anchorage, truly pumped. He'd found full transcripts of FPD's interrogations. That wasn't all: he and the court clerk's staff stumbled on the infamous footprint exhibit, sitting in a drawer for oversize files! They helped him separate the transparent overlay pages and make a full copy.

Hours later, Gary called back sounding changed, even distraught: That Vent kid admitted everything! He was guilty. Likely, all of them were, as Gary had long feared.

I hadn't read what he had in hand, but I'd heard Gary Cohn, Eric Nalder, and Maurice Possley, three of the best investigative reporters around, warn that claimed confessions aren't always what they seem. What matters is the order in which information first emerged and the source of incriminating disclosures. Did facts about the Hartman murder come from Eugene? Or did interrogators introduce damning details through their questions?

"Let's look at it together when you get back," I told Gary. "The main thing is you've found it."

MAIL CALL

Though details were hard to get because of domestic violence constraints on releasing information, Gary Moore persuaded courthouse staff in Galena, Alaska, to mail us the case file on Arlo Olson's epic blowup with Franklene. Kidnapping and other charges were still playing out.

Meanwhile, I encouraged Olson to seize the opportunity presented by his upcoming sentencing hearing to set the record straight on his Hartman testimony. "You know you weren't sure what you saw," I reminded him whenever he called.

The kidnapping case was unrelated, of course, but it would be a sworn statement to a judge, made under oath in an official setting. I figured that would add weight to whatever came out of Olson's mouth. And it just so happened the judge hearing the case, being familiar with the Hartman angle, might allow it. I hoped so anyway.

The day of Arlo Olson's sentencing, I watched from three rows back in the gallery, waiting to see what happened. Judge Richard Savell held the gavel, gazing down impassively as the squirrely inmate with dark-ringed eyes rose and began his pitch for mercy.

"A few years ago, I testified as the state's key witness in the John Hartman murder case," Olson said.

I could hardly believe my ears. Arlo Olson, coming clean!

"I did what I thought was my civic and patriotic duty," he announced. "Most of all, I did what I thought was right!"

No. No, I realized. This was a pity party.

"No longer am I welcome at Native gatherings, functions, places of work, and homes," Olson whined, urging the judge to consider his special burden. "Jail time imposed on me will be hard and unbearable. I'll have to do it in solitary confinement. I am known by everyone as a rat and as a snitch."

That much was true.

Judge Savell heard him out, then lowered the boom.

"What has changed," he asked, "since the first assault against the female in January 1996? I can't point to anything. No improvement, only escalation, increased frequency, and more of it."

He sentenced Olson to nine years in prison, suspending five years as incentive to reform.

Olson's dad, former Y-K schools superintendent Glenn Olson, rose as the bailiff slipped handcuffs on his son. "God love you," he called softly.

After it was over, I stood up and directly asked Judge Savell for a copy of the state's presentencing report, a confidential summary of the offender's broader history.

"Sure," he said, ignoring the prosecutor's heated protest.

Hardly believing this was happening, I walked right up to the bench. Savell handed over his own copy as the prosecutor stared.

Out in the hallway, I ran into Olson's father, the former school superintendent, and asked him for comment. He quickly refused.

"I'm just trying to understand your son," I said.

That stopped him. "So am I," he said.

That sentencing report proved to be a doozy. Between 1995 and 2000, Arlo Olson racked up seven convictions for assaulting the same unnamed woman. He'd also attacked others who tried to protect her. In 2000, he served time for hitting and choking the mother of his children. The following year, he was jailed for punching a Unalakleet woman. In August 2002, he'd been arrested for drunken driving, the second time within a month. In one of those DWIs, he had two of his young kids with him when he rear-ended the vehicle ahead.

All this preceded his November 2002 kidnapping case.

Any sympathy I might have felt for Arlo Olson died by the time I finished reading the confidential report.

He called me soon afterward. "So what about coming clean?" I demanded.

"I tried something," he croaked, sounding woeful, "but it didn't work."

Meanwhile, police confirmed the entire jury took part in that outdoors experiment. That was good news for Kevin Pease at least. His attorney, Lori Bodwell, was amped discussing his prospects for a new trial.

DIGITAL STORYTELLING

Professor Lisa Drew, a former magazine editor, taught *Extreme Alaska,* the department's capstone online publication class. Under her direction, students from all our tracks—print, photojournalism, television, and multimedia—combined forces, covering a single subject from multiple angles. She asked whether I was interested in partnering in a website focused on John Hartman's murder. Oh yes.

With our multimedia instructor's help, Jade, a slim, creative student with straight brown hair spilling over her shoulders, began developing an interactive graphic based on the notorious Exhibit #30, the footprint. She envisioned creating an interface enabling Extreme's online viewers to flip transparency sections of George's boot tread, comparing how well each matched up with Hartman's bruised face, essentially testing DA O'Bryant's theatrical performance during the first trial.

The online project was ambitious; so was Jade Frank, whose last name reflected her Athabascan heritage. No surprise, she'd done a stellar job profiling a Minto village elder for a previous class, capturing the woman's spirit and beautiful singing voice.

"NOW, THAT COULD WORK!"

APRIL 3, 2004

Marvin Roberts called from Spring Creek Correctional Center in a panic. He was listed for transfer to a prison in the Lower 48; he wouldn't get to see family and friends hardly ever. "Maybe you could tell them you're working on a story."

I tried. No one I talked to in Corrections was the slightest bit impressed by the UAF professor's call. That effectively closed the door on my efforts to arrange lie detector exams. Eugene and George were already incarcerated out of state. Kevin's initial lies about being with a girlfriend during the crucial hours stripped him of credibility. Without Marvin's participation, there was no point.

The next time Investigative Reporting met, I shared Marvin's update.

Mark Evans immediately offered to hit the road and interview both Marvin and Kevin before those transfers went through. It meant one hell of a road trip.

Spring Creek was in Seward, down near the Gulf of Alaska. A quick search pinned the distance just under five hundred road miles, each way.

Mark was a nontraditional student in every respect. A hair salon owner and a family man, closer to my age than any classmate, he'd returned to college with the goal of launching a new career in wildlife management. Being a curious soul, he couldn't resist taking my class. From what he now knew about likely injustice, he didn't intend to let the state get away with this.

A solo trip didn't seem realistic, I warned Mark and the class. Arranging media interviews took a lot of haggling, sometimes official letters. While walk-in visits were a better bet given Marvin's pending transfer, gaining access to a pair of prisoners was more problematic. A stranger with no family or legal association attempting to see both Marvin and Kevin the same day? That could draw flags.

Would it help, Casey Grove asked, if he accompanied Mark?

"Now, that could work!" I said.

Over the years since our encounter at the lumberyard before I started teaching, the kid with the ball cap had proved himself a dogged investigator. His latest project, Last Day, a multimedia website chronicling John Hartman's movements and encounters, reflected the department's new emphasis on digital journalism.

Casey's personal incentives ran deep; he and Hartman were the same age. Both grew up here. The teen's murder still loomed the summer Casey had a scary run-in with a trooper that could have ended far worse. The lawman, in plain clothes and on foot at the time, claimed Casey bumped him with his car in a parking lot. He subsequently chased Casey and his friends down, ordered the teens out of the car at gunpoint, and arrested him for assault.

Casey's mom taught at Howard Luke and knew some of the boys in jail for Hartman's murder. "I don't know what happened," she told him, "but that's why you don't run around Fairbanks at night with your friends making trouble."

When Casey bailed on the planned prison visit, Mark didn't blink. Even after authorities suddenly transferred Marvin Roberts to the Lower 48, it simply doubled his determination to hit the road and interview Kevin Pease.

Mark didn't mind driving solo. He was from California, where a car was part of every plan growing up. He'd once cruised five straight days on a whim. Indeed, he never mentioned it in class, but twice a month, Mark drove to Anchorage, a round trip of some seven hundred miles, checking on one of the hair salons he co-owned with his wife.

He rolled into Spring Creek about 4:00 p.m. that first Saturday of April 2004. Visiting hours stretched till 8:00. All good. The challenge came when he requested a sit-down visit with prisoner Kevin Pease.

"Is your name on his list?" the guard inquired.

"No," Mark said, explaining that there hadn't been time to write and let him know he was coming. Recalling our class discussions, he requested to speak to the shift sergeant. "It's my understanding," he told the sergeant, "that you can tell him I'm here and ask if he's willing to do it."

Visitation rules covered that much; the rest was human nature. Prisoners are generally lonely and curious, he recalled me telling the class, explaining that I'd never been turned away, not on an initial drop-in visit.

That got him in.

And there he was, facing the big, buff inmate with piercing eyes through a booth separated by glass. Mark hurriedly introduced himself, and he and Kevin Pease fist-bumped.

He asked Kevin about an odd encounter we'd heard about involving our lead suspect.

It happened back at FCC, Kevin confirmed. Word had just come down that the murder indictments set aside earlier had been reinstated. Out of the blue, a Fairbanks inmate he certainly knew of walked into his cell, offering to shake hands. "I'm Dale Depue," the guy announced, "and I want to say I'm sorry."

"Get the fuck out of my cell, or I'll kick your ass," Kevin recalled telling him.

Though irritated at the time, Kevin told Mark, he didn't read much into it one way or the other. "If Depue did it, he's kept it real close for a long time," he said, adding that he knew what it was like to be falsely accused.

Now that Marvin was gone, Kevin said he kept to himself. "I try to stay low-key in here. You have to be careful of rats."

While he didn't play basketball anymore because it hurt his legs, Kevin hadn't given up the game entirely; he'd coached the team that recently won the prison floor championship.

Kevin didn't testify in the 1999 trial. Mark asked if he planned to take the witness stand if they got a new trial, as I was predicting. Kevin thought for a while, then said, "I don't think it would be a good idea." His attorney, Lori Bodwell, advised against it when he last had the chance, and he figured the same considerations would apply. "I make a really bad witness," he said sadly. "Because I get mad and sarcastic, and my juvenile record's really bad. If I testify," he added, "the jury will get to hear all that, and they'd want to see me hang."

On the hour, a guard suddenly appeared behind Kevin and promptly escorted him away. Another guard on Mark's side of the glass tapped him on the shoulder, signaling time to go. Mark mentioned there was another guy he'd like to see after coming so far, but he doubted he'd get permission.

Not likely, the guard agreed as he and Mark wound their way toward Spring Creek's exit. After a pause, he added, "Come back at six."

"Why?"

"Shift change," the guard casually mentioned.

Killing time over a beer at a Seward bar, Mark kept replaying that encounter in his head. It was like that guard was saying, "There's a way around this, brother."

Dale Depue stood in the back of the booth, eyeing the stranger warily. He didn't return the visitor's wave and waited until Mark was seated with the phone in hand before approaching.

Like a cornered weasel, observed Mark. He plunged ahead, describing our efforts investigating Hartman's murder. He'd hardly begun with his list of prepared questions when Depue protested that he wasn't even in Alaska at the time. That took Mark by surprise; hadn't a classmate interviewed the woman living at Depue's house that night?

Mark persisted, citing several similarities we'd identified between Hartman's murder and what we'd heard about Chris Stone's beating some two weeks earlier.

That too happened while he was outside the state, Depue insisted.

Mark was flummoxed. Hadn't this come up during the trials? He wondered if Depue feared he'd incriminate himself.

By and by, the inmate loosened up, discussing rumors, joking about his claimed involvement—which he again denied—in the assault on Hartman's younger friend. "I even heard I was supposedly mad at Chris Stone because he was fucking my girlfriend," recalled Depue. "Shit, have you ever seen Chris Stone, man?"

Mark hadn't.

"He's a little pale fat fucker with fuckin' holes punched all over his face. I mean I'm not saying I'm the best-looking guy around, but no girlfriend of mine would ever fuck that face full of holes."

When the interview was over, Mark put his hand on the glass, as he had with Kevin, just being human. Depue failed to acknowledge it.

Mark's story memo on the prison run detailed both encounters, followed by his assessment of the suspects, and concluded with a broader observation about their natures and guilt. "Sociopath fits," he wrote, referring to Depue. "I believe Kevin Pease is innocent of the Hartman murder, but I'm not yet convinced that Dale is guilty of it."

Driving back north, Mark's thoughts returned to the guard's assistance subverting the rules. All boils down to life experience, he decided. He and that guard were kindred spirits perhaps. The guard, like him, came of age at a time when bureaucrats represented the enemy, gatekeepers who got off on stopping others whenever they could.

Probably he was just rummy, but for the first time since returning to school to finish his degree, being the oldest student in every class? That felt like a good thing to Mark Evans.

Whether our jury discovery would benefit Marvin wasn't clear. Though he and Kevin were tried and convicted together, Marvin's final appeal had been briefed, with a hearing date. His attorney, Dick Madson, requested permission to bring up the jury's street experiment during oral arguments, but he hadn't heard back.

When that day came, from where I sat in the gallery, it didn't seem to go well for Marvin's team. His famed defender was barred from even mentioning the panel's unsanctioned vision test, eyeing each other from afar on the street outside the courthouse. Instead, Madson's closing argument compared the state's case to Hans Christian Andersen's "The Emperor's New Clothes." A weak, recycled argument, it seemed to me. By comparison, the prosecutor's calls for conviction echoed like thunder.

Afterward, Lori Bodwell confronted me in the courthouse main lobby, demanding that I turn over our juror interview tapes. I refused. "This isn't a game," she shot back, threatening me with a subpoena.

We countered by publishing full transcripts of the students' juror interviews in the *Sun Star*, along with renowned justice professor David Blurton's assessment of the issue confronting the court. He pointed out that juries are meant to decide cases on the basis of the evidence presented in court.

I also encouraged Sharice and Tom to provide Kevin's lawyer with affidavits describing their reporting steps—if they chose to do so.

Both did. Yet for some reason, Bodwell remained furious with me.

That June, Marvin lost his final appeal; he faced transfer to a private prison out of state at any time. "My family won't be able to visit anymore," he griped when I next visited jail, sounding truly depressed for the first time. He soon brightened up, mentioning he'd be eligible for parole within a year or two. Now that seemed most unlikely. He'd served, what? Six years of that thirty-three-year sentence? But I didn't say anything. Why dash those hopes?

CLOSE SOURCES

Had he survived, John Hartman would be about twenty-two. Students raised in town were old enough to recall the 1997 murder's repercussions, like curfews and tighter security at high schools. Occasionally, local undergrads let me know they had connections to the guys convicted or others involved as witnesses. Most often, this happened following Mass Comm, an entry-level media literacy course satisfying a general elective requirement.

Sessions ran ninety minutes. I seeded our discussions about media's cultural influence by showing memorable TV ads, attention-grabbing film clips, such as Tarzan's jungle cry, along with serious works, such as Frank Capra's Nazi-bashing propaganda films and Leni Riefenstahl's Hitler-boosting *Triumph of the Will*. It always took me a while packing up, and that was where it usually happened: a student, generally white, would tell me they knew John Hartman's friends. Or a Native student would mention they went to school with *those boys* in jail. April, a young pregnant student, stood out in that she seemed to know people on *all sides* of the case.

Mulling over goals for the fall 2004 IR class, it struck me that we were too caught up in old legal battles. We needed to invest more effort interviewing kids who were out and about that night. And this campus was loaded with potential sources.

Drawing on what we'd learned, I began considering what we needed for a website examining holes in the case.

1. **Hartman's last night**
2. **Stone's assault**
3. **Other suspects**
4. **New self-assignment: Mary and the lost pants**

LEARNING CURVES

Teaching frequently reminded me of taking sled dog pups on walks; they want to smell or chew everything, every direction, all at once. A promising Investigative Reporting student went AWOL and ultimately dropped out of school. When he finally resurfaced, he explained that he'd been arrested for DWI and didn't make bail. "I had one free call," he joked, "and I didn't choose you."

Kelsa Shilanski at least left word when she skipped class for a Hawaiian vacation. "What's a gal to do?" she emailed, explaining a friend scored her a fifty-dollar round-trip ticket. I was irked, but what undergrad would pass that up? And such things happened around the bright-eyed, auburn-haired lass from Dillingham, a far-off fishing town north of the Aleutian chain.

Without even asking, school friends named their band KELSA. Her best friend Abbie, a top achiever in every respect, soon joined as piano player. Though she didn't play a lick, it was Kelsa who drew cheers when she joined them onstage, teasing Abbie about her childhood at a commune back east.

Abbie Stillie's father was a nondenominational minister from New England. She was eight when the family moved to Delta Junction, Alaska, a windswept crossroads town known for swaying fields of barley, located on the northern tip of the Al-Can, the state's lone road to the Lower 48.

The preacher's daughter was nervous the day she interviewed our chief suspect's girlfriend. The woman proved helpful. Dale Depue was broke when he left their place the night of Hartman's assault, she told Abbie, yet he came home $160 richer. She was sure of the date because that weekend marked Depue's birthday.

The woman was standing by to testify about that score during one of the Hartman trials, but the judge apparently blocked her from taking the stand. Why? Checking that was next on Abbie's to-do list.

Before his grad school–bound wife dragged him to Alaska, twenty-five-year-old Robinson Duffy, a quiet student with large round glasses and piercing eyes, collected a pile of credits as an English major in Wisconsin. He impressed me in News Writing and really shined as a *Sun Star* reporter, covering theater and arts—when he wasn't digging for answers in the old murder case. He and Abbie joined me interviewing former supermarket employees about Hartman's friend Chris Stone, another person of interest in the case.

The woman who counted nightly receipts in Foodland's high booth assumed they were being robbed, but it was just a boy bursting through the door that night, causing the ruckus. He appeared terrified. This also stuck in her mind: Chris Stone, that was his name, wasn't wearing a coat like you'd expect on a night as cold as that one.

Sheryl DeBoard, the manager on duty at the time, declared she'd never forget the fourteen-year old's startling entrance. Afterward, DeBoard called Stone's mother, then sent him home in a cab. That phone call and other aspects of the incident were documented in the Foodland logbook, she assured us.

I sent our best student cameraman to get the night manager's statement on video. "She threw me out," Dan Urquhart announced on his return. "She said she doesn't know me and will only talk to you."

Though I should have sent Dan right back with orders to apologize, plead, whatever it took to get that interview, I didn't want to risk alienating

Sheryl. Most of our sources were teenagers, Native activists, or lawyers on the defense payroll. Sheryl hailed from Main Street, Fairbanks. Her dad was a red-blooded Republican former state senator; she'd checked me out with him before talking to us.

And I knew Sheryl likely had cause for taking offense. Dan had a quick mouth and liked to use it.

"THEY'RE ALL BABIES!"

"All alibis aren't equal," I often reminded students, Shirley Demientieff, and others who took for granted that I'd chosen sides, fully embracing the innocence claims. The truth is individual timelines had potential gaps, and if the group convicted weren't cruising together with Marvin, all bets were off.

The Alaska Court of Appeals agreed to hear Kevin's challenge on the jury misconduct issue yet denied Marvin's, though the experiment likely tilted the scale against both. Afterward, I sometimes had trouble sleeping, weighing scenarios that held room for his involvement. Nor could we rule out George's participation, considering that foot injury. Stomping a person in the face isn't common, from what I'd read. Indeed, it seemed more like a message. We didn't have the details, but we'd heard that Kevin and Chris Kelly, the victim's oldest brother, were arrested together and locked up as juvenile offenders. What if they had a falling-out?

Passing sentence on Kevin Pease in 1999, Judge Esch had said "it wasn't a matter of whether you'd murder someone but when."

What if our discoveries freed Hartman's actual killer?

No matter how hard she tried, earnest, hardworking Theresa Roark hit dead ends. Feeling she hadn't done enough, she threw herself into mining old yearbooks for clues about relationships. School librarians helped her collect graduation pictures and individual shots of anyone with ties to the Hartman case back through middle school. Reviewing that gallery of faces associated with violence, drugs, and the night's dark events, she was surprised by what leaped out. They're all babies!

LESSONS ON THE ROAD

My thoughts often return to a tempting fare back when I spent nights chasing Manhattan fares in Yellow Cab 4H43.

"Where to?" I asked, pulling away from the curb.

"Florida," said a guy in a foreign accent I couldn't place.

He wasn't joking.

Cab 4H43 was a dented old rust bucket, but its karma was strong. I could have cleared it with the dispatcher. Such fares were legal and legendary. But something about that guy's vibes bothered me. You gotta listen when that happens.

Alas, this seven-hundred-mile fare wasn't on the meter. I was delivering students to the Alaska Press Club's annual conference in Anchorage. Beyond the Native village of Nenana, we pretty much had the Parks Highway to ourselves. I pointed out the abandoned igloo-shaped motel and tourist traps shuttered awaiting the return of Denali Park tourists. The radio fetched nothing but static once we left the park behind; I'd planned for that. "Better than music," I announced, popping in a cassette recording of the "The Case of the Flatted Fifth," an episode from *The Adventures of Harry Nile*.

Before long, the undergrads were as caught up in the radio detective's cases as our own kids on road trips, hanging on every word.

"Okay," I said, pausing playback at a crucial turn. "What's really going on?"

"It's the waitress," blurted Kelsa.

"The bar owner did it," her pal Abbie declared.

Nearing the Mat-Su Valley, I loaded a cassette of an Investigative Reporters and Editors national conference session. "Now we'll hear from the real detective who cracked the Starbucks murder." The recording came from a joint presentation by a DC homicide detective and the *Washington Post* reporter who covered the high-profile case. Students quickly fell silent, caught up in the pair's discussion of the coffee shop customer who gunned down three employees, confessing to other murders in the aftermath.

I paid close attention to my passengers' reactions, watching nods, catching eyes in the rearview mirror, as the detective and reporter touched on investigative considerations we'd covered in class. During the Q and A that followed, eyes widened as they realized that was me describing Eugene Vent's interrogation to the panelists. "What's your department's policy on interrogating drunken suspects?" I asked the famous DC detective. "Let alone an unaccompanied juvenile?"

"I can't believe that was allowed," the lawman said.

On the way back North, we took a detour, pursuing leads on Tony, a self-described "close friend" of Hartman's I'd found elusive to say the least. The one time I'd reached him on the phone, Tony was noncommittal. That number was no longer working. Students and I headed for an address associated with his latest court appearance.

Beware of Dog warned the sign posted on a chain-link fence surrounding the mobile home. The front door was about ten feet inside that fence. Students stood there mutely, taking that warning to heart, waiting to see what the professor would do.

"Anybody home?" I called brightly.

The curtain parted, and the exterior screen door soon rattled. A thin, sharp-featured woman cracked the door just wide enough to scrutinize us. "What do you want?" she demanded.

Abbie was nervous even before a big dark snout appeared by the woman's waist.

Hurriedly, I gave the spiel: UAF professor, these are my students, mentioning our investigation. "I've talked to Tony before," I said. "Would you be his mother?"

The woman folded her arms, frowning. That door was about to shut.

"We're hoping Tony can help settle questions," I added hopefully, "about Chris Stone."

"Oh?" the woman said, softening. "You all looked like Jehovah's Witnesses! C'mon in!" she said, shooing that big dog out of the way. "I always thought Chris knew more than he was saying about JG."

The woman proved to have more suspicions than facts but gave us some leads on Tony Argend's friends. The whole encounter had a bizarre edge, adding a giddy note to our long drive back to Fairbanks.

CHAPTER 6

BACKSTORIES

At this point, our Hartman project had seasonal rhythms: the *News-Miner* published our breaking news stories, and student discoveries were covered in more detail in weekly issues of the UAF *Sun Star*. Multimedia packages, featuring video and audio elements shared through the department's ExtremeAlaska.com website, prompted coverage by interns and staff reporters at KUAC-FM, the university's public radio station.

Emerging details about past events occasionally opened new lines of inquiry, sometimes reshuffling everything.

REWIND: FRIDAY, OCTOBER 10, 1997

Chris Stone, fourteen, began his day smoking meth with EJ Stephens, an older friend, in an apartment across from Lathrop High. By midmorning, Stone, who'd hadn't been to school in the month since he got his ass kicked near an abandoned gold mine outside town, wandered over to the McDonald's across from West Valley High school. That's where Stone chanced to run into his childhood pal John "JG" Hartman, sharing a booth with a girl Stone didn't know.

Her name was Sheva, and she was Hartman's new girlfriend. The young couple had just exchanged gifts celebrating their first month together. Her free period was nearly up, and she soon left.

Had he kept pace, John Hartman would have joined Sheva and other freshmen hustling back before West Valley's next bell. Instead, he'd been held back and was finishing eighth grade through a homeschooling program. Though they seldom hung out these days, he and Chris Stone were old pals; they'd grown up in the same trailer park. After Sheva left, the pair set off together on a somewhat chilly afternoon, roaming downtown on foot.

"Last Day," Casey Grove's online multimedia package, tracked John Hartman's movements and encounters over the final hours before violence struck him down forevermore. Drawing on interviews he and other students collected from schoolmates and friends and a thorough review of court testimony, Casey's investigation heaped doubt on Chris Stone's version of events, from the moment he and Hartman ran into each other at McDonald's that morning.

Stone alone claimed his thin friend Hartman showed up wearing his oversize blue corduroys. Even mentioned how well they fit. Stone claimed he hassled him about it: "Dude, like, you're going to give me those back, right? You know, you better."

From McDonald's, the pair walked to the Fairbanks main public library, then the big mall northeast of town, where they dropped by the pull-tab parlor run by Hartman's mother, Evalyn Thomas, who gave her son five or ten dollars to get something to eat. For a while, the pair hung out with other kids at the mall, according to Stone, grabbing a bite to eat at a different McDonald's.

Sometime after 5:00 p.m., Stone and Hartman caught a ride back across town with Jessica, another friend interviewed for "Last Day." She left them at Noah's Rainbow Inn, an old motel located right below campus. That's where EJ Stephens was babysitting for his uncle that Friday, a gig that quickly turned into a party.

Casey tracked down Trent Muller and others who were at that party at

Noah's. Muller and Hartman were close; they planned to form a band called the Sentinels, riffing on Marvel Comics' mutant-hunting robots. Muller and several others told Casey that Hartman briefly collapsed during that party at Noah's in what looked like a seizure.

When Hartman recovered, Muller and another friend took him outside for a cigarette, urging him to leave with them, Casey reported, explaining the friends feared, "Stone had his friend Hartman on 'a drug cocktail' or 'some mind-control drug.'"

Both recalled Hartman still wore his new camouflage pants.

Interviewed by police later, Stone blamed his friend's collapse on popping Wellbutrin pills. Forensic tests conducted after Hartman's death failed to confirm the presence of specific drugs, reported Casey, citing a disclaimer attached to results: "Specimens must be kept frozen to preserve the stability of this analyte. This specimen was received thawed."

Gary Moore tracked down EJ Stephens, living in Washington state. Interviews with him were short, rushed phone conversations. Hartman wore his new camouflage pants at Noah's, at least when he first arrived, EJ was sure of that. It could be he changed into the baggy blue corduroys during one of the many times he and Stone ducked out of the room.

EJ was pretty sure the pair were drinking somewhere else within the old inn. That was what stuck out, because both smelled of booze every time they came back.

With his mother's help, Abbie tracked down Hartman's friend Tony Argend, who described Chris Stone as a pudgy, younger kid with blue eyes who sometimes dyed his hair blond. Tony said he used to take care of Stone, no more. They had a falling-out over a car accident, resulting in a ridiculous, long-running insurance hassle.

As for our chief suspect? Dale Depue once landed in trouble for pulling a gun on another friend, according to Tony. Though it turned out to be a BB gun, Depue was not someone to mess with, he warned Abbie.

BATTLES AND OPPORTUNITIES

The attorney on the line had helped us before, representing the *Sun Star* without charge when the paper sued the university for video of a politician caught drunk driving on campus. Gaining access to the records should have been a no-brainer, except this arrest had a twist. Sources present at the scene alerted Sharice Walker, the *Sun Star*'s editor at the time, to check the condition of another passenger along for that ride, a line of inquiry that ballooned into a constitutional battle over privacy rights drawing national attention.

"The *Sun Star* not only wanted the audio and video tapes that were recorded by campus police at the scene," reported the Student Press Law Center, explaining we pushed for a precedent-setting agreement setting time limits on releasing information in similar cases.

Alaska's foremost media lawyer, John McKay, was among those urging the student paper to keep fighting. As he saw it, the case facts held promise for a ruling that shielded news outlets from censorship under the Alaska constitution's right to privacy provision.

After a yearlong battle, the student paper's pro bono attorney ultimately negotiated a compromise that opened select records of the politician's arrest, confirming his wife was the woman with him. *Sun Star* editor Robinson Duffy called the ruling a symbolic victory. The truth is we folded. That was my call as faculty advisor. Sharice, a hardworking single mom who'd already graduated, faced potential financial ruin if the paper lost; we never did get that video.

"You know I represent Eugene Vent," the caller now said. "I've been thinking about it, and giving you access to his records is probably the best thing I can do for my client." Eugene's long-running bid to overturn his

1999 conviction had recently landed in the lawyer's lap after a string of previous defenders bowed out. An appellate deadline loomed.

Was I interested? You bet! I recruited Robinson, Abbie, and a few other students. We grabbed the department's copier, several reams of paper, ink cartridges, and trays of blank cassettes, and borrowed an audiotape duplicator from UAF's library. Pilling into cars, we raced to the attorney's office.

The lawyer and I sat side by side on a little bench discussing Eugene's case. Students went through boxed files, bringing over folders that struck them as interesting. The lawyer blacked out addresses, occasionally names. As the pace picked up, he redacted less and less. Some cassette tapes were in folders, some boxed, rubber-banded together, or loosely stacked. I recognized the names of witnesses on some. A few were numbered police dispatch recordings. One set was labeled GRAND JURY.

It felt a little like we were doing something we shouldn't be doing, Robinson said later.

The next day, I called the lawyer back, requesting permission to bring a VCR and copy a motel surveillance video we'd come across and a few other things we missed.

"I guess so," he said, sighing.

TELLTALE GAPS

Most of what Kelsa Shilanski investigated hadn't panned out. Other than showing up for class, she remained one of my least productive Investigative Reporting students ever. I tried her hand at transcribing our growing stack of police interview tapes. Even with a good foot-pedal control, transcribing recordings sucks, so I offered to pay her ten dollars a cassette if she proved any good at it. No can do, Kelsa soon reported back; she'd tried, and the darn cassette was inaudible.

After grades were in, that term Kelsa used—*inaudible*—nagged at my memory. I'd come across something like that in the xeroxed paperwork. Flipping through defense team correspondence now organized in a three-ring binder by another helpful student, I found similar complaints leading up to the Hartman trials.

"Is there a recorded statement by Arlo Olson? In my reviewing, I couldn't find any reference to one. Am I missing anything in this?" Eugene's attorney, Bill Murphree, faxed Lori Bodwell in May 1999.

"Theoretically, tape 165, but it is not audible," Kevin's attorney faxed back. She included a scan of the defense investigator's note.

"There is a tape on Arlo Olson," Thomas Bole wrote, "but it is almost indecipherable."

Olson and I discussed this the next time he called from jail. "I said a beige car," he recalled, describing the day Detective Aaron Ring took him to the garage and showed him a blue car instead. "Then they brought me up and showed me Marvin Roberts's car. Then it was, 'No one else drove that car but Marvin Roberts.' You know? He [Ring] kept saying that. We went through those three or four times before he decided to put it on the record and tape it."

That interview was documented in Ring's page-and-a-half report summarizing his early follow-up efforts. The detective described his initial encounter with the suspects, Frankie Dayton's mugging, Olson's return to Eagles Hall, that party at the Alaskan Motor Inn, followed by Olson's wobbly return to his grandfather's apartment around 4:30 a.m. Fairly detailed, as such reports go.

I dug out our copy of police tape #165 for comparison. Detective Ring and Arlo Olson had barely begun talking when surging static and a loud hum swallowed his words. Skipping back and forth, I came upon a few sections with faint voices. Perhaps something audible could be filtered out; it didn't seem likely.

No wonder Kelsa quit on me.

Those convenient recording gaps caught Bill Murphree's attention.

Eugene's lawyer was a former prosecutor. He couldn't get over the police department's reliance on his young client's drunken confession, absent supporting evidence. That and the apparent indifference toward Stone's lies and self-serving confusion.

Still worked up about it when I reached out, Murphree and Bodwell both agreed to discuss the case with my students.

Murph made quite an impression, cracking jokes, raising his arms to demonstrate how he'd held up those pants found on the victim. Big baggy pants, he pointed out, that didn't come close to matching the notches on John Hartman's belt.

Yet Stone claimed his skinny friend praised the fit of those pants. Beyond absurd! the old lawyer said. And what else, Murph questioned out loud, did that punk leave out of his story?

LOST PANTS DANCE

The last time they saw him, Hartman's mother and several others told us, he wore his new camouflage jacket and matching pants. By the time medics arrived, he still had that jacket but was wearing baggy blue corduroys, much too wide for a young man as slim as John G. Hartman.

Testifying on the witness stand, giving depositions, and in other official settings, Chris Stone swore again and again that Hartman already wore *his* blue cords when they ran into each other at McDonald's. He even complimented Stone on the fit.

How did Hartman end up wearing Stone's baggy blue pants?

Well, Stone said, he'd left those with a girl named Mary about ten days earlier. Hartman knew her too. That had to be it, he insisted. As for the gal's last name? Stone claimed he'd forgotten it.

Poor suffering Theresa Roark hunted hard for Missing Mary. Yearbooks borrowed from Fairbanks-area students attending UAF yielded dozens of

Mary candidates, along with Marians, Marias, a Merilee, Marygrace, and Ann-Marie. Where to begin?

In hopes of at least narrowing the interview pool, I reached out to a local businessman with many interests. Mike Young had recently acquired Noah's Rainbow Inn, an infamous motel below campus, where Hartman and EJ Stephens supposedly spent a couple hours babysitting the night of Hartman's assault.

Mike was intrigued as I explained our interest in tracking down Mary No-Last-Name, a gal who may have even lived at Noah's back then.

If anyone knew her, it would be Corazon, the motel owner said, a former maid he now had managing the place.

Fresh paint and the new name—College Inn—hadn't changed Noah's clientele and worn hallways. Mike sat in on my meeting with Corazon. I'd hardly begun when both agreed this had to be a former tenant named Mary, who'd been the center of every party, likely involved in drug deals as well, possibly even prostitution.

That seemed like a stretch. Hartman was barely fifteen, I reminded them.

Well then, Mike said, that likely involved Mary's daughter.

Again, Corazon agreed.

The young lady apparently ran wild at the time. And even if it wasn't her, they assured me, that girl would know the other teens hanging out at Noah's back then. The family was still in the area, according to Mike; there was no mistaking her old gray VW bus, and he'd recently seen it south of town near Ester. There was more: Corazon readily identified the guys living on either side of that room where EJ Stephens's babysitting gig turned into a party spiced by teens popping pills.

These fresh leads exceeded my expectations. I hadn't ever pictured Noah's Rainbow Inn as a place with long-term clientele. It was a long shot, but I had to ask: Was there any chance a pair of pants, camouflage pattern, new at the time, might be sitting unclaimed in the motel's basement or storage locker? Mike smiled, perhaps recalling all those letters to the editor referring to Hartman's unexplained pants change. "We'll keep an eye out," he said kindly. "But abandoned property is generally tossed within a week."

———————

IR CLASS HANDOUT: APPLYING OUR TOOLS, TECHNIQUES
Court files tell us Mary Bigocci is now using the name Dupo, which is possibly her maiden name. In a 2003 collection suit over a trailer park squabble, the paperwork in the case noted that one Hal A. Brown signed an IOU guaranteeing Mary's debts.

Brown's cabin looked lived in but not recently, judging from little snowdrifts covering parts of the front landing. A burning light and radio blaring uncomfortably loudly inside did nothing to change my mind. I knocked on the door. Nothing. Likely the residence of a slope worker, commercial fisherman, hunting camp employee—someone out of town for extended periods.

I tested the latch. It was unlocked. And that gave me real pause. Who dials up the radio to discourage prowlers but doesn't bother locking the door? Could be an ill-fitting door that doesn't lock. Or maybe the place had been broken into so many times, the owner no longer bothered. Gripping the handle, I fingered the latch, hesitating. That loud radio creeped me out. Recalling a story involving a shotgun set to welcome intruders deemed to have received fair warning, I went looking for a long stick.

It was a single-room cabin equipped with a woodstove, refrigerator, folding card table, and a built-in counter with a sink and plumbing holes but no faucet. A "dry cabin," Alaskans call it. If you are away a lot and don't have dependable heating, water is more trouble than it's worth. Pipes, jugs, Coca-Cola bottles, pop cans, anything full of liquid exposed to cold invited hassles. I once returned home from an assignment to find my dry cabin splattered with ketchup!

Several coats hung on wall pegs. I considered checking pockets but didn't. The only copy of the newspaper was a month old. I quickly flipped through a couple of envelopes on the counter. None were addressed to a Mary or familiar last name.

A wooden ladder offered access to a loft. I'd pushed my luck far enough and left without exploring that. On the way home, I swung by Ivory Jacks, where I ran the names past Joni Ellsworth, one of the bar's longtime owners. She drew a blank but suggested that I talk to Richard Hall, the landlord for many similar plywood palaces, as she put it. The name struck a bell: most everyone living in Goldstream, Alaska, followed Animal Control's ongoing efforts to muzzle Hall's four-hundred-plus howling dogs.

There was no obvious house. Hall's muddy road wound through heaps of old cars, trucks, and snow-covered god-knows-what. I continued toward what appeared to be a combination shop-residence boasting a huge TV antenna and—the giveaway—smoke wafting from an old sheet-metal chimney.

No one appeared home. I left my card tacked to the door with a note scrawled on the back that I was working on a story about a murder case, please call.

He didn't.

In the morning, I went back. Hall welcomed me. He'd found the note and said he'd been weighing whether any current renters might be linked to a murder. He chuckled, recounting former tenants who'd figured as suspects in various crimes.

Hall remembered Mary all right. She lived in one of his cabins about a year before clearing out this past fall and still owed him eleven months' rent. At one point, the eviction process got heated, he said, and she had the gall to borrow his phone to summon troopers on him! She was short but not little, he said. Kinda stocky, with brownish hair. "And I wouldn't turn my back on her—or you'll be dead," he added, raising his eyebrows.

Mary's daughter didn't attend school regularly, appeared to sleep on the couch for want of any furniture, and generally seemed listless, according to Hall, attributing that to being drugged up or developmentally disabled.

And where could I find them?

One night during the eviction dispute, Hall recalled, Mary and her boyfriend appeared to be stealing appliances from their rental. He'd followed them to the grandparents' house.

I left with the crude directions; a quick tax records check gave me the rest.

No one was home at the apartment, so I left my card with a note to call. Bigocci soon got in touch. She and her daughter were home. I raced right over.

They lived at Noah's Rainbow Inn at the time, sure. And both seemed excited about being associated with the famous murder. They were cooperative, fielding question after question, yet had nothing of substance to offer about Mary, John Hartman, Chris Stone, or anything or anyone relevant. Really, really disappointing.

And sometimes that happens, I told students afterward.

JADE'S VACATION

The lady staffing FCC's front desk knew my face by now and was friendlier than most I encountered when visiting inmates. "Jade really enjoys your class," she said one day.

"You know Jade?"

Jade, I soon learned from her mother, wasn't related to the Frank family in Minto. She was adopted. That last name, her straight, dark brown hair, and slightly almond complexion? I misread everything about her, breaking journalism's cardinal rule: never assume!

Indeed, I soon realized Jade's dad was not only our kids' school bus driver and a local assemblyman, that meant her uncle was former state senator Steve Frank, past chair of the senate finance committee, a big player when Alaska had oil money to burn and one of my go-to sources covering the capitol.

Jade's mom let me know said she and Randy were proud of their daughter's efforts pursuing justice for Hartman and those boys. I heartily agreed.

At this point, only Kevin Pease remained incarcerated in-state. The other three had been transferred to a massive private prison in Arizona, shaving state costs. It just so happened that Jade's family traditionally vacationed in Arizona every spring, inviting a special assignment.

This time, old contacts in the Alaska corrections commissioner's office put in a good word, and we received permission for Jade to interview Marvin, Eugene, and George down at Florence Correctional Center. "I anticipate Frank will be bringing a camera, two handheld recorders, and a notebook," I wrote the warden, "for what I hope are individual face-to-face interviews. Each of these sessions should take no longer than twenty to forty minutes. Her first preference would be to conduct these interviews on Monday, March 22."

I don't know if it made any difference, but I pointed out her special training. "FYI, this student's mother works at Fairbanks Correctional Center. Her mom and I have both discussed with Jade how she ought to dress and conduct herself."

The motel in Arizona really gave Jade the creeps. That morning, she embraced daylight like a cherished old friend.

The Florence prison receptionist greeted her with a smile. Alas, the public information officer was off that day; no one had mentioned prearranged interviews, let alone by a student. Jade stood her ground, pointing out how far she'd come, insisting she was cleared for one-on-one interviews with all three Alaska prisoners—in a quiet room!

She got 'em!

FLORENCE, AZ, MARCH 22, 2004

Jade met with the three prisoners from Alaska one at a time, video recording each session with her smart phone. Each time, she began by asking those boys whether they knew Hartman or his brothers. None did.

What about our chief suspect?

"Dale?" George Frese said. "Never knew him before. I met him when he came to jail."

"And what are your feelings toward him?"

"I don't like him. That's about it."

"Do you feel he possibly killed Hartman?"

"I don't know," George said. "I don't know."

Marvin Roberts shared a story from an encounter back in Seward.

"You know they think I did that murder," Depue had crossed the yard to tell him, referring to an accusatory letter the *News-Miner* published back home. "I didn't do that murder," he insisted.

"I didn't say nothing," Marvin told Jade. "I just looked at him and said, 'Oh well.' And he said, 'See you later, Marvin.' And that was it. That was the gist of the whole conversation."

"So," she asked, "do you have any anger toward him at all?"

"Until there's some really solid proof. I don't have no anger at him. 'Cause I can see how people might think he did it, *but people think I did it*," he pointed out. "You know? I can't really put the blame on anybody until there is some good solid proof or a confession."

Eugene told Jade he still agonized about where he was that night, who he was with, and how he got places. Though adamant that he'd never had a gun, what he did during the hours that mattered? That remained a blur. "There was a point like after the Eagles Hall where I kind of went into a little blackout," he said. "Then I came out of it at the Alaskan Motor Inn, Eagles Hall, probably like five minutes, ten minutes, but that's like three a.m., after the dance closed."

The youngest of the Alaskans, now twenty-four, seemed homesick. He really missed his little brothers and sisters, he told Jade, and they didn't understand why he couldn't come home. He'd also heard his grandparents weren't doing well. That worried him, and there was nothing he could do.

As for rumors?

Eugene said he'd heard Black guys might be involved. "It was just somebody in Fairbanks talking, like I knew somebody they knew," he recalled. "It was a female, and she said that people were bragging about it on the south side." This was "back in '98," he added. He'd heard nothing more about it since.

Marvin too told Jade there were stories that maybe some Black guys did it. His mom was supposed to pass me a name.

George had a cellmate whose nephew claimed Hartman's friend saw the assault. *Chris Stone should know*, he told Jade. The name Nyrobbie had also been thrown out there.

Marvin and Eugene seemed generally upbeat and optimistic about their chances for early release. George recognized his future was darker, Jade later reported for the department's new *Extreme Alaska* site. "Frese has a 90-plus year sentence for Hartman's murder and an unrelated robbery, which appeared to depress him greatly. He was very shy, which made me a little uncomfortable, and there was a deep sadness in his eyes." Her final takeaway: "I left the prison with a strange feeling in my stomach. These guys sure didn't seem like murderers. They looked like three young Native guys from Fairbanks, guys who easily could have been my friends."

HARTMAN MURDER FILES

The mosquitoes were in seasonal retreat, along with the evening's roving yellow jackets. Carpenter ants were scouting wall cracks, rotten stumps, and other desirable winter quarters. Dorms, largely empty over summer, readied for the fall invasion.

Extreme Alaska served as an outlet for wide-ranging experiments in digital storytelling. Professor Lisa Drew's whole class contributed to it. The Hartman case section remained Casey Grove's baby. He'd polished his own account of the murder victim's last day. Summaries of all three trials were loaded for viewing. Jade's incredibly detailed "Wild Night" interactive map/timeline finally worked as intended. The last glitch was in the new website's landing page.

The site opened on a squat, black, single-drawer cabinet. Splashed across that front drawer in two decks of tall, bloodred text: THE HARTMAN MURDER FILES.

Topping that cabinet, in smaller type, Casey inserted what newspaper editors call a nut graph, neatly framing the issues for readers unfamiliar with the case.

> **Four young men went to prison for the 1997 murder of Fairbanks teenager John Hartman. No physical evidence put them at the scene. The four, three of whom are Alaska Native, are running out of appeals. Was justice served?**

Casey envisioned that big drawer rolling open when viewers landed on the site, displaying a set of rumpled manila folders, opened by clicking on the subject labels.

- The Accused
- Wild Night
- John Hartman
- Prison Interviews
- Did They Confess?
- The Trials

For weeks, the kid in the ball cap slogged away, rooting out coding errors and software bugs in a cabin with all but useless dial-up internet and no running water. That's right, no running water. Living off campus in a cabin without plumbing, feeding a woodstove for heat? That's practically a rite of passage at University of Alaska Fairbanks. But how many web designers lived this way? In the internet age? Anybody but him? Casey seriously doubted it.

When he finally got that virtual cabinet to open, the sliding-drawer action was agonizingly s-l-o-w. Fuck it. Casey deleted that whole string of buggy code, leaving the drawer sitting open, displaying his clickable subject folders from the get-go.

And that worked fine.

He barely slept and washed before UAF Journalism's new *Hartman Murder Files* site began racking up views and comments, notably a former jailbird's tip concerning a friend's utter panic that night.

"WHEN I'M SCARED TO DEATH"

You need to look at what he told troopers in my case, said Michael Grimes, who'd faced rape charges as a teenager a few months after Hartman's fatal assault. He got in touch with me after viewing the Murder Files site.

With Grimes's help, we got a copy of the old transcript. Chris Stone, by then fifteen, had been arrested for holding the victim's friend in another room. Though he'd duct-taped her arms and brandished a knife, he assured Trooper Lantz Dahlke the girl was just playing along.

"You ever been scared, Chris?" the trooper inquired during that March 1998 session.

"Yes, I have," Stone said. "I've been scared to death. I was scared when I was in jail. I was scared when I got the hell beat out of me. I was scared when my best friend died."

"So, you know what fear's like, right?"

"Yes."

"So," the trooper probed, "do you whimper or whine?"

"Yes, I do."

"Every time?"

"When I'm scared to death, I do," Stone snapped. "I'm not calm. I'm not just sitting there. I'm looking around my shoulder—I am freaking out."

I ran this by Sheryl DeBoard, the manager of the supermarket where Stone's panicked entrance caused such a stir. His description of fear stopped her cold. "That is what Mr. Stone looked and felt like when he walked—no, ran!—through that door," she said. "He was freaked out."

APRIL 29, 2005

An overnight email from another time zone had me scrambling:

Subject: Can I get a complete Copy?

I would very much appreciate a copy from page 1 to the very end of everything on this site. Some pages I'm not able to print out. I'd appreciate this very much.

Thank you

Though unsigned, this particular Yahoo account belonged to Hartman's mother, Evalyn Thomas. Oh, man. She'd moved, and her old email wasn't good anymore. But I hadn't tried that hard to find her before the *Hartman Murder Files* site went live. And the one thing she'd requested was no surprises.

The website wasn't designed with printouts in mind. Given the Flash-coded storytelling components, even copying text looked complicated. I had no idea how to respond until I talked to Casey or Ryan Long, another genius coder.

Within the hour, another email raised the stakes.

HOW DARE YOU SMEAR THIS POOR BOY'S MURDER ALL OVER
THE INTERNET WITHOUT THOUGHT OR PERMISSION FROM HIS
MOTHER! YOU LET THAT BOY REST IN PEACE AND YOU LET HIS
MOTHER LIVE OUT WHAT'S LEFT OF HER LIFE WITH WHATEVER
PEACE SHE CAN FIND!

The writer was just getting warmed up.

AS FAR AS I'M CONCERNED YOU ARE LOWER THAN A BOTTOM
SUCKING FAT FUCKING MAGGOT! IF YOU BELIEVE THAT
THERE'S A HELL, I HOPE THAT YOU BURN THERE PROFESSOR
NOSEYBODY I HAVE MORE RESPECT FOR SHIT-STAINS THAN I
HAVE FOR YOU.
                                     —A WOMAN YOU WOULD RATHER NOT FUCK WITH.

The tone was familiar. Likely, this came from a thin older woman who
seemed ready to take my head off during a recent drop-in visit with one of
Hartman's older brothers.

Robert Kelly was one of the twins, younger than Chris, a year or two
older than John, and very tight with Jesus. Before we even met, his pickup
drew my attention. I couldn't help but smile whenever I encountered that
rolling tribute, covered with ever-expanding, hand-painted Bible references.
When I realized who drove it, I already knew where the owner lived from
his parked prayer.

The day I dropped by and introduced myself, Robert remained wary.
He'd heard that I worked for Native corporations or the lawyers who defended
his little brother's murderers. I assured him my paychecks came solely from
teaching at UAF. These days, *News-Miner* stories published under my name

didn't bring me a dime. Just trying to answer questions about the case as a public service, I assured him. That's all.

Robert, like his mom, Evalyn Thomas, and older brother, Chris, had his own questions about Hartman's murder. He agreed that Chris Stone's mom, Maggie, likely knew more about her son's movements that night. I suggested that we visit her together. Robert seemed to be warming to the idea when a thin, older woman I took to be a friend of the family got in my face, practically chasing me out the door. Had I referred to the Murder Files website during that visit? Very possibly. That would explain where Hartman's mom heard about it.

I buckled down and knocked out a thousand-word status report, updating Evalyn on everything we'd found to date and still hoped to learn. "At this point, I sincerely believe Marvin's innocent and Chris Stone and likely [his mother] Maggie know what happened."

I let her know she wasn't the only one feeling stressed. "I really don't have time to pursue this. Kate is mad at the time I put into it. We still have the dog team, two boys, and a nine-month-old baby. Yet I can't sleep thinking how screwed up this is. And I'm stubborn. I'm the guy who finishes dog races days after everybody around me quits… Give me an address and I'll send whatever you want."

"I have a PC, a disk would be great," responded Hartman's mom a few hours later, explaining that she'd moved to the East Coast to take care of her own mother since we were last in touch. "I'm sorry, this all upsets me. You knew my son—he was a good kid that did not deserve what happened to him. I do believe Stone has hidden a lot. But I am hurt. Every time it's brought up, I get very upset. Can you blame me?" She closed with a familiar plea. "Though I get upset—keep me informed of stuff like this site—Instead of me finding it out not expecting it—so it turns into shock."

By midafternoon, Casey had a CD-ROM loaded with Extreme's Murder Files stories, videos, and interactive graphics. I let Evalyn know what we were sending her way. On further thought, I forwarded those disturbing emails without comment.

"Sorry about my friend Lisa," Evalyn responded the following day. "She got upset but doesn't know how to control her mouth sometimes. She was actually very close to my son and Chrissy. They helped her pack—move everything—and take care of her kids when she needed help once. My son was a good kid that cared for others. Just—yes—I'd appreciate a heads-up before anything goes public."

By then, the inbox held another blast.

FUCK YOU! YOU weren't there holding a dying boy in your bloody arms while his attacker was getting treated for a busted foot, he got kicking JG's head in.

YOU didn't pick his mother up off the floor when she realized he was dead. YOU didn't hear the confessions before they were tossed out of court. YOU have no right. It's NONE of YOUR business. DO NOT ever email me again you bottom-feeding gutter slug.

CHAPTER 7

VILLAGE DETECTIVES

Skeptics embraced the internet. "This is the seventh year of Marvin's imprisonment for a crime he had nothing to do with. We are determined that it will be the last," declared an unnamed blogger on the home page of a site named the Marvin Roberts Project.

A subsequent post denounced the court's fixation on procedural rules: "Because Marvin's attorney had filed previous action, the court determined that he had used up the one chance allowed under Alaska law." Dismissing that as "game playing and technicalities," the unnamed blogger cheered other developments: "Still, we are extremely happy that Kevin has been granted a new trial. For if the truth is finally told in Kevin's new trial, it will be very difficult for the Alaska legal system to ignore Marvin's innocence."

The *News-Miner's* coverage of Hartman's murder drew the blogger's predictable fire: "Since the articles appearing in that paper were simply recap of what the police wanted the public to believe, the average citizen was left with a wholly erroneous picture."

The Roberts Project posts stretched pages and pages when I printed them out. Though written from a singular perspective, references to setting aside workspace at "the village clinic" and other goals framed this as an organized group effort: "On a practical side we have decided on two wall displays. One will be an enlarged map of the city of Fairbanks on which we plot times and locations of various witnesses. The other will be a true timeline comparing statements of various witnesses."

Several posts faulted areas of police work my students and I also identified as problematic. No surprise in that. Another post, referring to individual assignments, pulled back the curtain on the group's membership: "Christine has made good headway in organizing the documents we have. Kathy has been able to gather specific information from a variety of individuals. Carla has written to the editor of *The Council* [the Tanana Chiefs Conference's broadly circulated newsletter] and will continue to post updates on the website. Curtis has submitted another Letter to the Editor."

Of course, Curtis Sommer would be involved! Reading further, so it seemed, was I destined to be: "We will also request that Brian O'Donoghue share with us the information gathered by his students."

The dean, an anthropology professor, picked up the tab for my plane ticket to Tanana, traditional home of the Roberts family, Marvin included, before his parents divorced.

Gazing down on endless green tundra, patches of trees, shimmering ponds, and a braided, muddy-brown river, it felt like the 130-mile flight had barely begun when the plane banked hard over the Yukon River, bringing a small grid of streets into view.

I wondered if Marvin was among the kids watching the visiting reporter fifteen years ago, hunched over a laptop in the village school gym. The assignment was Denakkanaaga, a Native elders conference. That 1989 gathering promised to be bigger than most because it coincided with a festival called Nuchalawoyya, better known as Nuch, the Athabascan term for two rivers meeting, a description that literally applied to the village overlooking a namesake tributary's junction with the mighty Yukon.

That two-day elders' meeting was informal; participants pulled chairs into a circle and shared their concerns, opening their hearts about many things. That year's big topic was alcoholism and other forms of substance abuse ravaging Native families. The testimonies came with a lot of tears.

Here's where it got newsworthy: leaders of three big Native organizations flew in together on Denakkanaaga's final day. The executives, all men in pressed suits, took seats on the school gym's stage, folded their arms, and settled in. One began summarizing current operations at his Native corporation's oil field and construction subsidiaries.

A big white-haired lady cut him off. "Everybody is talking about it, but no one is saying anything," declared Hannah Solomon, slowly rising from her chair. "So I will." The elder from Fort Yukon chastised the bigwigs for coming so late. "We say we want the young people to follow us," declared Solomon in a tone likely familiar to her dozen kids, forty-six grandchildren, and twenty-seven great-grandchildren. "This is not the way to lead them!" she declared, then turned and addressed fellow elders. "They should have been here to hear what those kids are saying!"

As other elders vented in a similar vein, all three big-shot Native corporation leaders hung their heads.

After dark, guitars were uncased, fiddlers began tuning up, and chairs were cleared away for dancing. Locals pulled the corporate executives and other visiting dignitaries onto the dance floor.

Gray-haired women pestered the visiting reporter to find a girl and join in. I politely declined; the News-Miner was holding space for what I'd convinced the editor was an important story. That 1989 assignment offered an early glimpse of the growing disconnect between Alaska's profit-centered Native boardrooms and rural shareholders struggling to uphold values beyond spreadsheets.

Reviewing that Denakkanaaga clip delivered a surprise. "The day's spiritual feast was matched by the evening's bountiful potlatch. Tanana's Curtis Sommer ladled out generous servings from three washtubs of moose soup." I hadn't realized he and I had crossed paths before those letters questioning the convictions.

WAR ROOM

Down in the village clinic basement, a half dozen locals were seated lining both sides of a brown folding table heaped with printouts, Doritos, and other chips in close reach.

Pinned to the wall by the entrance was a photo of Marvin leaning on the hood of his little car. A map of downtown Fairbanks was posted right under it. The place felt like a war room.

As I introduced myself, a muscular Native man in need of a shave emerged from a side office to listen. That was Curtis. Soon I was the one taking notes.

"Pongee," a woman said, prodding a hefty man sporting farmers overalls and curly gray hair. "Tell him about the window."

Arlo Olson testified that he saw Marvin cruising with Kevin, Eugene, and George twice that night. He claimed that during the first encounter, an hour or more before Hartman's assault, Marvin pulled over near Eagles Hall, leaving his engine running, and George, seated in the back seat, offered to sell Olson cocaine.

"He [Olson] said George leaned out that window," pointed out Pongee, eyes wide, letting that sink in. "How do you do that if that window don't open?"

Others gestured at the picture on the wall, showing the rear windows on Marvin's little hatchback model Dodge Shadow were fixed in place.

Could police, prosecutors, and all the lawyers over so many, many years have missed that? Sensing my skepticism, a big woman sitting nearby flipped through a binder and showed me Olson's sworn statement in the trial transcript.

"George leaned out the passenger side window and asked if I wanted to get high," Arlo Olson testified that day. During another appearance on the witness stand, he said, "He was kind of leaning up through the window."

My students and I missed this entirely.

Racism drove those verdicts! That was the Tanana village detectives' consensus. Notebook open, I asked for specific examples.

"Has anyone told you what Jeff O'Bryant said about Spartacus?"

Carla Klooster, a non-Native employee of the council and twenty-five-year Tanana resident, reached for a note pad and jotted down apparent homework: "Page 3145, line 17," referring to the Roberts-Pease trial transcript.

Marvin and Kevin stood trial together. The proceedings consumed the better part of July and August 1999, marked by testimony from more witnesses than the previous two trials combined. Thanks to Gary Moore's painstaking efforts on the courthouse copying machine, we had a hard copy of that transcript, filling half a dozen extra-wide, three-ring binders.

Klooster's page reference took me to a pivotal moment in prosecutor Jeff O'Bryant's closing argument in that final trial. "Mr. Roberts has got some problems with his alibi. He can't be in all those places at once," the DA reasoned, then took a Hollywood leap. "It reminded me of the movie where the Romans have a bunch of prisoners, slaves, and there's an uprising amongst the slaves because of the conditions. And the leader of the uprising, apparently, was Spartacus. When the Romans came looking for him, other slaves began standing up," as O'Bryant put it, "much like the alibi witnesses here. 'I am Spartacus,' the person behind him, 'I am Spartacus,' the person behind him, 'I am Spartacus,' 20 or 30 people said 'I am Spartacus!'"

"I am your alibi," the prosecutor continued, "because you gave me a ride to Goebel's. No, I am your alibi because you went to the store for pop. No, I am your alibi because we danced and on and on. That's the story that came to mind."

He'd borrowed from a scene in director Stanley Kubrick's 1960 Oscar-winning movie named for the Roman slave rebellion leader. Over the years, that cry, "I am Spartacus!" became an enduring American cultural reference, repeated in many popular works as well as scholarly essays over the years. My quick survey indicated the slaves' self-sacrifice is most often held up as embodying loyalty to one's leader or champion.

The prosecutor's theatrical argument for convictions in 1999 was taken differently in Tanana, observed Klooster in a follow-up interview. "It's basically saying the loyalty stems from cultural identity; that one Native will back up another Native." She called that "ridiculous," citing her experience as an outsider observing village life, "because it's absolutely not reflective of Native culture. Natives don't back up other Natives just because they're Native."

When the opportunity arose years later, I ran Klooster's comment by O'Bryant. He declined to discuss that 1999 slave-rebellion closing argument.

ANY HUNTER KNOWS BETTER

Before leaving Tanana that summer day, I sought out Marvin's father. Directions were simple: Just look for the house down near the water with two river boats hauled up.

Gerry Roberts, a tall, thin Athabascan with long dark hair, invited me inside. After he and Hazel broke up, Jerry remarried and had several younger kids. That complicated matters when Marvin returned to the village as a teenager, fleeing his mother's drinking.

For a while, Marvin ended up living with his aunt Kathy, who I'd just been talking to over at the clinic. That whole year was awkward, Jerry acknowledged. It wasn't until their fall hunting trip, in one of those boats resting in the tall grass outside, that he and his oldest son really got to talk.

Curtis Sommer turned out to be Jerry's best friend. They attended those trials together, all three of them. The outcome would have been different with a true "jury of peers," insisted Marvin's father, making a point I'd never heard concerning Arlo Olson's credibility.

With or without a scope, Jerry reasoned, any hunter who has squinted down a rifle barrel at twilight, trying to determine if he's looking at a legal bull, knows the absurdity. "Five hundred feet is a long way to see moose too, you know?" he said. "Somebody you could recognize?" Jurors from a village—white or Native—*would know better* than to believe Arlo Olson, declared Marvin's dad.

When I got the chance, I ran the villager's argument by a guy particularly qualified to assess that hunting angle and probability. "There's no damn way," declared Virgil Umphenour, a prominent hunting guide and decorated Vietnam-era sniper. "That's about 160 yards," he said, inviting comparison with Alaska's hunting standard for taking moose with antlers less than fifty inches wide. "For it to be legal in most areas, you've got to have three or four brow points," Virgil explained. "Those points or tines can be hard to discern," he said, "even with a scope in good light."

And eyesight wasn't the only consideration weighing Olson's claims, Virgil pointed out. "A person who is not impaired," he quipped, "and *he was impaired* at the time."

That wasn't all: O'Bryant later blocked Olson from testifying on what some would call a less serious matter impacting Interior Fish, Virgil's one-stop buying, processing, and marketing outlet for salmon, white fish, and other species netted throughout the region. It had to do with what Virgil characterized as a hatchery fraud down in Prince William Sound involving nightshift employees grinding up and dumping hundreds of thousands of pounds of salmon daily while keeping the valuable eggs.

Kelsa later dug into this, tracking down the Kaltag man who first tipped off troopers. The guy confirmed that Olson, then night manager of the hatchery, was the inside source regarding his employer's wasteful scheme. All this played out after the Hartman trials.

What galled Virgil was O'Bryant's refusal to prosecute. The DA informed him he didn't consider Olson credible!

"I've got that in a letter somewhere," Virgil muttered.

I'd asked Hartman's mom if she could put us in touch with Sheva, his most recent girlfriend. "Last I heard she was living in Anchorage," Thomas wrote, then veered straight into the twilight zone. "We both had the same dream for weeks haunting us right after JG was killed. The dream was that we were standing behind Chris Stone in the bushes across the field—like hiding—and *watching Chris watch* JG getting beat up because of something Chris had done. Who knows with dreams, but it still makes me curious that 2 of us had the exact same dream. Thanks for the tape and I will let you know what I think when I get up the guts to watch the whole thing."

"Most of what's on that disk shouldn't surprise you," I wrote back. "There's a decent profile of JG called, 'A Good Kid,' that you might even like, though I'm certain it's full of holes and doesn't do him justice. If there are other people to talk to for that let me know."

COURTHOUSE RUNS

Most semesters, I hauled News Writing students down to the courthouse at least once. If the clerk's office wasn't busy, I'd spend time bringing them up to speed on what we might find or hoped to learn through backgrounding new individuals of interest or updating files of known offenders' logs associated with the Hartman case. When the place was crowded, I simply handed out case numbers and pointed students toward the service windows.

The clerks at Rabinowitz Courthouse knew my routine. One or two remembered me from the *News-Miner*; generally, most went out of their way to be helpful and often commented that my students offered a welcome break from impatient attorneys, drivers fuming over tickets, poor souls caught up in divorce proceedings, and other legal hassles.

I'd look over students' shoulders as they reviewed file folders or microfilm, handing out quarters when we came across pages worth copying. On our way out, I'd reconvene the class in the lobby and quickly go through their printouts, summarizing what these documents signified in relation to Hartman's murder.

First and foremost, files gave us relationships and phone numbers. Who assaulted whom? Over what? What were the names of others riding in the car? How can we get in touch? If an individual had been picked up recently or had a hearing coming up? Bingo! We knew where to find them. And if charges melted away in what appeared to be a strong case, say, a guy pinched holding illegal drugs? That, I'd point out, likely reflected a deal or a snitch. Something unusual anyway. Worth flagging!

Students generally found courthouse runs empowering.

Truth can also hurt. If you really care about somebody, I warned, be prepared for what you might find checking the person's case records. That hit home when one of my aspiring world changers returned to the courthouse on her own and looked up her parents' divorce.

REWIND: JULY 16, 2004

"I'm your basic criminal type," declared Hartman's oldest brother Chris Kelly, a.k.a. Sean, grinning through the security glass at FCC.

School was out. Fairbanks had settled into bright blazing-hot days and sleepless nights, typical of interior Alaska summer. I'd tried to visit Kelly before only to be turned away for wearing shorts.

Kelly had reddish curly hair and skull-comic tattoos, and he seemed far more upbeat than I would have guessed listening to his 1998 police interview tape, part of that trove of material we scored from Eugene's attorney. Of course, back in January 1998, Sean Kelly had cause for despair: not only had he blown off a warning his brother might be in trouble at Noah's, but he also dwelled on the possibility a drug dealer he'd ripped off may have gone after his little brother in retaliation.

Detectives didn't follow up on any of that, I told Kelly. And there was no indication that police spent much effort looking into Chris Stone's beating. Eugene's sleepy apology at the jail, the one Kelly told police about, appeared to be the main thing case investigators were excited about.

He cheered up reminiscing about his little brother. "JG, he was kind of my favorite," Kelly said. Though seven years apart in age, he said they bonded over comic books. "I'd be over at someone's house and trade a lid of pot for a pile of comics and give them to JG."

I left FCC with a better sense of the victim and a fresh lead on the woman who called Kelly that night, warning that Hartman was in over his head at Noah's. "Her last name is Perrier," he said, "like the water."

We plugged the brand name into Motznik. No hits from the reliable database. We tried other search tools and directories; there wasn't a match in all of Alaska. Complete dead end.

A full year later, the paper's crime blotter noted the arrest of a young man with the last name Peryea. Conceivably that *might* be pronounced like the fancy water. A records check identified a pair of women with that last name, about the right age, apparently living in town. Their initial address proved to be a dead end, but we located a property down the highway associated with the women's mother. No phone number matched up.

Racing seventy-five miles, I located the property and a cabin.

No one was home. I left a message on the door. Liann Peryea soon called! She confirmed she and her youngest sister lived at Noah's Rainbow Inn back in 1997. In those days, she said, the motel was "not a great place for anyone to be hanging around." She was "pretty sure" she'd been the one who called Sean Kelly after running into Hartman there. "People usually like to look out for their little brothers," as she put it. Beyond that, she saw little point in dwelling on it. Anything that could have been done should have been done that night.

HOW FAR IS TOO FAR?

EAGLES HALL, OCTOBER 11, 2005

Ninety minutes past midnight on the eighth anniversary of Hartman's fatal beating, current IR students and volunteers from my other classes gathered downtown across from the big log cabin tourism center.

I divided everybody into two groups and explained Amy's role in directing tonight's reenactment. When everyone had a general understanding of the plan, I presented tall, curly-haired Brandon with the walking wheel, a long-handled measuring tool purchased for the occasion. From there, we all headed to Eagles Hall, the starting point for tonight's field test.

Inspiration for this came from a Minnesota journalist's presentation at the Denver 2004 conference of Investigative Reporters and Editors. "When you get stuck," *Star Tribune* reporter Paul McEnroe had advised, "go back to the emotional center." He'd been digging into Minnesota programs for individuals with intellectual disabilities. The sheer depth of institutional neglect he'd come across felt overwhelming. Where to even begin telling such a story?

Walking the grounds of what was officially known as a state home for "retarded children," he found himself passing through what he realized was a cemetery, though the markers only had numbers. Children buried there were stripped of the most basic form of personal identity, which he confirmed through a records request yielding their names.

When the time came to write, McEnroe said, it wasn't until he went back and stood in that graveyard that he found the words.

Tonight, Brandon Seifert set off with high-stepping flourish, pushing that walking wheel measuring tool across the Eagles Hall parking lot toward the approximate spot where Frankie Dayton was jumped. Robinson Duffy paced alongside, headlamp beam trained on the advancing roller dial, calling off distance. Dayton's stand-in followed, along with tonight's crew of jolly muggers.

Amy Hanson, Heather Taggard, and several other observers I could count on not to goof around remained with me, watching from under the hall's red-canopied staircase, the same place Arlo Olson swore he happened to be that night in 1997.

Exactly 550 feet away, Brandon and Robinson halted. They'd just passed the building named for Native elder Poldine Carlo. That matched Frankie Dayton's description of the place where he was jumped from behind, landing belly down on the pavement, where he never got a good look at the guys who plucked his wallet from a back pocket, raced to a nearby car, and fled.

We were here testing Arlo Olson's version of events the night of Hartman's fatal assault. Amy used her cell phone, directing the student playing Frankie to lie down at Brandon's precise mark, backside to the pavement, handing money up.

When everyone was in place, Amy cried, "Action!"

Our victim handed up her wallet, just the way Olson described.

Documenting this, cameras clicked, lenses were swapped, and zooms adjusted, capturing fresh 50-mm, 75-mm, 135-mm, and 200-mm perspectives on Olson's claims.

Next, Amy directed the group down the street to line up behind "Frankie," facing our direction. Again, shutters clicked under red the canopy.

"Okay," I said afterward. "Your eyes are younger than mine. Can anyone see faces?"

Heads, not faces, someone said. Nobody claimed more.

"Amy," I yelled, "tell your boyfriend to swing the car around, aiming his headlights toward 'em."

That left tonight's getaway car virtually blocking the street, spotlighting our assault in progress, as prosecutor Jeff O'Bryant suggested might have happened back in 1997, though no testimony supported it.

"Anyone see faces?" I challenged.

"It's just too far," observed Amy.

Take away Arlo Olson, and the state has no case, the prosecutor said during closing arguments in at least one trial. Did O'Bryant ever stand here himself at night, weighing the possibilities?

Our cheerful muggers and victim remained in place, ready to test Olson's other claim.

"Okay, let's hear it," I said.

Amy gave the cue.

From way down the street, our chorus obliged: "Give me your money, bitch!"

The words carried clearly but faintly.

"Seemed wimpish, didn't it?"

"You could tell what they're saying," a student offered.

"Yeah, but it's quiet tonight," I pointed out. "Picture a band playing inside the hall. We're standing in a crowd here, remember? Amy," I said, "tell them to try again, really shouting this time."

"GIVE US YOUR MONEY, BITCH!"

That was louder, maybe even plausible, we agreed.

Then again, the whole neighborhood was so dead tonight you could hear streetlights humming. How likely was that in 1997 when wedding guests crowded these same steps, cooling off, with that reception in full swing close behind?

———

Demonstrating the use of Vinelink.com, an inmate tracking site, in our computer lab that fall, I had students hunt for Hartman's childhood friend Chris Stone. We quickly located him serving time at a Washington state prison. Further searches showed he'd been convicted of check fraud and would likely be there for a while.

When class wrapped up, I dashed off a letter:

Chris, I'm sure you are sick of everything to do with JG's death. But it's not going to go away. Not the way things stand. Not until the day you fill in the missing pieces about what happened... The way I see it you were scared of somebody. Maybe you still are. It's no way to live.

So, here's my deal for you: I will fly down and interview you anytime, anyplace, and do the best possible job of setting the record straight on what happened.

Overnight, or so it seemed, the mailman delivered an envelope worthy of trumpets.

POSTMARKED: October 20, 2005

BENTON COUNTY CORRECTIONS noted thick black lettering in the upper left corner.

"I think maybe the Lord has set this up for you to help me," wrote Chris Stone, responding to my pitch for help settling questions about what happened that night.

Washington state corrections visitation policy didn't favor visiting professors lacking personal or legal connection with an inmate. Nonetheless, after six months of ongoing correspondence and calls, a guard escorted a tall, lanky, broad-shouldered inmate to my table in the ninety-five-year-old cafeteria within Monroe Correctional. For the moment, we had the place largely to ourselves.

"Just woke up," twenty-two-year-old Chris Stone said sheepishly.

Everything my students and I had learned indicated Stone was either with Hartman when the assault went down or heard something right after parting ways that sent him running for his life. Hartman's mom and his girlfriend had nightmares about it. Though Stone never owned up to it under oath, nothing better explained his panicked dash into the supermarket, running as if he was being chased, shocking night manager Sheryl DeBoard and other employees.

An hour into our interview, I battled panic of another kind. Though Chris Stone seemed earnest, the clock was running, and little added up.

"I doubt things," he said, describing the whole night as blurred. "I mean, I really even doubt that things happened the way from, you know, after we left the hotel. Just everything from when we left the hotel till my mom being in my face waking me up, telling me JG's dead!"

He blamed the memory gaps on the beating he'd received several weeks before Hartman's fatal assault at a mine north of town. "Between the ass whipping I got and those pills," he said, referring to painkillers he took in the aftermath. "Not only had me fucked up that night, but I've been fucked up since." He claimed he even had seizures: "I'm an epileptic. My brain is deteriorating."

The corrections staffer who'd put in a lot of effort on my behalf setting this up let me continue well past our allotted hour. I used every extra second, circling back to Stone's recollections about that party at Noah's, the cab ride after, and his stubborn insistence Hartman never changed pants.

As the interview stretched past ninety minutes, the escort caught my eye. "I think you've got all you're going to get here," she said.

Back at the hotel, I sat on the edge of a perfectly made bed, staring at curtains backlit by the setting sun. Gary Cohn had questioned my interview strategy. "I think you need more than one day," he'd warned. "You'll need to follow up after reviewing your notes."

I'd scoffed. He had no idea of the barriers I'd faced just getting this far as an out-of-state professor with no current media affiliation. Besides, Stone signaled he was determined to unburden himself. Requesting an extra day seemed pointless and expensive. And my ticket was already booked before he and I discussed tactics.

Stone had to know more than he realized; I'd been certain of that going in. Given his willingness to talk, I banked on scoring enough details, even memory fragments, that, combined with all we'd learned, would fill in the picture.

Six years into this, my best shot vanished in muddled fears and self-pity.

"I told you all I know," wrote Stone following my visit. "Maybe there were keys there and we just don't know it. Like I said in the interview, whoever hurt my friend, I want justice to find them—if it hasn't already."

Weeks passed before I could even bring myself to start transcribing the inmate's rambling, apologetic interview. I was relieved to confirm we at least covered this: "How the hell does John wind up in your pants?"

Stone chuckled. "I figured you'd get around to this."

Hartman's mom was infuriated by questions about where and when her son changed into Stone's blue corduroys. "My son also happened to slip in water after I saw him that day," Evalyn Thomas wrote in a 2002 letter to the editor. "One of his friends had a pair of Chris Stone's old pants at her house that she gave to my son, so he had dry pants on. What's the big deal?"

During the Monroe interview, Stone told me he left his new blue corduroys with a girl they both knew sometime around mid to late August 1997. He was sure of the timing; the Tanana Valley State Fair was underway at the time.

"So what was her name?" I asked.

"Mary."

"Mary who?"

"I don't know," said Stone. "Her dad's a cop."

"Her dad's a cop? Was a cop?" I found that hard to believe.

Stone insisted it was true, though it could be the guy retired. For all he knew, Mary's dad might have been a state trooper. "I'm not sure. I just remember him being a cop."

How Stone's pants ended up with this elusive Mary character we hadn't managed to track down offered another twist.

Christine, Hartman's girlfriend that summer, had a plane to catch, and they wanted to give her a memorable send-off, according to Stone. So they gathered at Mary's in advance and changed clothes. "We wore dresses to the airport!" That was what Stone told me, eyes wide, a huge grin spreading.

"You both changed into women's clothes?"

He swore it happened that way.

LOST FLOWERS

WEDNESDAY, APRIL 26, 2006

Though the group locked up for Hartman's murder retained broad support in Fairbanks Native households, other community losses from suicides and women feared kidnapped or worse commanded increasing attention as well. That April, Reverend Shirley Lee focused attention on those community heartbreaks through a ceremony staged along the Cushman Street Bridge.

As noon approached, organizers passed out long-stemmed flowers. When nearby Immaculate Conception Church's clocktower marked noon as usual, tolling a dozen times, Reverend Shirley led the way, tossing a flower off the bridge, paying tribute to a lost loved one. One by one, others followed suit. Some flowers landed on the icy edges of the river. Most were swiftly whipped away in the Chena River's dark, flowing current, carrying hopeful messages to lost souls on a chilly day.

Stone and I remained in touch for several months. I strived to keep correspondence interesting by including copies of the student paper and other articles of interest. Sometimes that triggered censorship. "The *Sun Star* issue they wouldn't let you see had a female body builder on the front cover," I wrote him that May, joking about the dangerous nature of the banned material.

Make good use of your time: that was the general thrust of my letters. I encouraged him to take UAF classes, relaying how-to steps from Monroe's prison education coordinator. "The letter needs to state that you are requesting a school transcript to be sent to a specific address. (I get the impression the coordinator's not going to spend time looking anything up.) So give her the address of UAF admissions, or whatever you decide to apply."

I hoped our correspondence might unlock memories. Stone had asked about the Peryea sisters. I filled him in, then asked if he might have run into them at Noah's that night. "I wondered if maybe the party taking place away from EJ's uncle's room might have involved them?"

And I made a point of reminding Stone that life holds more than the next score, even when it hurts. "I'm hobbling today from my first ever freaking hamstring pull," I wrote. "Got it last night playing driveway softball with my kids. Great way to start the summer."

CHAPTER 8

"WHO SAID THAT?"

REWIND: SPRING 2004

I had a puppy pen to build for our unplanned litter of Alaska huskies. My pregnant wife was anxious to finish the cabin's interior before the baby's arrival. But Dick Madson wanted a face-to-face meeting, very unusual. That was the only reason I put away tools and hit the road for town.

We'd covered Marvin's faltering appeal. My eyes were on the door.

"This probably isn't anything," the old defender began, finally getting to the point. An investigator from Oregon had tipped him that a current inmate at FCC was shopping information about the Hartman case. DA O'Bryant apparently wasn't buying. "The way it was described," Madson said, "is he was there or knows who was and what happened."

He had a name for me: Jason Wallace.

A quick search of Alaska's court database yielded two full pages of cases involving a trio of offenders named Jason Wallace, middle initials varied. Narrowing the search to Fairbanks cases gave me several involving twenty-four-year-old Jason T. Wallace. His most recent court beef involved a civil action filed in Anchorage, likely domestic. Skipping over that one, I saw Jason T. also had an active 2003 criminal case filed here in Fairbanks. The docket link opened with a click. Bingo! Jason T. Wallace, born November

28, 1980, faced a pile of serious charges: first-degree murder, first-degree arson, and three counts of conspiracy.

An internet search flagged "Police: Tacoma Man Confesses," a *News-Miner* story published the first week of January 2003. Details were intense: this Wallace guy murdered a Fairbanks woman with a hammer, then set fire to an apartment complex trying to cover it up. He apparently confessed. All of it figured in a big Fairbanks drug dealer's arrest for several murders Outside, as Alaskans refer to anyplace beyond the forty-ninth state's borders.

I happened to mention the case to our department admin, and it turned out her husband, Mark, a volunteer fireman, took part in battling that intense blaze a few miles southwest of town. Searching online archives turned up vivid accounts of what amounted to a bloody attempted drug-ring takeover and ensuing arrests.

Holy hell! How did I miss this?

Kate later reminded me that we spent that Christmas with my family back in DC.

FAIRBANKS CORRECTIONAL CENTER, MAY 28, 2004

I recognized the slim, handsome Black man from the news photos as he neared the visitor's room. He appeared startled when I waved from the other side of the glass, gesturing toward the stool opposite mine.

Jason Wallace sat down and picked up the phone, studying me without a word.

I hurriedly introduced myself, explaining as I had so many times that I'm a professor at the U, investigating whether guys convicted of an unrelated murder are innocent. Blah blah blah.

The inmate noticeably stiffened when I mentioned I'd heard he might know something about John Hartman's murder, something our district attorney apparently refused to consider.

"Who said that?" Wallace demanded, not loud yet forcefully, repeating the question several times.

As a journalist, I protect my sources, I stressed, and I'd protect him as well. Assuming there was anything to this. And if I wrote a story? Well, that might prod the DA to listen to whatever he had to trade—at least open that conversation anyway.

Wallace leaned back, nodding, occasionally mumbling. After a long pause, I caught the words "may have something to say," followed by "I need to pray on it first."

"Sounds good," I said, striving for calm, feeling anything but. "You do that," I added and signaled the guard I was ready to go. "Pray on it. I'll be back," I assured him, churning within. Clearly, the inmate knew *something* about Hartman's murder.

Visiting hours at the jail varied according to the day of the week, the alphabetical order of the prisoner's last name, and custody status. I missed several early chances, and a full week passed before my next visit.

"Swung by again today," I wrote afterward, documenting both encounters in our case database. "Jason was escorted to the call-window room but hung back. Seeing me, he made a slashing sign across his neck and backed away. I nodded and shrugged."

That second encounter really left me guessing. The window separating prisoners and guests ran the length of both open rooms. If, say, only two or three prisoners had visitors, you could space out for privacy. More often, seating was elbow to elbow, making it hard to avoid catching pieces of nearby conversations. And it could be Wallace didn't want to be seen talking with a skinny, white, bearded dude clad in a plaid shirt and blue jeans, a guy nobody would take for a lawyer.

It wasn't a huge stretch to imagine the guy heard something on the street. Why wouldn't the DA at least listen to whatever he might have to trade?

It happened that I knew Wallace's public defender from past service on a jury. Geoff Wildridge's client beat up a girlfriend in what sounded like a horrible drunken brawl. Both were Native. Each landed their share of blows, bruising, scratching, and generally marking the other up. One huge difference: the client went for the woman's throat.

Most jury members were ready to convict Wildridge's client. I held up the verdict for several days before agreeing to lesser charges. When the defender heard that I'd been the holdout, he got in touch, questioning why I caved.

They probably both should have been charged, I said, but he did choke her. Wildridge seemed ready to retry the case there and then. What you'd want in a defender, I guess.

Again, I reached out, requesting the lawyer's help arranging a jailhouse interview with Wallace, pitching it as a way to get the DA's attention. Though he flat refused, Wildridge held my eyes, then added: *Keep asking questions.*

Dear Jason,

I figure you had a good reason for declining to talk this week. Maybe your lawyer told you not to. Maybe being seen talking to me could cause you problems. Like I say, I figure you had your reasons... You told me you need to pray about what to do. That's always a good place to start. While you're at it, ask yourself what it would mean to free people jailed on a bum rap. Correcting an abuse the powers that be don't want to admit. Why should you care? There's no easy answer. The world is a hard place and tears each of us down if it can. I think there's value in deciding to be a person deserving of respect and settling for no less. Sometimes that means taking a stand against what's wrong.

In a week or two I'll send someone else by to feel you out.

Newscaster Darryl Lewis recalled that big Ester fire right away. He'd never forgotten how the station's radio scanner erupted that morning, all the chatter among fire crews responding to that old row-house blaze. D-Lew grabbed his big TV camera and raced over in time to catch an array of professional and volunteer fire battalions battling the flames. Dramatic stuff. He got video of displaced families standing around shivering. Conditions were brutal! Hell, yeah. Late December in Fairbanks, Alaska!

Back at the station, the TV reporter caught fresh scanner traffic about an arrest underway at Fairbanks airport. D-Lew dashed over with his camera. Recalling how that bust went down, he snorted, wide grin spreading. Get this: Our boy Wallace showed up at the ticket counter, highly agitated, trying to change his ticket for an earlier flight. Happens every day, right?

So what drew attention?

Not only was this anxious traveler scorched, he stank of gasoline! Got arrested on the spot. Choking with laughter at the memory, D-Lew readily agreed to visit Jason Wallace at the jail and see if he'd open up, brother to brother.

I should have seen this coming. Being a TV guy, Darryl applied for a formal sit-down video interview. FCC inmate Jason T. Wallace refused.

MARY'S GUY FRIEND

JULY 27, 2006

Closer reading of my rambling interview with Chris Stone paid off with a name; Mary Reynaga and I arranged to meet on a beautiful July afternoon at a children's playground behind Radio Shack. When we weren't watching her daughter's hesitant advance toward bigger kids playing in the sandbox, Mary shared stories about a coolheaded guy who went out of his way to make her smile.

John Hartman wasn't just funny, he was fun to hang out with. Mutual friends set the young teenagers up about a year before he died. They would have been only thirteen or fourteen at the time. We know someone who'd be great for you, friends assured her. And it proved true.

"He was my best guy friend," as she put it, "and I'd never really had a best guy friend before. He was someone you could trust." She described Hartman as a guy more likely to calm situations than get in anybody's face. "When he did get pissed off, he'd just go sit quietly and steam about it. Then he'd just be done. You know? I never saw him fight anybody. I never heard him say he wanted to fight anybody. He wasn't that type."

That didn't mean Hartman backed away from challenges. If someone said they could do something? He'd say, "I can do it better." She laughed thinking about it.

It wasn't really a boyfriend/girlfriend thing. After Hartman hooked up with Sheva, Mary hardly saw him at all. You know how new couples are.

She and her guy friend last hung out together in early September 1997, spending a whole day chasing dreams at local car dealerships. They discussed getting a Jeep with zipper windows. Or a van with a bed in back so you could, you know, have parties. Maybe an extended-cab Ford truck. They cruised that car lot, picking them out.

Her little girl was circling back from the sandbox. "She just wants me to come play," said Mary Reynaga, smiling as she watched her approach.

I recognized that stage, curious and increasingly self-assertive without being demanding, a tender period that doesn't last long. Her daughter had a couple years on Rachel. Somewhere between the ages of Rory and Robin, the summer Kate and I were the sole customers at the boys' lemonade stand located deep in the woods behind our cabin.

"I'll come play in a second, honey," Mary called. Her daughter paused, looking at us.

"She's pretty good," I said, watching her running toward that pair of potential friends. "Mine would be worse."

"She's actually being really good," Mary agreed.

About those blue corduroys: Mary confirmed the pants were Chris Stone's. JNCO was the brand, she was sure of that, and one of the pockets might have been torn. Stone left them at her house after getting soaked in a water fight, she recalled.

Several weeks later, Hartman happened to mention that he liked corduroys, so she passed them on. He didn't mind the loose fit, she said. "He always wore big clothes."

We were on borrowed time: Mary's little lass had returned. She shared the bench for a bit, then rooted around in the grass. Hurriedly, I recapped what we knew about that party at Noah's, Hartman's bad reaction to whatever pills he'd taken, combined with drinking, and how the Peryea sisters urged Kelly to come get his little brother, warning he was in over his head. He blew off their message that night, then tearfully described it to police that winter.

By then, I pointed out, though lab results on the crime-scene evidence were coming up negative, police and the DA ignored tips about the party at Noah's and anything else that conflicted with the state's case.

Mary wasn't surprised to hear Hartman's older brother feared the assault might have been payback for ripping off a cocaine dealer. John was the exception in that family, she said. All he ever did was smoke pot. He wasn't interested in all that other stuff.

Though he'd been held back in school, that fall, Mary helped Hartman with his math makeup class. For sure, he would have graduated from high school or gotten his GED, she said, and done whatever it took to land a decent job.

EJ Stephens was the one who told her Hartman had died. She didn't believe him because they'd recently broken up and hated each other for a while. Following Hartman's death, she and other friends gathered at the Boys & Girls Club and walked to where he had died, placing candles there. All these years later, that memory made her smile.

The assault still made no sense to her. What did they do? Just stop and ask him for money?

I had to ask: "Any chance Hartman crossed paths with Dale Depue?"

"Yeah," Mary said, "they all hung out at the fair together."

That took me by surprise.

It wasn't just Stone and Stephens who associated with both, she explained. A whole group of friends hung out at the state fair that summer, including other girlfriends and Depue's stepbrother.

Any bad blood between Hartman and Depue?

Not at all, she said. They were all pretty chummy.

Depue's 1999 arrest for stabbing that cab driver to death came as a shock, according to Mary. For a while, that changed perspectives among Hartman's friends. "Everybody said it was Dale," she recalled and gave me the name of a mutual friend I ought to seek out. "He was like, it was Dale, blah blah blah."

"Go play with your daughter," I said, processing it all.

"I think that I will," Mary said, chuckling. "Thank you."

MISSED OPPORTUNITIES

By all accounts, John "JG" Hartman, the youngest child in a hardscrabble family, impressed people as an upbeat, easygoing soul. Mary's testimonial added to that. As far as I was concerned, she'd settled how he ended up changing his pants for the blue corduroys. Stone claimed Hartman already wore those blue corduroys when he showed up at McDonald's earlier that day. I didn't buy it. You gotta go with a mom's account of the last time she saw her baby boy, and Evalyn Thomas never wavered from her fond recollection of Hartman dropping by her pull-tab shop later that day wearing his "birthday suit"—that camouflage-style jacket and pants.

Why and where did Hartman change into Stone's pants?

Detectives Ring, Geier, and Keller, Officer Peggy Sullivan, somebody working the case could have—should have!—nailed that down. All these years later, as Stone put it during that Monroe prison interview: "It's a fog."

Course plans for fall 2006 reflected my intent to publish a definitive series making the case for Marvin Roberts's innocence. The to-do list combined follow-ups and planned multimedia elements.

- Whom did George Frese kick?
- What's the story behind the FPD tactical squad call?
- Convert interview tapes to MP3s for podcast.
- Photograph Calvin Moses at the intersection where he found Hartman.
- Find and interview Jessica Wyman, the driver who gave Hartman and Stone rides to Noah's Rainbow Inn.
- Identify "Hassan," Wyman's (boyfriend?) companion in car.
- Write letters to inmates who might know something, in particular Jason Wallace and Depue's codefendants.
- Scan docs, photos for use on website.
- Background Stone's 2004 forgery case.
- Dupe Hartman news clips, place the folder/binder in reserve at the library for class reference. (This will take a good hour or two.)

Tips kept coming. A rapper known as "Red Dot" was rumored to be mouthing off about Hartman's murder. When the woman who supposedly had heard him brag about it finally called me back, she insisted she had no idea who I was talking about. None. All I had to go on was her voice, though, and I couldn't read anything from that. She stayed on the line with me far longer than I'd expect from someone truly clueless. I hadn't identified my source, of course. Yet right away, I heard from April, my former student with connections on all sides. The woman I talked to was apparently terrified this would get back to the guy she'd denied knowing.

Another lead regarding Red involved a woman I tracked down through her ties with a distant mining camp, down near Wrangell-St. Elias National Park. She too claimed to have no idea who or what I was talking about.

Working for news organizations instills a sense of security. It's wishful thinking maybe, but editors theoretically have your back. Our broadcast professor heard that I was interested in Redd Dott, correcting me on the rapper's nickname, apparently a riff on illuminated gunsights. He knew an investor in Redd's studio and took it upon himself to set up a meeting.

Up until now, our serious suspects were all locked up. Digging into a murder case as an academic suddenly left me feeling exposed. I nixed the meeting and, just in case, prepared a detailed summary of our Hartman Justice Project, pointing out holes in the evidence and problems with Chris Stone's story, listing our alternative suspects, including the rapper. "That's what I'm looking at now," I concluded. "At the risk of sounding melodramatic, I want all this on the record in case my work on this case is interrupted under circumstances inviting suspicion."

Nutball stuff. Feeling foolish, I mailed the letter to the FBI's Anchorage office.

At this point, I had a four-drawer file cabinet stuffed with student story memos and other Hartman case files. Folders on potential suspects and other individuals of interest nearly filled two of those long drawers with no end in sight. Many of these characters were repeat offenders. Recent courthouse trips mostly involved updating individual files, an increasingly frustrating process as paper documents from the closed case were sent away for conversion to microfilm. Backgrounding new suspects, even keeping tabs on repeat offenders, often took months.

Lazily reviewing an updated batch of folders, Dale Depue's ticket for a 1998 traffic stop made me sit up straight. April, the young mother with connections everywhere, was listed as a passenger in Depue's car. She'd seemed so genuine, praising my efforts for those boys, sharing tips. Was she playing us all along?

Shirley Demientieff suffered a stroke. She hadn't died, but her condition reminded me of my dad's final days. By the time I made it home, labor lawyer Patrick C. O'D was hospitalized, bedridden, and struggling to find words. His failed attempts to tell me something the night before he died haunted me still. Native communities throughout the whole region were really going to miss Shirley's constructive badgering and laughter.

I was completely unprepared when I spied her at a Nanook hockey game that fall, beckoning to me between periods. Dashing over, I gently took her hand. She was all bundled up. Her face didn't look quite right. I didn't know what to say.

Leaning forward, the grand old soul rasped, "So what are we doing about the boys?"

We both laughed really hard. Shirley Demientieff hadn't lost her sense of humor or fighting spirit. I began filling her in on the crazy rabbit trails opened by Chris Stone.

She stopped me as I began describing his dramatic Foodland entrance, declaring she too was in the store that night. She'd seen that boy's fearful state. Or thought she had. She shopped there late all the time. Maybe not that night. She really wasn't sure.

She'd never mentioned this before. Not to me. It didn't matter one way or the other. There were plenty of other witnesses to Stone's wild entrance. Her uncertainty: that made me sad. But we hadn't lost her. That was all that mattered.

Shirley Demientieff, fifty-six, died of lung cancer New Year's week 2007.

RALLY AGAINST INJUSTICE, OCTOBER 12, 2007

Approaching noon, Marvin's mom, Hazel, and sister Sharon scrambled getting ready in the parking lot alongside the Tanana Chiefs Conference's new tribal hall, a huge, log-cabin structure perched overlooking the Chena River downtown. Stacks of well-used, handmade protest signs awaited pickup from the Robertses' wide-open trunk. A line of eager takers soon formed, and those signs went fast.

Streaked lettering on old signs reflected past service in all kinds of weather. Newer signs emphasized the timing of today's protest. A DECADE OF INJUSTICE MUST END declared one, the last two words triple underlined. 10 YEARS, NO JUSTICE proclaimed another sign, gripped by a Native man wearing a Doyon Native corporation ball cap.

With students on spring break, I'd brought a ten-year-old helper raised in the shadow of this case. On the way into town, I briefed our oldest son on what to expect: Marvin's mom, maybe his grandmother, and a few others would take turns pleading for justice, followed by a prayer from Reverend Shirley Lee or Father Scott, possibly accompanied by singing. The whole thing wouldn't last longer than lunch hour, I promised, ensuring attendees made it back in time to deliberate and vote on resolutions up for consideration during the Tanana Chiefs Conference's annual meeting.

I happened to mention my interview with Chief Peter John, the man that new tribal hall was named after. Rory's eyes widened hearing that Chief John lived to be over one hundred years old. Our son loved magic, and his eyes grew even wider as I described an encounter with a Native lawmaker in Juneau who'd wondered whether I'd noticed Chief John making clicking sounds when I interviewed him. If so, state Senator Georgiana Lincoln told me, Chief John may have been "casting spells" meant to influence the outcome. "Go back and listen to your tape," she said.

Waiting for things to get started, my attention switched to the tall Native man with loose graying hair stretching past his shoulders slowly making his way toward the protest leaders. Jerry Isaac, a tribal member of a small village closer to Canada than Fairbanks, had recently been thrust into the presidency of the Tanana Chiefs Conference by his predecessor's death. He stopped alongside Reverend Shirley Lee, one of the organizers, and began surveying the crowd, hands dug in pockets of his open brown jacket.

Was Chief Isaac speaking at this protest? If so, that promised to be newsworthy. I handed Rory the family video camera and put him to work. Eyes barely visible under his fat wool hat, he knelt in the snow behind Darryl Lewis, shooting from under the big TV reporter's shoulder camera.

"We call forth and challenge the legal community and the institutions to revisit this case," declared Isaac, citing the prosecutor's use of "question-able evidence" in those Hartman trials. "It is wrong," Isaac declared. "It is inherently wrong to convict on hearsay."

He'd just become the first Native leader of statewide consequence to take a public stand supporting the boys.

When Reverend Shirley Lee's turn came, she talked about time lost to injustice, referencing those new signs. "We asked them to send us a picture and they sent this," she said, holding up a photo showing Kevin and George standing outside, with Marvin and George kneeling in front. "They're still strong young Native men who need to be helped," added Lee, addressing cameramen large and small.

I assumed from the landscape the prisoners were still in Arizona, but I'd lost track. Wherever it was looked hot as hell, even in the shade. All four wore white T-shirts and white shorts. Marvin, smaller than the others, wore shades.

Chief Isaac's stand confirmed what I'd been telling the publisher and anyone else who'd listen down at the *News-Miner*. This case wasn't going away, and the verdicts were a festering wound, undermining Native faith in Alaska's whole justice system. If the town's stodgy paper got behind this, opening eyes throughout the region? That was a potential game changer.

Managing editor Kelly Bostian was in my corner, but it was on me to satisfy city editor Rod Boyce, an editor who enjoyed playing devil's advocate. Bostian figured the scrutiny would temper internal opposition from the guy who first hired me, Dermot Cole, a popular columnist and former editor. Cole put his faith in the jury process and saw nothing to be gained in reopening the case.

He wasn't wrong there.

With Bostian's encouragement, city editor Rod Boyce and I began mapping out a series reexamining the Hartman verdicts, though the paper hadn't committed to publishing a word.

Through spring and summer 2007, emails ricocheted between the newsroom and campus. Most reflected Rod's emphasis on balanced reporting and context. "Indicate that the study of false confessions is an emerging field and that there are people with widely differing views on the subject," he wrote following a morning meeting in late November 2007. "Something I forgot to bring up this morning," he added. "Is it correct to use the word 'interrogation' all the time?" He suggested "questioning" or "interviewing" as alternatives. "Just want to make sure that 'interrogation' is the word you want."

It was. I did.

REWIND: SENTENCING HEARING, FEBRUARY 2, 2007

Nearly four years had passed since that Christmas bloodbath in Ester. The clean-cut, hard-to-read Black inmate I later visited, the wide-eyed guy who kept asking where I got his name, carried himself differently.

Jason T. Wallace, twenty-seven, now wore eyeglasses. A fuzzy little beard jutted from his chin. Sitting alongside his lawyer in the courtroom downtown, he appeared fully engaged, leaning forward to catch every word as the judge and attorneys discussed his fate. When he spoke, it was "Yes, Your Honor," "No, Your Honor."

He'd already pled guilty to murdering a young woman with a hammer, stabbing another friend in the neck with a screwdriver, and torching a row house to cover the tracks, describing it all in detail as required. All that was part of the case record, as was his testimony implicating William Z. Holmes, another member of a Tacoma gang.

As far as the state was concerned, one question remained to be settled: what did Wallace, Teacka Bacote's confessed killer, deserve for his help putting away his drug-ring partner?

The way I saw it, Wallace's undefined association with Hartman's murder mattered more in a real sense since it might have some bearing on the plight of innocent men locked up without evidence. It could be Wallace simply crossed paths with Hartman's muggers that night in 1997 or later heard something with trading value in jail. Whatever the reason, the sentencing for his own murder spree kept being put off, year after year.

After the hearing, I confronted his lawyer in the hallway. "I've got a lot of demands on my time," I told Geoff Wildridge. "I need to know where your client fits. Just tell me, is there something there?"

"As his attorney," the tall, lanky defender said calmly, "I don't want you talking to my client." Then he added in a firm tone, "But keep asking those questions."

Jason,

I'm that journalism professor who came to see you a couple summers back. I was in court for your sentencing the other day sitting in a back row...

When I was young, I admired Malcolm X. He took charge of his life and improved himself during a prison stint...

Given a choice, I believe most people will do the right thing... Do you ever think about the Hartman case? That white teenager's fatal beating in 1997? I've heard from several odd directions that you know something about it, something perhaps the DA didn't want to discuss... [If] the day comes you feel like talking about it, I'm ready to listen.

Once more, I got no response. I took that as a message in itself. When I wrote inmates, I generally included a clip, transcript page, calendar, or a copy of my Iditarod book, something to prompt a reaction opening or sustaining a conversation. Wallace's failure to write, call, or send messages via a third party, which sometimes happened—all of it further set him apart. Could be I had the address wrong. I was looking into that when one of my letters was returned with a notice that the content violated institutional rules!

He might be tearing them up without reading a word, but he was getting them. I'd put money on it.

Another year slipped by, still inching toward publication of the Hartman series. The latest holdup: privacy concerns. City editor Boyce worried that identifying alternative suspects and others associated with the old case invited lawsuits. The last week of February 2008, he copied me on his request for legal opinions on references to seven individuals he feared might sue under the Alaska constitution's right to privacy clause. While I was pretty sure the reporting wasn't libelous—most references to individuals named in the series came from court testimony or direct interviews—it wasn't unreasonable to get an opinion, but he'd even included both O'Bryant and our main suspect, public figures by any definition.

"Any concern about the following," Boyce noted in an email, "since it seems to suggest a failing by the district attorney?"

The offending paragraph noted nobody was in a better position than Jeff O'Bryant to weigh Dale Depue's possible involvement in both Hartman's 1997 murder and the slaying of cab driver Maurice Lee Smith a year later. The first was investigated by city police, the second by state troopers. "I believe there was an inquiry," I quoted him saying. "Not obviously that night, but later when that information surfaced. I believe there was an inquiry made. To what extent? Or how in depth? I don't recall."

My reporting showed that O'Bryant ignored Roberts's alibis, convicting the four without a shred of physical evidence, based on hearsay and discredited confessions. If any of that was off-limits, kiss journalism goodbye.

Boyce and I met with the paper's lawyer in the same old library room where I'd first pitched the value of revisiting the Hartman case. I'd brought printouts of the draft series, Boyce's legal queries, and folders stuffed with documents I anticipated might be useful.

Attorney John Burns immediately raised a point I hadn't even considered: "Why are you doing this? You don't even work here anymore."

"It's important," I argued, pointing out the ten-year-old case still drew letters to the editor.

Like Boyce, the newspaper's attorney was mostly concerned about the series final piece, "Unopened Doors," which made the case that police ought to have investigated Dale Depue's possible involvement.

"Doesn't that invite a lawsuit?" he asked.

I was incredulous. The first hurdle in a successful libel action, as I understood it, is demonstrating quantifiable financial damage. A story error that costs someone their job, that attaches dollar signs to reputational damage. As part of his own plea bargain, Depue described, under oath, how he and his half brother lured a cab driver into the woods for a drug deal, then chased him down, stabbing and kicking the guy before their older partner finished him off. Nothing I'd written suggested anything worse about the guy's character.

I'd feared the lawyer might dig in his heels over aspects of the series that were less clear-cut, yet off he ran, researching precedents involving libel actions by murderers. Lo and behold, he concluded that a convicted murderer's reputation wasn't likely to suffer quantifiable monetary damage from implied association with another murder. Thus, a libel claim founded on such grounds wasn't likely to find traction in court, he said.

. That didn't mean the *News-Miner*'s attorney was entirely at ease. "So," he said, "you two believe this is the guy. You're satisfied that Dale and his friends killed Hartman. There are no other suspects?"

I glanced at Boyce. He appeared tense, perhaps sensing where this could go.

"Actually," I said, "my reporting shows police should have looked at Depue. The fact they didn't—and we know that—shows the holes in FPD's investigation. There's this other guy I visited in prison," I continued, feeling a grin spreading. "A guy whose name keeps coming up. I've kept Rod up to speed on this."

The lawyer appeared more and more uncomfortable as I described my disturbing visits with inmate Jason Wallace and very relieved to hear that we weren't printing his name.

Letters to the editor and online comments hashing over recent developments helped make the case for publication of the series.

"Saw it this morning and felt amazed by the timing," I emailed Boyce and Bostian, citing the response sparked by a recent letter to the editor referring to the twelve-year-old murder. "Just now peeked at the comments; reactions really frame the significance of the confessions, pro and con."

We were still haggling over the series title. The current favorite didn't satisfy Kate, who now made a pile more money than any of us, applying her PR smarts as public affairs director for Alaska's whole university system. "She loves the font, overall old-time news look, as well as the John Hartman Murder Case logo," I emailed the editors. "She isn't sold (and I'm being kind) on titling the series 'Ten years of why?'"

Naysayers were silenced by a timely assist from the courthouse: Superior Court Judge Ben Esch had scheduled a hearing on Eugene Vent's long-running final appeal for the second week of July 2008, adding currency to that old murder downtown.

CHAPTER 9

"DECADE" ROLLS

Managing editor Kelly Bostian and I stood side by side watching newsprint flashing jumpsuit orange. The color reflected tomorrow's main front-page photo. The continuous sheet of newsprint threaded other rollers and printing plates, collecting additional colors before the A-section's pages were automatically sliced, folded, and assembled, wrapping sections B through G of the next day's paper.

Mark, the pressman in charge, threw the brake as the first Sunday edition copies landed on the conveyor belt on their way upstairs for sorting and delivery. I took a picture as he grabbed a copy and snapped open pages, checking for glaring printing flaws warranting plate alignment or ink adjustments. When he was satisfied, the pressman took my camera and got a pic of Bostian and me holding up Sunday's fat edition.

A teaser of new Wimbledon champ Venus Williams topped the page, racket in hand, swatting through the *News-Miner*'s masthead lettering. Directly below, Sunday's main headline in bold black type: "Decade of Doubt," Kelly's final choice for the series title.

My eyes dropped to the old photo of the four suspects, all young, all wearing those bright orange jumpsuits, shackled together for inspection by a court officer prior to their 1997 arraignment. George Frese, then twenty, appeared to faintly smile as he took in the situation, both wrists cuffed to his waist.

The jumpsuits worn by Mark and the other pressmen scurrying around tonight were nearly identical, but theirs signified good-paying jobs and freedom.

Below and to the left of the inmates, the page featured what had become John Hartman's iconic image, grinning at the camera, kneeling on one leg, clutching a football. One last image introduced the series kickoff coverage: Heather Taggard's 2003 photo of a young Native girl, face largely concealed by her pink and blue winter coat, leading a crowd of protesters, walking alongside the late Shirley Demientieff, steering the little gal with her free hand, holding up a handmade sign with the other. ALASKA NATIVES STANDING UP FOR JUSTICE.

Fierce and formidable as I will always remember her.

An accompanying editorial explained the paper's partnership with the university, the investigative efforts of students and this professor, outlining the project's goals and limitations.

> This seven-part series offers no proof of guilt or innocence. It documents gaps in the police investigation that raise questions about the victim's last conscious hours. It points out the group convicted of the teen's murder may have been prosecuted with forms of evidence identified in national studies as contributing to some wrongful prosecutions elsewhere. And it shows how rulings from the state's courts have undermined Alaska Native confidence in the justice system by keeping juries from weighing all that's known about the crime...
>
> The result, by many accounts, has been a decade of doubt.

110 PERCENT CERTAIN

He'd been drinking for hours by the time he claimed to see four guys fleeing a robbery, the boys who would later, the prosecution claimed, beat John Hartman and leave him for dead. Those standing alongside later swore they didn't notice the crime unfolding more than a block away. A perception expert argued that no one can recognize faces at such a distance. Yet jurors believed the man from Kaltag. Arlo Olson sounded *that* good on the witness stand.

After the final Hartman trial in 1999, an assortment of offenses landed Arlo Olson behind bars for weeks, then months, and more recently years.

At least twice while incarcerated, Olson disavowed portions of his trial testimony: first with George Frese's defense attorney, Robert Downes, who now serves as a judge, and later with an investigator working for Marvin and Kevin. Both times, he declined to be tape-recorded.

Detective Aaron Ring soon visited. Olson told him he was talking about recanting in order to be released from incarceration.

———————

Former student Robinson Duffy, the *News-Miner*'s new website editor, had created an online site offering the full print series, enhanced by audio clips of police, trial testimony, the shaky video of Marvin Roberts's graduation, and excerpts of Chris Stone's prison interview and a link to Extreme's "How Far Is Too Far," the audio slideshow from our midnight field trip assessing Olson's superhuman vision.

Departing from tradition, the entire series was published online that Sunday while print installments were pieced out daily. That was the managing editor's call based on recent research about digital reading habits and active engagement tools.

FEEDBACK

Sherry 29: I still remember watching the news reports about this attack it was so upsetting and truly a turning point for our town. This boy was so young and looked like the "All American Boy" in his photos. He reminded me of my brother, and I cried for him and his mother while I watched. We found out later that this boy was getting into trouble, just like the boys that are accused of this... I know that with everything that I have read (and I am white) I could not have convicted some of these boys!

Olddog: To all the wannabe detectives out there. Is it possible to stomp a person to death and have no physical evidence on you or in your car? Not only no physical evidence on you but the other people convicted in this crime. What are the chances of that? One would intend to think that with all the blood on the victim there would be at least one speck of the victim's blood on the accused or at least in the accused car.

JB: The confession that occurred for the third time after sleep, family counsel and food... they got the right kids. From how the body was found, it sounds like they "curbed" him. Chris may have been the mark, but John was killed. This is a story of bad DAs and judges not racism, and not having the innocent in prison.

Akguy: Looking good DNM—I bet the racial tension you are stirring up with this makes you proud! Hope the bottom line is looking good over this sensationalism. None of you really knows what happened that night—for you were not there! Enough with the "crime they did not commit" statements if they didn't commit the crime, find those that did. Until then, the criminal justice system has deemed these youths guilty, and they are where they deserve to be—nothing more, nothing less... I would think the same no matter what their race, color, or Creed. I do think, however, that if another ethnicity would have been convicted, this story would not have been dragged off the shelf as it has here!

Dove: Exactly Olddog. It is difficult to believe that the prosecution got a conviction with zero DNA and zero forensic evidence. The evidence is purely circumstantial. The suspects were drunk. The witnesses were drunk. Who can remember any facts accurately when you're drunk? The interrogation, and not to ridicule are Fairbanks police, should never have occurred while the suspects were still under the influence of alcohol. It seems the confession was forced with intimidation and lies. Granted one or two of these four young men had some criminal history, but so do many other Alaskans... I'm not convinced the suspects received a fair trial or that they are guilty. I vote "yes" for a new trial.

Duff: Poor taste and will aggravate old wounds. I'm not entirely convinced the four guys in jail are guilty of murdering John Hartman. They certainly were on a bad path Oct. 11, 1997. Whoever did this to John frankly deserves the same done to them. My kids won't be out on the town after dark!... Bless you, John Hartman.

Fbkreader: A few months ago, a letter to the editor ran. It was from one of the young men in prison for this crime. I followed this case back when and his letter was so filled with hate and disdain and disregard for the victim and his family and so filled with selfish statements to help get out of jail. I had no doubt that even with the inconsistencies in the prosecution, we have one of the murderers behind bars. Please pray for all the families involved it is a hard time for all.

paramedic9708: Justice for these murders would have been the death penalty. I believe that they did it and I hope one day they will tell the truth... I wish these guys would get what they deserve... A long drawn out beating until unconsciousness sinks in and they need a machine to keep them alive... This is only my opinion.

Curt J: Anyone who kicked up someone in the snow will have blood, tissue stuck to their shoes, clothes, and jackets. Anyone who ever butchered a moose in the winter will know. As far as I know, Marvin had ALL his footwork confiscated. No blood was found on his shoes, clothes and, most importantly, his car... The boys were railroaded, and justice not served on the real murderers or for the murdered white boy whose real activities are concealed behind a picture of a young All-American boy in a football suit versus continuous pictures of sullen young Native men... The DNM is as much as much to blame as the justice system!

north_pole79: Curt J you should read the story—John Hartman died of internal bleeding So, your rant, "anyone who kicked up someone in the snow will have blood, tissue and hair stuck to their shoes, clothes, and jackets. Anyone who ever butchered a moose in winter will know" Is invalid. As are the rest of your arguments.

Dove: Not true NP79. Anyone with any criminal forensic knowledge will tell you that blood spatters, even the smallest drops, would show up in testing. I have to remove myself from this sensationalized drama. It's simply too painful, period! I pray justice can somehow be

truly served here. Big error on DNM's part to publish this article. BIG
MISTAKE!

Fifty comments, many of them critical, were posted within the first
hour. Despite the outcry, Bostian stuck with the plan, running the second
installment, "A Cry in the Night," as prominently as the first. Gutsy call! I
was grateful.

Online comments and downloads demonstrated readers were interested
in source documents. Robinson, who helped collect much of the material as
a student, now provided tech support delivering it.

Robinson Duffy: Some of the related documents are thousands of
pages long. PDF was the only way to package them so that most
people could read them and so they would be searchable. My
suggestion to anyone having trouble: save the document to your
computer before opening it with your Adobe Reader.

JB: Go read the confessions! Vent names everyone, not in the first
confession but in all three. I am sorry, the article can argue the details
of how an interrogation are performed but the reality is that these are
confessions that were not coerced with details of the acts of violence
against the victim... I was at the Eagles Hall that night and don't
remember seeing any of them there, but I do remember when word
spread about the fight outside. There were close to 600 people there
and unless someone spent the entire evening sitting and talking with
Roberts there is no way anyone [will convince me] they can vouch for
his presence in the party that night... One more question, I see a lot
of "Native pride" stickers on the back of vehicles since then. What
would I be called if I had the same thing on the back of my truck
saying, "White pride?"

SadinaAk: I don't understand what the point of this story is. This is not journalism. You can't tell me the person that wrote this story didn't let their opinion show here. Was the point to make us all feel so bad for these boys that we would let them out of prison? I knew Marvin in school, and I liked him. I also knew JG and all I can say is that at least Marvin is still alive. Was there a point to posting a video of his graduation? I don't see how it fits into this story except to remind me that he got the chance to graduate. JG never did... As I sit here, I feel sad and sick all over again, thanks guys for making this a little harder on everyone for no reason at all.

Born and raised: These trials, the witnesses, the interrogations, the fact that there was NO HARD EVIDENCE.........it screams CORRUPT! I tell you what, for all these people saying that this is not journalism, if it was MY CHILD in this situation. God bless ANYONE that would bring attention to this travesty!!! My prayers are with everyone involved.

Readers flagged a pair of errors: we miscalculated a person's age during past run-ins with the law. The second error drew gleeful rebuke from the former captain of the Howard Luke Hawks basketball team: "George never had the grades to make the team!" Marvin Roberts pointed out, calling from jail.

NESBETT COURTHOUSE, ANCHORAGE, JULY 8, 2008

Eugene's long-delayed hearing on postconviction relief pitted defense attorney Colleen Libbey against William H. Hawley Jr., a graying prosecutor with brows that literally arched when he demanded justice.

The hearing was strictly procedural. I was weighing whether it even warranted a story when I ran into Bill Oberly, director of the newly formed Alaska Innocence Project, a lawyer I'd been itching to meet. I immediately bent his ear, rattling off problems in the case, unaddressed in the verdicts.

"It's got my attention," the slim, weary-eyed, graying attorney assured me.

State Senator Al Kookesh, a Juneau power broker of Tlingit descent, asked Alaska's Department of Law to respond to the Decade series findings. He forwarded to me Deputy Attorney General Richard Svobodny's eight-page critique, discounting virtually every aspect of my reporting and even defending the jury experiment. "I cannot speak of the legal issues of this appeal because it is presently before the Alaska Supreme Court," he wrote the senator. "However, I believe it is appropriate to say that only one person in the experiment could not identify a person from the distance Olson was, and six jurors could."

Once again, he was ignoring the fact that those jurors were sitting together in court for days on end before the unauthorized daytime experiment. And unlike Olson, they were presumably sober.

The fact that no trace evidence of any kind linked the four boys to Hartman or the crime scene seemed to make no impression on the justice official. "Apparently," Svobodny sniped, "the *News-Miner*'s position is there can never be a conviction without DNA."

Wherever Alaskans were incarcerated, copies of *Decade of Doubt* soon turned up inside jailhouse walls. Twenty-seven-year-old Eugene Vent, subject of the hearing that spurred the *News-Miner* to let the big press roll, heard something new on his cell block: *You guys really are innocent.*

ALASKA SUPREME COURT, FEBRUARY 17, 2009

A piercing squawk halted discussion. The three justices present swiveled in unison, gazing down at the student wearing headphones. "Sorry," said Jenny Canfield, wincing.

Seated alongside, I smiled and recalled the written assurance accompanying my request for permission to shoot photos and record audio of today's hearing. "Anyone I bring will be coached on the importance of remaining as unobtrusive as possible."

Kevin Pease, now in his early thirties and facing fifty more years in prison, was presumably listening in from a cell block in the Lower 48, though I hadn't heard clerks announce he was on the line. His longtime defender Lori Bodwell and prosecutor William Hawley Jr., who at least kept hearings lively, took turns at the podium up front. The only other observer present, photojournalism major Cassandra Johnson, sat by her camera tripod farther back. She hadn't taken a single photo, fretting how shutter clicks might echo.

The issue before the high court's five-member panel concerned intent: what were jurors testing back in 1999 when they left the courthouse while still deliberating verdicts in the third and last Hartman trial? Were they testing Arlo Olson's claim that he recognized the guys mugging a guy way down the street, or were jurors weighing an expert witness's experiment involving subjects trying to identify a famous movie star's photo from two hundred feet away? Either way, our discovery about the jury's unauthorized sojourn figured prominently.

"What troubles you most?" Chief Justice Dana Fabe asked Kevin Pease's lawyer. "Is it the fact they did it as a group? Or the actual nature of it?"

"Both," said Bodwell. She argued that jurors eyeballing fellow jurors on a bright afternoon simply can't be compared to midnight observations from more than a block away by a guy who'd been drinking for hours. "They took one of their own, somebody they'd spent weeks with, and watched him walking down the road." If that experiment influenced even a single juror, she branded the verdict corrupt.

Assistant Attorney General Hawley appeared to be hardly listening. He'd slumped back, both wrists draped over the chair arms, and didn't seem to be watching his opponent or the justices.

Where was the fire I'd seen at earlier hearings?

When the state's turn came, Hawley spoke deliberately and rather softly. "I was just struck sitting here a minute ago. What we're talking about doesn't make a difference in determining human rights or what standard of review should be applied. We are dealing with the death of a fifteen-year-old who was kicked in the head and died for no apparent reason."

Here it comes, I thought.

"The jury wasn't checking Mr. Olson, the eyewitness's testimony," the prosecutor continued in a monotone without his usual kinetics. "Only checking it to the extent that Doctor Loftus was challenging it." Recognition at one hundred to two hundred feet away. That was all the jurors were testing, he said, referring to a vision expert's testimony. He calmly reminded the court of the sworn statement from the juror with poor eyesight who first mentioned the experiment to Tom Delaune years ago. "It confirmed what he found was hard," the prosecutor said, "but was fairly able to do."

Chief Justice Fabe challenged that, pointing out that the juror said he couldn't recognize anybody and relied on others who said they could. She quoted that juror's statement to authorities after our 2003 story broke. "It removed the doubt that one might have that it's impossible to see someone or identify someone at five hundred feet."

Hawley jumped in. "And he went on to say, 'it would have been hard for me to positively identify the two jurors who walked down there.' He didn't say he couldn't!" He cited the same juror's response to another follow-up: "The question is, 'with your bad eyesight,' and I can relate to that," Hawley quipped. "My view," he summed up, "is he didn't say he couldn't. He just said it was hard."

Justice Fabe read from another section of that same juror's statement: "At least half the people said, 'Oh, yeah, I can tell that it's so-and-so. That made it believable to me that it's possible. It removed the doubt that one might have. That it's impossible that someone can identify someone at five hundred feet.'"

On rebuttal, Kevin's lawyer Bodwell directed the court's attention to another exchange: "Your eyesight wasn't such that you could see the people?" a juror had been asked during the hearing. "Yeah," that juror confirmed. "My eyesight's not that good."

"So," Kevin's attorney argued, "he clearly stated he could not see what other people were seeing."

Another justice brought up Olson's claim that he saw all four up close earlier that night, cruising together in Marvin's car.

I sighed; it was that old lie about George leaning out the rear window of Marvin's car.

Bodwell, unruffled, emphasized Olson's condition and the recollections of another witness. "The fact of the matter was, it wasn't just his eyesight, it was his eyesight at 550 feet in the dark while drunk, while under the influence of drugs," she pointed out. Along with the fact that "his testimony conflicted with that of the victim himself."

The hearing on the jury's ten-year-old sojourn lasted just under an hour.

Cassandra Johnson's photo of black-gowned justices peering down on the attorneys topped the *News-Miner*'s front page. Public radio stations across Alaska aired Jenny Canfield's neatly wrapped two-minute, forty-seven-second audio report. "The Supreme Court still has the power to overturn Kevin Pease's conviction and order him a new trial," she concluded, "but there is no time limit on that decision."

"'97 Murder hounds journalist who followed it," headlined the big Anchorage paper's follow-up. "Sure, maybe O'Donoghue is slightly obsessed," journalism alum Jade Frank conceded. She didn't see that as a fault. "Students would rather research a murder than cover 'news' stories about a building dedication or politician's visit." Mark Evans, another former student, told *Alaska Dispatch News* that if I reached out, he'd drop everything and help me again.

Kevin Pease's attorney sounded butt hurt that I hadn't turned over the interview tapes and generally frustrated. "We interviewed those same jurors," Lori Bodwell recalled, "and they never mentioned it."

ADN's reporter kindly gave me the last word: "It really has been a Kafkaesque situation of retracing things that would have been easy for police to look into at the time."

FOLLOW-UP QUESTIONS

Readers often stopped me to discuss those boys. Nearly all had the same question: "So you think they're innocent?"

It wasn't that simple. All alibis are not equal, I found myself repeating; detectives didn't appear to have nailed down anyone's movements. That left alternative scenarios wide open. The bigger issue, I stressed, is nobody in America ought to be locked up based on the state's case. And with all we'd learned, I told anyone who asked: If they get a new trial? They're likely walking free.

Former students remained discouraged. Kelsa Shilanski, for one, had pictured Chris Stone coming clean and helping us solve the crime. "The kids would get out of prison, and everything would be great," she'd assumed. "Yeah, and it just didn't happen."

CHAPTER 10

OF WAR AND WAITING GAMES

DIYALA PROVINCE, IRAQ, JULY 2009

"The air is hot and thick in the high-ceilinged room as the man shuffles forward. Sitting at a desk in front of him is a gray-suited official with a folder who glares and starts asking questions. The next few minutes will determine whether he goes free or vanishes into the Iraqi prison system," reported Tom Hewitt, a student journalist embedded with the Twenty-Fifth Infantry's First Stryker Brigade.

Observing the tension between local police and a delegation of visiting Iraqi officials weighing accusations against the detainees, Tom suddenly got it. This was what the colonel was going on and on about our first night embedded in Iraq.

Colonel Bert Thompson, commander of the U.S. Army's Fort Wainwright–based brigade, greeted us warmly, somehow more at ease wearing a camo-pattern uniform in the desert than the summer he and I often chatted on the sidelines of our son's soccer games. Back then, deployment was on the distant horizon. Thompson's four-thousand-member brigade now had ten months on the ground in war-torn Iraq. Our mission: sharing soldiers' experiences and challenges with readers and viewers back home.

The colonel cleared his calendar and generously made time for an impromptu press conference, fielding questions from UAF's embed team: *Sun Star* editor Tom, aspiring public radio reporter Jenny Canfield, video ace Jessica Hoffman, and this professor.

"Restoring rule of law," Thompson kept emphasizing. We heard the words but didn't know what he was getting at.

Seventeen suspected terrorists faced questioning by a visiting government minister the day Tom and Jenny covered the processing of detainees. All but one man facing an active criminal warrant were freed. On that day, authorities even kicked loose a guy who refused to directly answer whether he knew a local al-Qaeda member, claiming he'd been locked up so long he no longer remembered.

"The first couple times we did this," Colonel Thompson told Tom, the police chief played some games. "I said, 'Hey, wait a minute. It's been two weeks, and you didn't release these guys. Where's the warrant? Release 'em now.'"

The visiting Iraqi official conducting the review had been jailed by former Iraqi leader Saddam Hussein. That was why he got the job; he knew what it meant to be a political prisoner.

Tom Hewitt's dispatch, "Facing Iraqi Detainees," concluded with a jaded observer's prediction. "One of the American soldiers watches as the former detainees walk off. 'I'll give it two, maybe three weeks before we're dodging their IEDs,' he says, turning away with a shrug. 'I'm a realist.'"

At this point in the Iraq war, most news organizations had cut back coverage, citing declining public interest. Our mission was cooked up by University of Alaska president Mark Hamilton, a former U.S. Army two-star. He reckoned the publicity surrounding UAF's undergrad embeds would raise awareness about the ongoing contributions of active-duty service members. He foresaw lasting lessons for my team as well. "Their stomachs will pitter-pat a bit," the retired general told the *Alaska Dispatch News*. "Not a bad thing for a journalist to feel."

These days, Kate oversaw the university system's communications, working directly under Hamilton. She was horrified when the general floated the idea; she knew I'd be involved.

As a young photojournalist, I aspired to be another Robert Capa, one of the most famous news photographers of the twentieth century. The closest I got was covering Egyptian-Israeli peace talks in 1979 for UPI. For years after, my wire-service photo of Moshe Dayan, Israel's one-eyed former general, glaring at the Egyptian delegation in Cairo, opened doors back home.

When I began teaching, I regularly placed my journalism students in war games, staged out of Fort Wainwright, role-playing aggressive reporters.

Only Rachel, six, remained unaware of the strife brewing over the potential Iraq assignment. Her older brothers were worried, I knew. Kate remained furious, though her tight goodbye hug signaled hope. After dropping me off at the airport, she bought a trampoline, something I'd always nixed for the kids as too dangerous.

Yet Daddy seemed to think it was fine to cover a war?

Kate might never get over it, but I'd been losing my mind waiting for the Alaska Supreme Court's decision on Kevin Pease's final appeal.

"Alaska appellate slip opinions week ending 8/14/09," stated the incoming email's subject line. Internet bandwidth was limited in the media tent at Forward Operating Base Warhorse in Diyala. The Alaska Supreme Court's ten-page court decision took forever printing out.

Skimming the contents, I noted that a pair of justices dissented. No surprise, given a five-member panel. I scrolled like mad till I found the actual decision: "The petition for hearing, filed September 25, 2007, and granted February 8, 2008, is DISMISSED as improvidently granted."

What?

Returning to the two dissenting opinions: "The identification evidence was critical to [Kevin] Pease's convictions," wrote Justice Robert Eastaugh.

"The experiment was flawed. And there was at least a 'reasonable possibility' it affected the outcome."

Justice Daniel Winfree went further, criticizing the trial judge and the appellate tribunal, arguing the jury experiment warranted a full hearing. He also flagged the significance of the state's witness to the supposed warm-up crime. "[Arlo] Olson was the only one who identified the defendants as Dayton's assailants and one of only a few who placed the four together on the night of the crimes." That "magnified the unauthorized experiment's impact," reasoned the justice, arguing for a new trial. "The court cannot find that an experiment that attempted to resolve the validity of this difference [between Olson's and Dr. Loftus's testimony] was not likely to have influenced the verdict."

The three prevailing justices didn't bother explaining their reasoning.

Our land o' the free felt darker than when we left. The rule of law, America's supposed gift to Iraq, apparently didn't apply in Alaska courts.

"GIVE ME THAT VIN"

Richard Norgard called that July, introducing himself as Bill Oberly's investigator. Might I be available to discuss the case? That sounded great to me, and about time! We'd been in touch several years earlier when the Alaska Innocence Project was getting off the ground. He reminded me I helped draft the press release announcing the organization's launch. My interest waned when the Alaska office, like the national group, prioritized cases with untested DNA evidence. That scenario didn't really apply with the Hartman case, where the convictions rested on liars and drunken confessions, absent tangible proof of any kind.

The short, sturdy, former army investigator with light brown hair parked himself in my old leather swivel chair and began flipping through binders of court transcripts, police reports, and other documents students had collected over the years, mostly indexed, bearing labels such as ROBERTS-PEASE I-III, PRE-TRIAL, HJP, and STUDENT STORY MEMOS. He marked whatever caught his attention, and I shuttled back and forth, making copies. In between, we hashed over alternative suspects, debating motives and weighing who seemed to be hiding something and who hadn't talked but might still, given the right approach.

"If you've got other names," I stressed before Norgard left, "we've probably got something on them. Let me know." For the first time in many years, I felt momentum.

Norgard tagged so many items for copying that I returned that weekend with my six-year-old pal Rachel. Setting her up with a computer game, I continued duplicating the police report binder. These pages had seen lots of use. Edges were worn, had little tears, or were folded for ages, and had to be straightened by hand. The stack feeder kept jamming, so I shifted the binder from side to side for each exposure and flipped pages. As copies piled up, I shuffled between rooms, using the department's manual hole puncher, then transferred them into old three-hole binders. Tedious work, but it kept everything in order.

Duplicating Exhibit #30 required thought. Still tucked in the khaki-green hanging folder Gary Moore brought back from the Court of Appeals, the exhibit consisted of eight transparent layers overlaying a life-size close-up of Hartman's bruised face. The top layer displayed a black-inked tire tread impression from Marvin's car. "Right Boot Evidence Item No. 6" noted the white label on the bottom right. When I looked it over, my eye jumped straight to the dying kid's facial close-up. The image, taken in the ICU, was hard to look at, and our copy was black and white; jurors viewed the color photo version.

That upper layer featured a see-through six-inch ruler positioned across John Hartman's bruised chin and lower cheek. ALASKA SCIENTIFIC CRIME LABORATORY read the label, implying experts put this together, as if there was anything scientific about detectives playing cut and paste with the lab's photos. Such a lie!

I began taking apart the transparency layers for copying one at a time. The sheets displaying sections of boot tread kept slipping on the department copier's worn rollers. I repeatedly stopped the machine and fished them out.

Rachel's patience was wearing thin. So was mine. Distracted and rushed, I reassembled the darn exhibit. By the time I finished, I wasn't sure the pages were in order, not that it mattered.

CORNERSTONE PLAZA, FAIRBANKS, SEPTEMBER 2, 2012

Walking toward the student union, the circular array of flags grabbed my attention. Pennants from all fifty states waggled and snapped in the wind, hoist ropes beating on the poles. Winter felt near. Freshmen moving in today, unloading suitcases and bags by the dorms, might not get that, not on a sixty-degree day. But fall wind signaled change.

The first chance I got, I emailed the Alaska Innocence Project's investigator.

Richard,

I need the details on that car. We've got Wallace's old addresses and identified junkyards and other disposal sites worth checking. What are we looking for? A Monte Carlo? Old tickets show Wallace drove a Mazda 2-door.

My spirits had soared the day Richard Norgard called requesting help finding an old red muscle car, possibly red, driven by Jason Wallace. That name! It was the first indication the Alaska Innocence Project suspected his involvement. Sure, we'd help, I said. Backyards in Fairbanks were full of old rusting cars.

Soon after fall classes started, I took News Writing students to the courthouse. The records-checking session yielded a ticket Wallace received back in high school, driving a Mazda two-door, color unknown. Back in the lab, I had my IR students collect high-resolution Google Earth satellite images of Wallace's old neighborhood in South Fairbanks. We identified several cars stored in backyards as well as a sprawling wooded church property on a nearby parcel that might be worth exploring. In addition, we discovered that Fairbanks North Star Borough not only routinely disposed of abandoned vehicles, but it also kept records on the vehicle information number (VIN) of each. Before we spent a lot of time on this, it made sense to check whether Jason's Monte Carlo had ended up in the crusher.

There were seasonal considerations as well. "Once snow falls," I pointed out to Norgard, "it's far less likely we'll stumble across that coveted abandoned heap."

He emailed back, vowing to check his storage unit for paperwork noting that old car's VIN, required on a sticky manufacturer's label posted inside every U.S. vehicle.

Students piled into Kate's mini-van. Consulting the satellite photo printouts, we cruised Wallace's old neighborhood. We identified plenty of boats, campers, wood piles, and sheds too small to matter. We didn't find any red muscle cars or likely two-doors inviting closer inspection. Howard Hardee, a smooth-swinging homegrown baseball phenom, pointed the way to party spots and other places known for abandoned cars. We visited a few of those. No dice.

Before calling it quits, I pulled off on the shoulder of the Parks Highway west of town and pointed out a car driven or pushed off an overlooking ridge, now lodged in heavy brush about three-quarters of the way down a steep, rocky hillside. The boys and I had been tracking its slow-motion descent all summer. Hardee, among others, agreed that the ridge looked like a sweet place for bonfire parties. From where we stood, no one could identify the vehicle's color, much less model. We piled back into the van for a look-see.

A big power intertie, linking utilities in Anchorage and Fairbanks, ran along that same ridge. We followed a dirt access road to a clearing overlooking the whole valley. Tire tracks in the mud and campfire rings confirmed this was indeed a regular party spot. Gazing down off the edge, scrape marks and gaps in the brush pointed straight to the car. Rust and mud obscured the color, but this old wreck lacked the width and sharp tail lines of a Monte Carlo, and it didn't appear to be a two-door. Oh well.

Norgard finally got back to me with that VIN. A student checked with a junkyard; Wallace's car hadn't been "parted out" in Alaska, according to a commercial database. Nor had it been picked up for disposal, according to borough records. How complete were these records? "That's anyone's guess," I told IR students, emphasizing we'd at least taken this as far as we could.

Steve Hormann, a merry-eyed Native elder and former laborer majoring in journalism for the hell of it, caught wind of our efforts. "Give me that VIN," he said, grinning. "Some of my relatives are criminals. I'll check the property north of town. We've got a pile of old cars up there."

TIPS AND CONFRONTATIONS

SEPTEMBER 2010

I'd been teaching long enough that Casey, Sharice, Russ, and a boatload of other former students were making their marks as working journalists and other career pursuits; many were following case developments, occasionally passing tips.

"I'm not sure where you are with your John Hartman research," a former student pursuing a career in law wrote on September 17, 2010. "The investigator told me that the men convicted for the crime are innocent and was pretty sure he knows who committed the act. He said those involved were indeed rolling people that night for their PFD money."

The former student's source in the public defender's office "hinted" that a local lawyer represented the "true murderer."

Pulling likely records, I couldn't connect the lawyer he identified with Jason Wallace, Dale Depue, Redd Dott, or any of our other suspects. However, the guy had briefly represented a witness who testified against Kevin Pease, another case file worth reviewing.

Colleen showed up at the courthouse late. No surprise. Rushing downtown with a carload of other News Writing students, we all watched her miss the turn exiting Cushman Street Bridge. Classmates were already pulling files when she rushed into the clerk's office. I handed her the case number for Wallace's 2003 murder case. "Look for whatever's most recent."

I shuttled among students, handing out quarters and helping identify arrest narratives and other pages worth copying. Colleen, who'd finally caught up in time for this, returned with the microfilm in hand and a question. "They told me the machine is in use."

"There's more than one," I snapped, then apologized when I saw the available viewer had an "out of order" note on front. My eyes settled on the tall, lanky guy with the Beatles haircut using the adjacent reader. "How are you doing, counselor?" I asked Geoff Wildridge.

Wallace's public defender glanced up, took in the students milling in the background, and nodded in what seemed like approval.

"News Writing students," I added. "First time most have ever set foot in here."

The lawyer faintly smiled.

"You and I need to talk," I said pointedly.

Wildridge's expression tightened. He said he hadn't changed his opinion or something to that effect.

"I need to fill you in on where we are," I said. "What we've come up with."

The public defender shrugged; clearly, he knew what I was talking about and wasn't about to open that conversation.

On the way home, I stopped to pick up meat at Safeway. Brooding over the lawyer's stubbornness, I ran into Reverend Scott Fisher. "Father," I said, "I need ideas about lawyers and ethics."

"Oh?" he said, pausing in the aisle, mustache lifting above his spreading smile.

I unloaded: "A public defender's client secretly confessed to Hartman's murder. What he said was confidential under attorney-client privilege. His lawyer has the discretion to come forward but won't. As far as he's concerned, the privilege trumps the injustice of leaving those innocent guys in jail."

He stared, slack-jawed, processing this; first time I'd ever seen the garrulous man of God at a loss for words. After a long pause, he said, "You're telling me this attorney could come forward, but he won't?" He answered that himself. "But he has to!"

"That's what I think," I declared, nodding in agreement. "How do I get him to do the right thing?"

Father Scott said he'd pray on it.

"THAT WAS HAWK'S GIRL"

REWIND: CHRISTMAS WEEK, 2002

First came a terrific "whoosh," the woman told the 911 operator. Right afterward, she and her husband "felt the floor lift." Now it was smoky. He was pounding on doors, warning everybody to get out.

That call, logged at 8:03 a.m., Friday, December 27, came from a small apartment complex a few miles down the Parks Highway south of Fairbanks.

Trooper Scott Johnson heard the blaring sirens and radio traffic en route to Fairbanks Memorial Hospital, where doctors were working to save a young man stabbed in the neck.

Twenty-six-year-old Corey Spears was headed for the recovery room when Johnson approached his girlfriend Jackie at the hospital. Spears was really, really lucky, she told the trooper. Apparently, no veins were nicked. His windpipe wasn't touched.

The injury turned out to be nothing to do with a knife; some kind of crazy accident involving a screwdriver, Jackie assured him. That's right, just a misunderstanding. A friend from out of state was sleepwalking when he hurt Spears. When he realized what had happened, he drove them both to the hospital.

And that friend's name would be?

Jason Wallace.

And where was he now?

Jackie couldn't say. After dropping her off, Wallace borrowed their car and left.

When firefighters got the Ester fire under control, they found the body of twenty-five-year-old Teacka Bacote in the same apartment where that blaze apparently started. Another trooper working the case alerted Johnson that his stabbing victim—Corey Spears—was named on the unit's rental agreement.

The sleepwalker was from out of state and wasn't staying long, troopers learned from a friend keeping vigil at the hospital. A quick check with airlines confirmed that Jason Wallace had changed his ticket for an earlier flight, departing that afternoon. Trooper Johnson notified the airline to hold the passenger should he appear and cruised to Fairbanks International Airport.

An airline employee directed the lawman to a slim Black man in the boarding area. Johnson immediately noticed the guy's knit hat appeared singed; the back of one hand looked scorched as well. The trooper took the twenty-two-year-old visitor into custody, booking him on assault. The paperwork didn't reference that suspicious fire.

While being processed at FCC, Wallace confided to a nurse that he couldn't stop thinking about a friend's recent death; he'd even had thoughts of killing himself. A guard overheard the conversation and placed Wallace on suicide watch. Under the protocol, his street clothes were confiscated; he received a thin gown and blanket, unsuited for hanging himself, and he was placed in a cell equipped with a camera with orders for visual checks every fifteen minutes.

Later that same day, a staff member escorted Wallace to an interview room where Troopers Johnson and Lantz Dahlke, a stout, hard-nosed lawman with a thick mustache, joined the scorched suspect for a recorded interview.

"Justin, how are you doing?"

"Justin? I'm not Justin," the suspect protested.

Johnson realized the printout had it wrong. "Do you go by Jay or Jason?"

"Jason," corrected the prisoner.

"I'm not here to talk about why you're here right now," the trooper assured him. "What I wanted to talk to you about, uh, another matter we touched on a little bit today. And that is being out at Teacka's house."

The suspect muttered, saying nothing intelligible.

"Okay," Johnson tried again. "Were you ever out at Teacka's last night?"

"Not last night," declared Wallace, adding that he and his friend Corey were at Jackie's all night long.

Trooper Johnson reminded Wallace that didn't square with what he'd said earlier. Hadn't he and the man he later stabbed driven around "quite a bit" that night?

Wallace mumbled that he "didn't remember," then briefly fell silent. "In my fucking mind, it's gone," he suddenly blurted out. "Once I heard what happened."

Hakeem Bryant, a tall, Black military kid, first drew attention as a quarter-back whose evasive steps and powerful arm kept drives alive and Fairbanks fans cheering. Skilled and competitive, the "Hawk" wasn't easy to coach or particularly loyal. Entering his final year of eligibility, he bolted West Valley High for archrival Lathrop, ditching his Wolf Pack yellow-and-red jersey for Malemute purple and gold.

After schoolboy games ran their course, Hawk dealt drugs with bravado, encroaching on the notorious Coffey family's turf. In the fall of 2002, Hawk scored a kilo of cocaine in Washington, which proved particularly lucrative split up for resale in Fairbanks.

Emboldened, Hawk soared even higher, flying south with several close associates and a pile of borrowed cash to invest. Christmas Eve was the last anyone heard from him, Wallace told troopers.

That Friday, word spread that Hawk's body, along with another, turned up alongside a road in California. Wallace said he and Spears were up late trying to make sense of it. "Happened so quick," he told the lawmen crowding his cramped little room. "One day we seen him and the next we get a call like that."

Wallace insisted he never meant to hurt Spears: "I just woke up and just thought he was trying to kill me," he told troopers, then mimicked his friend's response: "Hey man, it's me! It's me, Corey! Man." Afterward, he said, he just lost it. "I started crying. Started crying like hell."

"Sure," Trooper Johnson said kindly.

Wallace accepted there would be consequences. "I'll probably be doing a year, maybe two years over [this] shit. I don't even know what caused my emotions. I can't handle my emotions."

"Everyone deals with stress differently," the trooper acknowledged.

Wallace mentioned legal counsel early on but didn't press it. Instead, he rambled, alluding to the murders and money Hawk was carrying. Yet he was evasive. "I don't know, sir," he told Trooper Johnson. "How do?" he began, then fell silent. "I'll put it to you, sir. If I knew where they were going…I probably would have been with them, and I probably would be dead too."

Trooper Dahlke was forty-five miles off the grid, working his trapline, collecting pelts from marten and other valuable little furbearers, when the brass yanked him back to town. When his turn came, the savvy investigator set verbal snares. "Now, Scott and I came here to talk to you about the fire."

"There was a fire," Jason Wallace slowly acknowledged.

"Yeah," Dahlke said. "Well, you know Teacka?"

"Yeah, I know Teacka."

"Well, we think Teacka died in it."

"Man," Wallace cried out. "What tha' fuck, man! Oh, man, are you sure of that? Fuck!" The shouts were followed by a moan captured on the trooper's recorder. "I mean, I need to see a counselor or something! Going crazy, man!"

"Listen to me for just a second," Dahlke coaxed. "You know where she lived? Did you ever go out to her? To her pad?"

"No, sir," Wallace protested, voice fading. "I just…"

"Never been to her crib or anywhere out there?"

"No, sir. No, sir," Wallace repeated. "That was Hawk's girl."

"So any reason why Corey would say that last night, at 4:00 a.m., you and he were out at Teacka's place?"

After a long pause, the suspect said quietly, "Not that I remember."

Wallace's mood swings, the personal appeals and tears, none of it fooled the lawmen. "He was probing what information we knew," Trooper Johnson later testified. "What we knew about his wife's involvement. If we knew the truth about what had happened."

By then, Alaska troopers were in touch with authorities in several states investigating a spate of related drug-ring murders. Two days after interviewing Wallace, Johnson caught a jet to Seattle with intel about a known associate of Hawk's placing calls from Wallace's apartment.

"Wild Bill" Holmes, a notorious Fairbanks rapper and drug dealer, was arrested without incident leaving that same apartment in Seattle. Wallace's eighteen-year-old wife greeted the lawmen like liberators. Several days earlier, she told the lawmen, Holmes had showed up in the middle of the night, desperate for shelter, then refused to leave.

Johnson had phone records that put a different spin on her actions, revealing Wallace's wife drove 140 miles and picked up the big rapper after he'd burned a car to destroy evidence. As the trooper later put it, "Ms. Wallace changed her story several times."

"GOD IS TELLING ME"

FAIRBANKS CORRECTIONAL CENTER, NEW YEAR'S EVE 2002

Johnson and Dahlke dropped by for another chat with Wallace. "I got back first thing this morning," Johnson told him. "Some things came up I wanted to talk to you about."

"Yes, sir," said the prisoner, who hadn't heard back on his request for a public defender that holiday week. He asked if he was facing third-degree assault or second.

"Before I can answer that question for you," Johnson said calmly, "because you're in custody on that charge, we need to read you your rights. Okay?"

"How is my wife, sir?"

"Well, like I said," Johnson began, then stopped and assured him his wife was all right.

Dahlke jumped in. "You know this is a technicality," he said, "so just bear with me, okay? You have the right to remain silent. Anything you say can and will be used against you in a court of law…"

Johnson stood up as the familiar advisory continued, certain the suspect was going to end this.

"Should I have a lawyer present?" Wallace soon asked.

"I can't make that decision for you," Dahlke said quickly, wondering why the prisoner had a blanket on. "What I have to do," he continued, "we have to do is get through this. And now, ah, having these rights in mind, do you wish to talk to us?"

"What's it about?" the prisoner persisted.

Dahlke referred to Johnson's trip to Seattle. "We need to talk to you about everything involved there."

"So," Wallace said, "can I ask you a question, and you be honest with me. Do I? Should I have a lawyer present when I answer these questions?"

Dahlke and the suspect, still on suicide watch, kicked around the ramifications.

Eventually, Wallace asked, "Does the lawyer know what you guys know?"

The trooper shook his head. "No, he does not," Dahlke said firmly. "He doesn't."

"So, what's the purpose of me even having my lawyer present then?"

Wallace kept tearing up, at times openly crying. Eventually he came around, turning toward Johnson.

"I'm going to trust you," he told him. "I ain't trusted no one in my life. I looked into your eyes, and it was like some reason, God is telling me, 'you can trust this guy right here.'"

HOW IT WENT DOWN

The attempted drug-ring takeover took root that November, Wallace told troopers. That was when Wild Bill Holmes, one of his old friends back in Fairbanks, proposed ripping off Hawk the next time he left town for a big score. Wallace, who was living out of state, agreed to fly north and kill Spears and any others loyal to Hakeem Bryant who might cause trouble.

That Christmas Eve, Holmes sent Wallace a pager code signaling he'd taken out Hawk. "That means I gotta do what I gotta do," Wallace told the troopers. Yet he didn't lift a finger for three days, not until Holmes upped the pressure, sending that selfie photo seated alongside Wallace's wife in their own home down in Tacoma. The apartment fire and Teacka's murder were the result.

"Did he tell you to kill Corey and Jackie too?" Trooper Dahlke pressed.

"He told me to kill everybody, sir."

"We understand there was a hammer on the seat of the truck," said Dahlke. "Was that what you used to kill Teacka?"

"It wasn't me," Wallace said.

"The person that?"

"It wasn't me."

"The person at the time?"

"It was not me," he repeated like a chant.

"We understand what you're saying, Jay, about—"

Wallace cut him off. "It was not me."

Questions followed by denials continued as the lawmen sought to make sense of the suspect's surreal denials.

"I feel like I see I didn't because I–I–I'd be lying."

"So it was almost an out-of-body experience?"

"I didn't do it."

"You were watching someone else do it at the time."

"Yes, sir."

Wallace had no trouble describing his own burns, and he whined about Holmes's instructions for pouring gas throughout the apartment, soaking Teacka's body, then igniting the blaze. "He didn't tell me to go outside first or nothing!"

"Did it burn your hands?" Dahlke inquired.

"Got one of them," Wallace acknowledged, showing them the marks.

"Oh, you got burned pretty good," the trooper said.

"I didn't know what I was doing, sir. It just—"

Johnson interrupted. "Were you actually standing in the apartment when you lit it?"

"Yeah."

"With fire coming all around you?"

"All the way around me," Wallace confirmed. "Thought I was gonna die."

———

Though a judge assigned the Public Defender Agency to represent Jason Wallace, another week passed before anyone from the agency followed up. Meanwhile, the distraught suspect remained on suicide watch, segregated from other prisoners and clothed like a large infant. Not only was he estranged from former Alaska friends, but Jason Wallace also lacked a credit card for long distance calls, blocking him from contacting his wife or family in the Lower 48.

Local calls were a different story. Wallace had Scott Johnson's number and called so often they had what amounted to an ongoing conversation.

NEW YEAR'S DAY 2003

Clad in real pants for the first time since his arrest, Jason Wallace took a little show-and-tell ride with Troopers Dahlke and Johnson. In the parking lot of Justa Store Liquor and Fuel, Wallace pointed out the dumpster where he chucked his scorched clothes. Next, they visited a weigh station on the Parks Highway a few miles south from his old Ester apartment. Leaving Wallace cuffed in the truck, the troopers poked around the field he'd identified and eventually located the hammer he'd used bludgeoning Teacka Bacote.

"I appreciate you coming out here and showing us," said Johnson in a conversation recorded that day.

"It all had to come out, Scott!" Wallace agreed.

Afterward, the troopers took the helpful murderer to McDonald's and bought him a meal, pausing at the prison gate to release his hands so he could enjoy it.

"His big concern is he didn't want me to think of him as a murderer," Johnson later testified. "Because that isn't the type of person he is."

Early that January, Geoff Wildridge registered with the court as Wallace's public defender. He met him once, then summoned the agency's new investigator. He figured Thomas Bole had the background to evaluate the client's unexpected reference to the Hartman case.

CHAPTER 11

THE AFFIDAVIT

APRIL 2011

It felt like skipping class. Alaska Press Club's morning panels in Anchorage sounded interesting, but the students could find their way around without me. More important, the Alaska Innocence Project's director had something he wanted to discuss.

Speaking just loud enough to carry over clattering plates and silverware at Snow City Cafe, Bill Oberly opened up: Jason Wallace was directly involved in John Hartman's murder. That wasn't all; Wild Bill Holmes, Wallace's partner in the 2002 Christmas week murders, was also directly involved, along with several other former Lathrop High students.

I was floored. "You're telling me Bill Holmes grew up in Fairbanks? Both went to Lathrop?"

"That's our information," Oberly said.

We'd been looking into Hartman's murder for years. Half the students who'd worked on this came through Lathrop High, Fairbanks's largest school. At the time of his arrest, Holmes was characterized as a Tacoma drug dealer. Could we have missed this?

My skepticism grew as Oberly indicated John Hartman just happened to be in the wrong place at the wrong time. Really? Experts I'd interviewed held that beatings as violent as Hartman received are usually personal, somehow arising from Dale Depue's long history with Kevin Pease for example. What Oberly described echoed FPD's random-spree-of-violence mantra. I didn't buy it.

"We have a source who was at that party," Oberly said softly, then shifted the conversation to people the Alaska Innocence Project needed help finding. By then, I had my notebook out, taking names.

Follow-up call: "Hi, Bill, it's Brian. Got a few minutes?"

"I do," Oberly said. "Let me put my lunch down. Had it in my fingers."

"We've gone through the yearbooks at least once. This is the '96, '97, and '98 yearbooks from Lathrop. Fleshed out some of the names on our list. Double-checked on connections. Pulled files on some of them."

Lathrop had a thousand students in that era, half as many as the school handled in the 1970s, during construction of the Trans-Alaska Pipeline. These yearbooks reflected calmer times. Student photos and club activities were even indexed, albeit with numerous errors and omissions. Rashan, last name unknown, wasn't listed among members of the Malemutes team, as Oberly's tip indicated.

"There was a student at Lathrop in '96 through '97 named Rashan Brown," I pointed out.

"Okay, yeah," Oberly said. "That's it."

And that was super, because this Rashan worked on the school newspaper, which gave the names of other staffers he likely knew.

Continuing down Oberly's list: "Matt Ellsworth showed up in yearbooks. '96, '97, '98," I reported. "Photos indicated he might have Native or Asian heritage. He was part of a cooperative education program. That looks like the kids who are borderline. Could be problem kids." I had a teacher friend looking into that.

"We've found Ellsworth," Oberly announced. "He's in North Pole."

I smiled. We'd already printed a Google map of the family's residence in the nearby Christmas-themed town, founded on selling personal letters from Santa.

Oberly was coming up for a bar association meeting. We made plans to interview Ellsworth together.

There was something else I wanted to address. "Davison is referred to in the '98 yearbook," I said quickly.

"Referred to?" Oberly caught my drift.

"Yeah," I said, explaining that when kids only turned up in the indexes with no page references, it was usually because they barely participated, if at all. Scott Davison's earlier yearbooks reflected more involvement overall.

"Scott Davison?" asked Oberly.

"We pulled his criminal stuff," I said pointedly, aware he was likely Oberly's main source concerning Wallace. I described the note we'd found in the case file that cautioned against holding Davison in Fairbanks, indicating he'd made some enemies.

Oberly characterized it as activity some thought helped authorities in a drug investigation.

"Snitch-type thing?" I asked.

"Exactly," confirmed Oberly, who'd been holding back. "Just so you know," he announced dramatically, "we just visited Davison at the Anchorage jail. We have his affidavit."

"Wow," I said, reeling from the implication if the Alaska Innocence Project actually had an insider's sworn statement challenging the verdicts.

Perhaps sensing my doubts, Oberly offered to email a copy. "If you want me to?"

"Oh yes," I told him.

"It won't be a signed one."

"That's okay," I assured him. "If you could email it, that would be great!"

I struggled keeping my thoughts straight. He'd asked me to track down a guy named Harold.

"We're still looking," I said, reminding him we didn't have a last name or high school for that matter.

"I would reeeally like to find that guy," said Oberly, chuckling nervously.

An email from info@alaskainnocence.org was waiting in my inbox. "He lined through the words 'and take his money' on line 3 of page 2," noted Oberly, referring to the attached affidavit. "Other than that, he signed it as written."

> **SCOTT S. DAVISON, BEING FIRST DULY SWORN, DEPOSES AND STATES AS FOLLOWS:**
>
> That I am the above-named individual, Scott S. Davison. My date of birth is March 5, 1979.

Blah blah blah. My eyes skipped ahead.

> During my time at Lathrop High, I became acquainted with an individual named Jason T. Wallace. Mr. Wallace is an African American male. Jason Wallace and I were in classes together.

Now we're getting somewhere. What had the Alaska Innocence Project dug up?

> Having been in Fairbanks in October of 1997, I was aware of the assault, and subsequent death, of John Hartman...
>   A day or two after the assault, I was riding in the car of Matt

Ellsworth, another friend from Fairbanks. Jason Wallace was also a passenger in the car. This was during the school day, and we had skipped school. We were driving around and smoking marijuana.

We were riding around Fairbanks when Jason Wallace said to Matt and me that he had been involved in the attack on John Hartman. Wallace further said that Bill Holmes, who I also knew from Lathrop High, and an individual named Harold, had attacked Hartman. I don't remember Harold's last name and don't think I ever met this individual. They had been driving around in Harold's Ford Tempo when they spotted Hartman and decided to assault him and take his money. Jason said he and Bill Holmes got out of the car while Harold remained in the car. They approached the individual on Barnette Street, beat and kicked him and left him on the side of the road.

Jason Wallace then said if we told anyone about what he had said about the Hartman assault, he would kill both of us.

That wasn't all: Davison said they never talked about the case again. He claimed he'd been "living with the knowledge" four innocent people were imprisoned for the crime.

FURTHER YOUR AFFIANT SAYETH NAUGHT.
DATED this _____ day of April 2011, at Anchorage, Alaska.
statement _____

Assuming Scott Davison had signed this, and Oberly assured me he had, the sworn statement seemed powerful and weighty. Would a judge read it that way?

Of course, I agreed to help vet Scott's claims.

Matt Ellsworth's criminal history proved extensive. Barely out of his teens when arrests and charges began piling up. Busted some two dozen times by his midtwenties. A felony assault charge involving a gun. All of it contributed to the stiff fine and multiple citations Ellsworth racked up driving a truck with false plates at eighty miles per hour.

When I had a free minute, I jumped in our old pickup and went looking for the home address cited on Ellsworth's most recent traffic tickets. The place was outside North Pole city proper, down a gravel road. I wouldn't have found if I hadn't printed out the borough's tax lot map. That guided me to a long A-frame home in a peaceful, shady spot.

A sturdy man with a white beard greeted me on the doorstep. Matt wasn't home, Mike Ellsworth said. Did I mind telling him what this was about?

So I did.

Ellsworth's dad proved to be a good listener. He'd heard about that Hartman case and didn't seem surprised to find me on his doorstep. He couldn't speak for his adopted Asian son but promised to let Matt know that the Alaska Innocence Project hoped to talk to him.

Following up on a related lead, I dropped in on Dan McKinney at FCC. The short, sturdy inmate, more Black than Native in appearance, picked up the phone across from mine without a word and stared hard as prisoners often do confronting strangers. His glare softened as I explained our efforts investigating Hartman's murder. Eugene turned out to be Dan's cousin on his mother's side. He is probably innocent, McKinney declared, adding that he appreciated my efforts. He told me to put any further questions I might have in a letter.

McKinney seemed ready to end it, so I dived ahead. "Did you know Jason Wallace?"

Oh yeah. McKinney explained that he generally hung with Black inmates in prison and knew them all. He didn't bat an eye when I mentioned we had a fresh lead suggesting Wallace was directly involved in the Hartman murder. The other rumor—that McKinney heard Wallace admit to it? That rattled him.

He and Wallace didn't hang out. McKinney hotly repeated that several times.

We talked about twenty minutes. I emailed Oberly from FCC's parking lot, recapping the interview and what I'd learned about Wallace's old girlfriend Kealoha. McKinney said he didn't know a lot of Lathrop kids, I summed up, explaining he'd spent two years at Fairbanks Youth Facility rather than conventional high school. McKinney stressed that Wallace didn't hang out with military kids. I didn't fully grasp the significance, but clearly that meant something to him.

"I can't read the guy," I told Oberly, but I assured him I'd keep talking to McKinney.

Later, I dashed off a letter to Eugene regarding his cousin. "He expressed sympathy for the four of you. Said he wasn't sure you and he'd ever met, but cited the family tie."

I suggested that he write McKinney ASAP, encouraging him to share whatever he may have heard or know.

———————

My years teaching proved this much: young inquiring minds can't resist playing with Court View, the state's trial database. After giving News Writing students a quick tutorial in the computer lab, I turned them loose, looking up charges and other details in cases involving friends and relatives. That bought me precious time hunting for Harold No-Last-Name. Searching Alaska criminal case records for "Harold" along with "A" for the last name yielded Harold Amber's 2004 domestic violence case, a 1992 civil action brought by a group including Harold Andrew, and a pair of 1993 small-claims actions initiated by Harold's Maytag Home Appliance in Anchorage. Harold Amber appeared to be the best prospect and a feeble one, lacking his birth date and other details kept in a courthouse some five hundred miles south.

Onward I charged, searching Harold Bs and Cs…

The lab, hallways, and nearby parking lot were deserted by the time I reached Harolds Zenger Sr., Zimmerman (two of them), Zinger, and Zsedny, who apparently died in 1998. All their cases involved estate settlements. Only one of the Zs had more than a traffic ticket, a misdemeanor misconduct with a controlled substance that smelled like a marijuana bust.

All told, my alphabet quest netted four Harolds with cases of interest in the years immediately before or after the murder. Most were a bit older than Wallace. The most promising Harold was a student enrolled at the university's Anchorage campus.

UAA's directory yielded an email address but no phone number; neither approach seemed realistic. "Your name has come up investigating an old murder. Is it possible you were driving the getaway car?" No, this warranted a face-to-face approach. Even a knock on the door, identifying myself and getting right to the point, would provide an opportunity for observing reactions. Dream on. I had a stack of Mass Comm papers to grade and IR reports to edit. Final exams were on the horizon. No way to squeeze in a 750-mile Anchorage run.

I moved on, checking local Lathrop High yearbooks for administrators and teachers worth tracking down. Two names leapt out; Bill Bodle topped the list. Back when our sons were in middle school, short, stout, Harley-riding Vice Principal Bodle maintained tight control of the school's bus lanes and hallways.

Not surprisingly, the old disciplinarian possessed total recall of every hard case he ever came across in classrooms and coaching football at Lathrop High. His take on Bill Holmes: "Always somewhat sullen and quiet," he said, praising the "huge" kid's efforts on the field. I was surprised to hear Holmes played football, which hadn't been referenced in any yearbook. Bodle said the big man likely "didn't have the grades" to officially suit up, but that wouldn't have blocked him from the practice squad.

"What about Daniel McKinney?" I asked.

"Now there was an intelligent kid," Bodle said. He simply couldn't keep out of trouble. Though younger than the others I'd mentioned, he assured me McKinney would have possessed situational awareness of fellow Lathrop troublemakers.

He couldn't place Jason Wallace at all, which was consistent with yearbooks; Wallace's name was listed with his class, nothing more. When I mentioned Rashan Brown, the old disciplinarian looked sad. Bodle's son Barry and Rashan were very close. The boy spent a lot of time at their house, he said.

Brown's later involvement in a double homicide? Entirely out of character, Bodle assured me, attributing it to drugs and/or mental illness. If the kid was headed down the wrong tracks at Lathrop, he would have noticed. Brown's troubles began after he left Alaska, Bodle said, recalling the boy's mother, a school counselor, spent a lot of time in his office weeping.

She still believes her son is innocent.

Dale Depue wasn't on Oberly's list, but I had to ask.

Hearing the name, Bodle locked eyes with mine. Depue was the reason he got a handgun and began carrying, he said.

Kate later pointed out we met Brown's mom when she was a counselor at the boys' middle school. The hardworking, outgoing, single mother's civic interests led her to run for local office.

"THEY GET MORE BRAZEN"

INTERNATIONAL KARATE ASSOCIATION, FAIRBANKS, MAY 2011

A flashing sign emblazoned with an approaching tiger signaled the driveway turnoff to a big house.

Charles Scott, head of the local martial arts college he founded in 1972, greeted me in a loose white robe. The former Lathrop High principal was shorter than I recalled from the era when his competitive feats regularly made the paper's sports page, but time couldn't diminish the sturdy Black man's sheer presence.

Mr. Scott, as he was known, grinned and invited me in. "Excuse me. I just finished working out," he said. I followed him into a pastel-hued living room, bathed in light from tall windows, where he pointed to a chair. He settled into another and nodded as I got out my little cassette recorder.

Mr. Scott prefaced the interview stating that he strives not to remember individuals by what they did as children unless it continues. For the pair I was interested in, Wallace and Holmes, their drug-ring murders canceled any clean slate. "This Holmes," Mr. Scott recalled, studying a yearbook I brought with me, "he always had big smiles."

The portrait captured a husky young man who seemed primed to make his mark. A wide, confident smile topped Holmes's strong chin. His eyes were narrowed yet inviting. Studio lighting emphasized those big shoulders filling his dark-colored polo shirt.

Holmes was no trouble at all, Mr. Scott assured me. "Most of that came from wannabes," he said. "They wanted to be punks, little gangbangers. They were playing the tough guy and all that. And it escalates." As for Wallace, "When Jason didn't have anything bothering him, he was all right," he said, grinning anew. "But you knew Jason had a fly temper. He had a fly temper!"

Serious problems in that era mostly filtered up from Alaska's largest city. On one occasion, Scott intercepted a carload of Anchorage hoods who'd cruised up to settle some beef. He faced them down outside Lathrop's main entrance.

"They were coming up looking," he said, flashing a smile. "That was '96, '97, right in that era. That was a crazy era."

Though he never had a problem keeping order himself, he accepted that you can't be everywhere or assume you'll hear what transpires when you aren't looking.

"You hate to make assumptions," said Mr. Scott, reflecting on the possibility Wallace and Holmes's drug-ring murders weren't their first. "Sometimes violence perpetuates itself," he mused. "There's a chance it may not be the first time. And they just didn't get caught. So they get more brazen."

Later, it hit me: those brazen kids roaming Mr. Scott's hallways chalked up at least six more murders after high school.

———————————

Ashley Briggs had serious senior fever. Her final piece for *Extreme Alaska* hadn't gelled at all. She still needed the class to graduate, and that gave me leverage for a story assignment we couldn't publish yet but ought to get ready.

> Ashley,
>
> I just sent you a pile of regional articles on the Jason Wallace-Holmes murder spree... Your assignment is roughing together a full story about who Jason Wallace was and is.
>
> For media: We have yearbook photos, the newspaper pages/photos, and, perhaps, tapes of Wallace's confession. (The judge allowed them into the evidence. I'll pursue copies at the courthouse.) We are uniquely positioned to do this because the Ester homicide was covered well up here...
>
> When the Innocence Project proceeds with its action targeting Wallace, our piece will be ready to go with a splash.

Ashley kicked it into gear. By the time she lined up for the university's cap and gown procession that May, her profile on Jason Wallace was loaded in Extreme's new "Crime & Punishment" section, a mouse-click away from publication when this story broke.

———————

I was on the East Coast visiting family following UAF's 2011 commence-
ment ceremony when a former student's email caught up: "I read the
material on *Extreme Alaska* for the first time," wrote April Monroe Frick, a
young mother whose connections on all sides of the case sometimes worried
me. In addition to the new last name, she had other surprises. Not only
were her father and a sister attorneys, who might assist my efforts, April,
now president of the Greater Fairbanks Board of Realtors, offered to assist
with fundraising. "I remember how surprised I was to see a college professor
fighting for four Native kids," she noted, observing that business isn't done
that way in our town. "It stands out and I would help any way I can."

———————

SEPTEMBER 2011

Dan McKinney left word on my office phone, encouraging me to visit him
at Northstar Center, a halfway house across from the Blue Loon Saloon.

Greeting me like a prospective business partner, he led me outside to a
fenced area, continuing past empty picnic tables to a far corner. Satisfied that
we were alone, he said he had a message for the Alaska Innocence Project:
Wallace did it. He'd heard him boast about it. He could testify to that, but
the reward needed to be a whole lot bigger!

We were off the record. I'd agreed to that walking in, meaning this
conversation was strictly for background; I couldn't publish a word. That
didn't stop me from trying to change his mind.

Let me report this, I urged him. Get it out there. People will support
you. The reward ought to apply.

McKinney scoffed. Did I not understand the risk? He wasn't coming
forward for "chump change." He had a kid to think about.

"Give me an example of what you know," I said, "what your testimony
might cover?"

Jason Wallace bragged that he stomped that kid so hard his head rebounded off the pavement, he said. "Like a basketball," McKinney added, raising his foot knee high, acting it out.

I agreed to pass on his message to the Alaska Innocence Project, but I needed something from him. "One question," I said. "Still off the record."

He remained noncommittal but didn't walk away.

"Anyone involved in this still out on the street?"

McKinney nodded.

I pushed for more. "Someone like that would have a lot to lose."

His lips tightened, nodding again.

Implications expanded by the mile driving home. I needed to completely rethink student involvement.

When I mentioned McKinney's interest in that reward, Oberly immediately began speculating what it might take for him to come forward. I cut Bill off. "As a journalist, I don't pay for information, and I'm not going to be involved."

CHAPTER 12

THE POWER OF STORIES

NOVEMBER 2011

"FREE THE FAIRBANKS FOUR" proclaimed blue letters on black, beside the silhouette of a man gripping the bars of a prison window and gazing at angry ravens. "It is hard to introduce a story so specific yet universal," wrote the unidentified blogger. "So young, yet so old. It is not enough to say that this is a blog about four young Native men wrongfully convicted of a brutal murder. It is not enough to say that this blog is about racism or hate, or faith or hope. This is the story of Alaska. Of America. A story of injustice, a plea for help, for understanding, and above all a story of faith in the power of stories, of the truth.

"Writing this blog is an act of faith, a testimony to the power of the truth, spoken, read. We may not be experts in journalism, in law, or many other things. But the contributors here come from Alaska, from a culture that has a long tradition of storytelling, and a belief that the truth holds incredible power. This is a long story, and we will have to tell it the old way, the slow way, in pieces as they come."

Beautifully written and powerful, the unsigned blog served as a call to arms, elevating the plight of Marvin, Eugene, Kevin, and George into a statewide movement embraced in urban areas, villages, anyplace with a modem or cell.

Who was behind this?

It proved to be April, that News Writing student from a few years back, a formidable woman, then working part-time in hotel management, an old friend of George Frese and others on all sides of the case. She'd apparently remarried, and Monroe was her last name now.

Clearly, I misread her from the start, unsure what to make of her tips that Alaska Redd was somehow involved. Or the woman April referred me to, who denied knowing who or what I was talking about. Though I hadn't disclosed my source, I soon heard back from April: the woman had called her, fearful Redd might come after her. I didn't know what to make of it.

Then came a class field trip to the courthouse, where we turned up a damning pair of tickets. In January 1999, April and Dale Depue, then sixteen and seventeen respectively, were both cited for underage drinking on the same night in the same car. For a time, I feared the young mother was deliberately steering us away from our main suspect.

Instead, April resurfaced as the blogger seeding a movement supporting the so-called Fairbanks Four. A pair of tech-savvy Native activists were apparently involved as well, notably website designer Misty Moon, another young mother fed up with racism, and digital graphics whiz Skye Mal. Virtually overnight, the trio launched an array of Fairbanks Four social media channels.

It didn't stop there. With her husband's band heading the bill, April's Fairbanks Four team staged fundraisers, packing new financial heft behind the Alaska Innocence Project's fight. They also stepped up pressure on prominent Native leaders and politicians to get involved in reopening the case.

"Friended" by April's team, students and I now had access to their private Facebook group, putting me in touch with the Fairbanks Four's expanding network of urban and village activists, including Ricko DeWilde, a fashion-minded ex-con and a school friend of Marvin and the others.

Ricko peddled signature swag, outfitting Fairbanks Four supporters with hip-hop-influenced liberation-themed hoodies and T-shirts.

The week before Christmas, April forwarded an "action plan" from the so-called Free the Fairbanks Four committee. She and ten others were designated as "core leaders of the movement," the plan stated.

The media outreach section called for developing press kits for celebrities and conventional media organizations. Letters to the editor fell under section C, noting the importance of sharing templates and suggested topics. Section D hit close to home, pledging continuous efforts to take full advantage of our personal relationships with local/state reporters.

"All interesting and encouraging," I emailed April. "Wish Shirley D was around to see this."

Blog updates on the Fairbanks Four were cross-promoted through a namesake Facebook page, where followers soon numbered in the hundreds. Another Fairbanks Four private group handled coordination of protests. I joined both to keep tabs on what was happening.

Support on the streets didn't carry much weight inside the Fairbanks courthouse or Department of Law offices. All Bill Oberly had in hand was a jailbird's sworn statement that fifteen years ago, while skipping school and driving around sharing a joint, a friend bragged about ripping off John Hartman. Matt Ellsworth, the one person we'd found theoretically in a position to confirm this, denied even knowing Scott Davison.

Oberly kept harping on the importance of getting Ellsworth on board. I'd called the kid on and off for months. He was holding back; I was sure of that from the way he occasionally answered and listened to my pitch for coming forward. But listening was as far as he'd go. Not once had Ellsworth conceded he was even there.

As for Harold, the person Scott Davison claimed was driving the car that day? I'd left messages for a UAA student we suspected might be our Harold. When he finally called back, the guy seemed genuinely bewildered.

April Monroe and other Fairbanks Four supporters were pressuring Oberly to challenge the convictions in court. In the best of circumstances, I knew the Alaska Innocence Project was a year or more away from even a preliminary hearing on reopening the case, let alone presenting convincing evidence warranting the exoneration of Marvin and the others. Mounting political pressure from fired-up activists wasn't enough.

NAMASTE

I'd taught at UAF for ten years, the longest stretch working for any organization. I remained a journalist at heart and sometimes felt like a fraud in classrooms. Yet I now qualified for a sabbatical in the coming year. Aiming high, I applied to be a Fulbright scholar in India, which I'd last visited on SS *Sam*. Kate was on board. The university's new president was another retired general, an Air Force four-star. She needed a break from old generals issuing orders. Rory, fifteen, was in sophomore year at West Valley. If I got the Fulbright, we'd be back in time for his senior year. Meanwhile, the whole family would share an adventure.

Just before Christmas 2011, word came down that I'd cleared the first hurdle. The kids were horrified. An entire year stuck in India? Bad Dad!

Spring break passed without any word on my application. At home, the dreaded trip began looking more like a gift swiped before it was even unwrapped. The boys even suggested we better not let Mom see *Slumdog Millionaire*.

FOUR MONTHS LATER

"Greetings from United States-India Educational Foundation. I am delighted to formally welcome you to the Fulbright family and hope that your academic experience in India will be rewarding."

Subject: NAMASTE

Brian-

Do you have contact information for Matt Ellsworth or Daniel McKinney? I am hoping to get in touch with them soon. If you have any thoughts on that please let me know.

Bon voyage, my friend.

Bill Oberly's note regrettably confirmed my pessimism. Despite support out on the street, the Alaska Innocence Project's court case was spinning wheels, sliding sideways, if not backward.

We'd partnered in this justice quest, and a temporary change of address didn't change that, not in this internet age. On the way out of town, I launched Dissenting Opinion, a new website intended as a clearinghouse for Hartman case documents. Visitors had access to audio links ranging from Detective Aaron Ring's interview with Chris Stone to hearings, transcripts of 1998 trooper interviews, police reports, court records, more than a dozen criminal justice studies about wrongful convictions, and new standards adopted elsewhere in the country for interrogations and lineups.

As hoped, April's team posted links, seeding discussions on Fairbanks Four social media channels.

Within a day of arriving in Mumbai, sensory overload kicked in. We marveled at the flowers and lavish ornamentation coloring a joyous wedding. The groom, Samir, was the son of a UAF petroleum faculty member who helped line up my Fulbright gig at Symbiosis Institute of Media and Communication, a top graduate school. The bride, Tulsi, was the daughter of a former UAF engineering professor. Chet, a UAF graduate, was our guide, alerting us it was time to congratulate the bride and cheer a game involving the groom. Rachel, our picky-eating little seven-year-old, recoiled from the fancy platters. Without a word, Chet dashed away and reappeared with plain white rice.

We were feeling dazed yet worldly as Chet bid us goodbye, pointing out our hotel, an easy walking distance from where we all stood. The monsoon unloaded as we were crossing the street, literally blinding us. Dodging three-wheeled auto rickshaws, we stumbled into a dim, crowded pedestrian tunnel where everyone stared at the dripping Americans. Peeling off wet clothes at the hotel, Rachel laughed along with everyone else at her bloodred streaked skin; the dyes used in her dress weren't monsoon quality.

I was teaching in Pune, a sleepy town, as Indian colleagues described it, with a population of five to seven million. The Symbiosis students were sharp and highly motivated to explore new forms of journalism. Before long, I had them producing an online weekly paper.

Our first night at our dusty Paradise Society rental, a rat squeezed through an impossibly tight crack under the front door. As Kate and Rachel screamed, I grabbed a bucket and chased the sucker across cool marble flooring and slammed the bucket down. Gotcha! The kids fetched cardboard. I slipped it underneath, flipped the bucket over, dashed outside, and hurled the invader toward the street.

Another scream from Kate punctured my triumph. "It's coming back!"

I slammed the door behind me, blocking the invader's return.

Kate glared, unimpressed. "I don't know why you didn't kill it."

"Babe, I'm barefoot."

Once again, a bolt from the blue landed in my inbox.

"It's been a very long time since we've talked and hopefully you remember me. Your voice mail message says you're in India for a year. What an exciting adventure that must be... The reason I'm writing is to pick your brain on the 'Fairbanks Four.'"

During my two-year fling as a TV reporter covering Alaska's capitol in Juneau, Steve MacDonald doubled as the anchorman and news director at KTUU, our company's big Anchorage affiliate. Every day, we discussed political developments and other story ideas along with what I had coming for the nightly newscast.

I put him in touch with April, assuring her he was a pro.

"Several hours into the interrogation, Detective Ring upped the pressure when he revealed some startling information about evidence gathered at the scene," the off-screen narrator told viewers watching *The 49th Report: The Fairbanks Four*, MacDonald's new hour-long documentary.

"See the problem is your footprints in the blood. Okay. So the fight already happened, and you stepped in it. Okay?" the unseen narrator continued, reading from the transcript of Ring's interview with Eugene Vent, the source of the text superimposed on the bottom half of the screen, last names identified in bold yellow-face type. "That's the problem we have and that's the problem you need to help me with. Okay. Because it's your foot in the blood, not somebody else's."

The video cut to footage of young and lean Eugene, full head of black hair, dressed in a clean white shirt with big cuffs. He looked worried as he swiveled in what I presumed was a courtroom chair, eyeing something happening off to the side, as MacDonald continued reading from that 1997 interrogation transcript.

"I can tell you a big lie and you still wouldn't believe me. I could tell you the truth and you still wouldn't believe me," continued MacDonald, reading Eugene's reply.

"He tells Ring that he can't remember details from the night before," summarized the broadcaster, skipping ahead, "because he blacked out from all the alcohol he drank, but the detective doesn't buy it."

"Okay," Ring replied. "That type of thing just doesn't happen."

And there he was, Detective Aaron Ring, looking younger than I ever recalled, dark hair showing above close-trimmed sideburns, lips flapping with silent questions spelled out on the lower portion of the screen.

"Just stand up for what you did and say hey, this is how I screwed up."

"I tried to," Eugene said. "I told you I was drunk, and I just don't remember."

"What was it that you did to take part in this?" Ring asked.

"Probably kicked him. Probably hit him too."

"Well, it wasn't probably," Ring said. "Let's get specific about it. Okay, you hit him with your right hand? Left hand? Or both?"

"I don't know. Probably hit him with both," Eugene said.

As I watched from India, MacDonald's documentary, loading in chunks, kept freezing up on my office terminal, yet I couldn't turn away. The historic footage included scenes from the original trials I hadn't known even existed. Incredible!

There was George, fresh-faced, with a short 1980s-style bowl haircut, wearing a blue button-down shirt and dark vest. The camera zoomed in, catching him gazing down at his lap, smiling to himself, and shaking his head as the judge sentenced him to serve forty years. Leaving the courtroom under escort, George paused before the door, spun around, and raised his shackled hands, giving gallery watchers the finger.

Another old sentencing clip showed Eugene reading from a written statement. "Yes, I'm sorry that such a tragic thing ended this young boy's life," said the young man in the blue prison jumpsuit. "I'm also sorry that I'm being blamed for it."

Though Eugene and George were convicted, the last pair to face trial had reason to be optimistic, MacDonald reported, setting the scene for his own recent interviews. "We had good alibi witnesses that weren't drinking. That knew times that night. That seen me," said Marvin Roberts, facing the camera in a well-lit white room, head shaved, clad in an orange jumpsuit. "They seen Kevin. They seen all of us at certain times that night."

But those jurors had also heard Arlo Olson's version, emphasizing that other mugging down the street from Eagles Hall, the broadcaster reminded viewers, cutting to another old courtroom clip showing the clear-eyed, cleaned-up star witness in action. "I remember seeing George and Eugene punch him," said Olson, testifying from the witness stand. "Kevin jumped in… I remember seeing Frankie pushed, getting kicked in the head."

Kevin told the broadcaster he always figured he'd be convicted. But hope surged when the jury foreman announced the panel turned thumbs down on the first-degree murder charge. "My heart was beating, beating really fast. I mean I can feel it in my chest," he told the broadcaster, pounding his chest. "Big, big sigh of relief," he recalled, taking a deep breath. "And then went to murder two. And they found me guilty," Kevin said, raising his brows, staring at the camera slowly zooming in on his wide-open gray eyes. "And the rest of the charges just kept coming. It's like I just went deaf," he added. "I couldn't even hear nuttin'. Tears start running down my face."

"Kevin Pease received sixty-four years behind bars," reported MacDonald. The scene cut to footage showing the big defendant leaving the courtroom under escort, when he suddenly turned back.

"How's it feel putting an innocent man in jail, Jeff?" Kevin yelled at the prosecutor, voice wavering.

Next came a hallway interview with Marvin's longtime defender. "I did my best," said Dick Madson. "Evidently it wasn't good enough, so I'll assume responsibility for that." For Hartman's family, he added, "I just hope the truth comes out someday."

KTUU's special offered my first glimpse of new Fairbanks police chief Laren Zager. "The staying power of the case" baffled him, he told MacDonald, yet the town's top cop insisted he remained open-minded. "I have no personally strong feelings about it. I don't feel defensive about it or anything. I would under the right circumstances reopen that case or portions of that case."

I hadn't wasted any time with FPD since Scooter Welch retired, but this Zager guy seemed worth a conversation when I got back.

PUNE, INDIA, THANKSGIVING 2012

The kids and I stared as Kate pondered the scrawny turkey she'd specially ordered from a market catering to foreigners. Though totally plucked, the bird's feet and head remained attached. We'd invited Indian friends and other local Fulbright scholars for Thanksgiving. The Americans, us included, likely wouldn't have much of an appetite if she served that bird with its head on.

There was a lot to celebrate this year, as I shared with Gary Cohn, Maurice Possley, and other friends from Investigative Reporters and Editors. First, the big news from home: Eugene Vent was granted a new hearing on his bid to exclude his drunken juvenile statements. My students were making plans to cover it. We were also involved in the documentary recently aired by Anchorage's top TV station. A former student shifted the fight for justice to the internet, raising a whopping reward for new information through her *Free the Fairbanks Four* blog and related Facebook group.

I also noted that we were getting plenty of downloads on justice studies on exonerations available on the UAF's Dissenting Opinion website. Best of all, Bill Oberly hinted that the Alaska Innocence Project was about to challenge the verdicts.

Symbiosis students were enterprising and fun to teach. Among the instructional innovations any professor would appreciate, I had a big persuasive student at my beck and call, ensuring classmates kept pace with assignments!

We truly had a remarkable year. Kate got into serious yoga. Our kids gained confidence dealing with crowds and traffic and made a lot of friends at their international school. The firsthand exposure to poverty's many faces reminded us all what a gift it is to be an American.

That said, the festering injustice back home was seldom far from my thoughts.

STREETS OF ANCHORAGE

JUNE 2013

Kate and the kids raced around the house, comparing notes about the renters' lingering imprint, that cracked window, the garden going to seed, dandelions on the rebound. On the upside, our renters left behind a full-size exercise treadmill!

We'd been home less than a week when I blasted down the Parks Highway in our nearly new black Toyota Tacoma bound for a Native powwow in Anchorage.

Hunting for a parking space, I passed protesters unpacking signs along several uptown streets. Drumbeats—no kidding—led me to the assembly point, a courtyard among tall buildings. From there, the procession took off, winding along the extra-wide sidewalks of Alaska's largest city on a rare, truly beautiful day. Some Fairbanks Four supporters were dancing single file in a weaving line. Larger clusters of protesters took their time stopping traffic, garnering waves and what seemed to be supportive honks. Little kids riding in backpack-style baby carriers took it all in wide-eyed.

The atmosphere reminded me of a procession of face-painted anarchists I once covered winding their way through the Lower East Side, playing homemade instruments. This day's tone was jovial as well.

Nearing a tall, empty stage set up overlooking Delaney Park's west-end grassy urban meadow, marchers melted away, mingling with friends. By and by, I bumped into Casey Grove, now working for the *Anchorage Daily News*. He was interviewing Bill Oberly.

"A fifty-to-sixty-page brief for postconviction relief is in the works,"

Oberly said. He declined to get into details but alluded to recently discovered discrepancies in the judicial process.

Asked who he faulted for the convictions in that final trial? Oberly observed that clashing cultures certainly figured. "The alibi witnesses were all from the Native community, and the prosecutor kind of pooh-poohed 'em."

Casey got sharper quotes from April Monroe, the event's main organizer. "Institutionalized racism!" That was how she sized up the case. "This is the type of corruption that stole people's children."

Music and speeches came next. When Hazel invited me to join her onstage, I hesitated only a second. "They will go free," I assured the crowd, "when all that's known about this case becomes public."

"Marchers Aim to Free the Fairbanks Four," headlined Casey's front-page story.

The movement to free four men whose supporters say were wrongfully convicted of killing a Fairbanks teenager in 1997 took to Anchorage's streets Saturday...

Fifteen years later and 360 miles from the scene of the crime, those attending the Free the Fairbanks Four rally were convinced more than ever that Roberts, Frese, Pease and Vent are innocent.

Support for the four men has grown slowly but steadily since their convictions. On Saturday, that grass-roots effort culminated in the Anchorage march. About 150 people with signs saying "Truth and Love Will Prevail" and "Release Them" marched from Town Square to the Delaney Park Strip where more supporters joined them.

CHAPTER 13

BYLINES AND HALLWAY SECRETS

The stakes 'r' high.
You gotta, get in, get out, make moves,
Strategize!
'Cause the stakes 'r' high!
The stakes 'r' high!
You gotta, get in, get out, make moves,
Strategize!

The tune, cut in 2002, according to the liner notes, featured Alaska Redd, a local studio owner, and Dolla-B, a.k.a. Wild Bill Holmes. Both rappers traded vocals throughout "The Stakes 'r' High" and other cuts on their *Clearer Than Black & White* CD. The pair also contributed cuts on *Interior's Most Wanted*, a double CD collection that featured more than three dozen staccato, rapping, grunting offerings by local bad boys.

Dolla-B's signature low guttural voice was apparent on at least three cuts, usually trading lines with Alaska Redd, including the rappers' tale of stalking a rival gang.

"One, two, three, four, five, six, seven," called Redd. "I got the shot."

"I got the MAC-eleven," rasped Dolla-B, referring to a submachine-gun pistol.

Though Redd owned the studio, he and Holmes clearly partnered producing *Clearer Than Black & White*. The CD case pictured the pair crouched back-to-back, each leaning away from the other. Redd was a fresh-faced white kid with red hair pulled back in tight rows. Dolla-B looked nothing like his smiling senior-yearbook photo; this sullen man glared at the camera, massive arms resting on his legs, hands draped over his bent knees. He wasn't frowning, but those eyes warned against testing him.

As the song continued, Dolla-B and Redd joined for the chorus, then took turns expanding on the theme. Redd was quicker with the phrasing, Holmes's voice was deeper, his pronunciation looser, storylines darker.

"The stakes 'r' high," he rasped.

But I still gotta try
to get the stake befo' too much time pass by.
My number one rule is dough or die,
for a piece of the pie!
Sometimes I ask myself why I ever decided to cross the tracks.
I knew I'd get lost and could never come back.
But I wasn't tripping,
'cause at the end of the road
I saw a pot of gold,
money fold, pockets bold!
Nights were cold.
Better yet they were freezing!
If money's not in my pocket,
I ain't sleeping.
I'm out strategizing,
watching myself breathing, unleashing!
Trying to find the reason that I'm so broke.
Life's too short.

A nigger like me gotta do the most,
coast to coast!
I mean I'm into fast.
Fuck with the slow.
Gotta get dough!
Rookie, I'm a pro!

Eyeing that CD cover, I studied Holmes's face. The guy vowing to do whatever it takes, and we now knew *already had* when this disk was cut. All but declaring it.

The studio's connection with Hartman's murder wasn't Wallace or apparently Alaska Redd. It was the big man who'd lost that smile Mr. Scott and others still talked about.

Timing indicated the young gangbanger was just getting started when I was still a reporter. That brought to mind the day a local police official dropped by the newsroom, warning reporters that Fairbanks had a gang problem. I figured it was malarkey.

Avoiding alleys and streets with poor lighting was second nature when I lived in New York and Baltimore. Gang problems in Alaska in the late 1980s and '90s seemed laughable, a figment of police union negotiators arguing for bigger budgets or better staffing.

The stakes 'r' high.
You gotta, get in, get out, make moves,
Strategize!
'Cause the stakes 'r' high.

All this needed context. Who better to ask than Holmes's former collaborator in music and who knows what else?

In classroom discussions, I always stress the value of interviewing people in-person, preferably at the subject's workplace or home, wherever they're comfortable. With Alaska Redd? No way. Too many jailbirds and disturbing lyrics were associated with his studio. Besides, knocking on doors for answers was old school. I simply friended him on Facebook.

"I'm working on a year-after update on events unleashed by Bill's confession," I messaged Redd, explaining I needed to draw on his artistic memory. "For example, how should I refer to him as Dolla-B, Dollar Bill... By the way," I pointed out, "'The Stakes 'r' High' comes up in the trooper's interview with the prison guard," adding that I hoped to include a prominent link to his studio when I reported the story. "You might see some business."

A few minutes later, I dangled bait again, "If you've got an email, I'll shoot you that interview transcript that mentions 'The Stakes 'r' High,' Mafia moves, staring down rivals, it's wild."

Redd's email address was waiting for me when I got back from class.

He politely declined requests for an interview about Holmes. When I asked about Lathrop kids, he pointed out that he never attended the school. "Maybe down the road," Redd emailed.

More often than not, Redd simply acknowledged my messages through a time-stamped profile image of him, leaning back on stage, both arms cocked as if double-punching the sky, right hand angling that mic by his lips.

The *News-Miner* hadn't committed to running my Holmes story. I kept promising that it would, pointing to possible benefits, attempting to draw him out. "Get ready for a sales bump."

"No problem," the rapper responded. "I'm just trying to take this all in at the moment. Just not sure how I want to go about it yet. Keep in touch."

Nearing the second week of October, city editor Rod Boyce was pushing for specifics.

"Who wrote lyrics to 'Stakes are High'?" I messaged Redd. "Bill's part fits what's been known about the 2002 drug conspiracy. Either way it's a fine tune. Supporting music is perfect."

That prompted two punches and an actual response: "We both wrote our parts."

"Thanks," I responded. "I'm working on this as time permits. Was listening to the song and it seems to foreshadow his moves against Hakeem."

Six minutes later: "I'm not sure," messaged Redd. "We wrote that song probably a year or more prior to the Dec incident."

Alaska's oldest student newspaper, the *Paystreak*, took its name from Italian immigrant Felix Pedro's 1902 gold strike on the Chena River. That pay dirt near a trading post prompted the gold rush to what's now known as Fairbanks, incorporated as a town the following year. These days, Lathrop High's paper was produced by a class taught by former *News-Miner* reporter Tim Parker.

School was out for the summer the day our footsteps echoed off the walls as Tim guided me through the maze of corridors, attesting to years of renovation at Fairbanks's largest school. He set me up in a free classroom with a stack of back issues and wished me luck.

We'd identified sources by mining yearbooks. I figured the *Paystreak* might offer more about student interests and concerns during the era shaded by Hartman's murder.

Long shot? Oh yeah.

I'd hardly begun flipping pages when a September 1997 headline slapped me in the eyes.

"DO STUDENTS THINK GANGS ARE COOL?"

When the word gang is mentioned what is the first thing that pops into the mind? Probably Crips, Bloods and Los Angeles, right? There are now students in Lathrop claiming to be in gangs. Teachers might not notice the gang members, but some students find them impossible to miss. Many students think gangs are uncool and want to rid their schools of them. According to senior Bill Holmes, "Gangs in Lathrop are wannabes."

Incredibly, Jason Wallace's drug-ring partner made an entrance!

Holmes does not believe that it's necessary for a person to be in a popular group at school. "They shouldn't make it a part of life," he said.

Plowing through back issues, I found the same reporter quoted Holmes's complaint about exit exams: "No matter what form the test is given in, it will still hold many hardworking students back from pursuing other goals after graduation." And a few pages later, she had him commenting on a rap star's new release. "I really enjoy listening to Tupac's music, but I refuse to pay $25 for a CD!"

More incredible, Holmes wrote for the paper as well. He'd been a *Paystreak* sports reporter, collecting bylines in several issues.

"The Lathrop Malemute Track and Field Team is off to a slow start because of the weather," he wrote for the May 1997 issue. The story included his event-by-event assessment of Lathrop's prospects, characterizing squad members as individually skilled on a team that lacked depth. "We have the talent to go to state, just not enough people," he quoted a junior saying. Sportswriter Holmes assessed the situation as a rebuilding year. "They have the talent; they just have to put it together."

A solid article. Holmes appeared to be a better-than-average student reporter. Clearly, the guy had more going for him than you'd expect from a cutthroat drug dealer.

Sharing the same page, I found a story by Ty Keltner, the former manager of KSUA, the student radio station on campus. He'd later worked for local TV, where he eventually realized his communication skills were worth more than our local news organizations. I found him working as a state agency spokesman.

"A cool, upbeat dude that no one could help but like," Keltner said of Holmes.

The big guy's impact on the sidelines of a basketball playoff game stood out. A player from archrival West Valley had just sunk a three-pointer with only seconds left, putting the Wolfpack ahead of the heavily favored Malemutes.

Lathrop fans fell silent.

"Wild Bill stood up," recalled Keltner. "'We got this!' he shouted. 'It's going to happen!' He puts his arms up, crying, 'I got faith!' and everybody started screaming!" Though Lathrop lost that game, it didn't diminish that moment for Keltner.

As for the rest: "It's a shame what happened to him," he said. "People get wrapped up in bad things."

That applied, I soon learned, to Ahisha, the student reporter who interviewed Holmes about gangs. She later married Hakeem! Yes, Ahisha's husband was the rival cocaine dealer Holmes later robbed and shot to death in California, along with another guy who happened to be "in the wrong place," as the big man later put it.

The Lathrop circle deepened. Several yearbook photos credited Rashan Brown as staff photographer. Not only was his byline on several *Paystreak* articles, two of them quoted Jason Wallace's girlfriend Kealoha.

From my experience, student reporters, especially new ones, invariably interview their friends. It wasn't proof, but none of these felt like chance connections. The group Holmes now claimed were involved in Hartman's murder hung out together back in the day.

The student newspaper's former advisor, a retired teacher, had trouble accepting Rashan Brown had it in him to later kill two people in Oregon, let alone take part in Hartman's murder during high school. "He was a very nice young man. If he actually did this," Fran Hove said, "it's got to be something very traumatic that happened to him."

If Lathrop had a gang problem in the late 1990s, local journalists—me included—missed it. The only time I recall even discussing gangs at the *News-Miner* involved a published photo of kids goofing around on the front stoop of a house downtown. One of them was flashing a gang sign, insisted a police official, who showed up in the newsroom. The offending page had a photo of a kid staring at the camera with one palm open, showing fingers oddly splayed. That was it. From what I'd seen and reported living on Manhattan's Lower East Side and Fells Point in Baltimore, this claimed proof of gang problems in Fairbanks seemed laughable.

Likewise, the *Paystreak*'s former editor remained skeptical that Lathrop had a gang problem in the late 1990s. "I never felt any reason to take it seriously. It wasn't like it was a scary situation," he said. The man who ruled the hallways made sure of that. "No one messed with Mr. Scott. He caught arrows!"

THOUGHT I KNEW THIS TOWN

A quick search using Motznik linked Scott Davison to a statistics expert I often quoted covering economic development issues in the 1990s. Approaching Janet Davison's house, I dreaded how this might go.

Scott's mom greeted me warmly. Her face fell when she grasped that I was investigating her son's possible involvement in that infamous murder case. All positive, I stressed: "The way I see it, Scott's emerging as a hero in this thing."

She stared like I was crazy.

The poor woman fell silent, devouring the affidavit her son gave the

Alaska Innocence Project. She finally looked up, face pale, no fight left in those eyes. "This is a death sentence," she said.

I hurriedly explained her son's courageous statement reinforced what we'd discovered about the Lathrop Murder Circle, as I'd begun calling it, and warranted praise and support.

Janet's analytic skills kicked in as she reflected on Scott's troubled path through high school. Though he came from an upper-middle-class white family, Scott gravitated toward the rap music crowd she clearly found distasteful. Slumping grades, skipping school, her son's drug use and related crimes, all that contributed to ugly rows with his father and the breakup of their marriage.

She questioned whether Scott's statement was even accurate. It could be he was locked up at the juvenile facility at the time.

All that needed checking, I agreed, along with Matt Ellsworth's insistence he didn't even know her son Scott. Hearing that, Janet grabbed my arm. He and Scott were such close pals, Matt practically lived at her house. And to this day, she said, whenever she ran into him, Matt hugged her.

She's coming around, I told myself as I left, perhaps even proud her son chose to come forward. Yeah, right. As if Kate and I wouldn't be terrified if one of our boys put their lives on the line like this.

Matt Ellsworth and I chatted several times that summer. "He's at least listening," I told Bill Oberly.

TWENTY-FOUR WORDS

SEPTEMBER 2013

The email carried a single-word subject line: "Draft."

> For your eyes only. Since you have probably the best handle on the
> factual nature of these cases I am wondering if you could review this

pleading and give me any feedback you might have... This is not yet a public document and must remain private until it is filed.

Thanks,

Bill

Clicking the attachment opened a PDF copy of Marvin Roberts's forty-seven-page motion for postconviction relief. That title, though thrilling to behold, didn't ensure anything. What did Oberly have that the justices hadn't heard before?

Flicking through legalese blah blah blah about constitutional rights and appellate decisions and rehashing events the night of the murder, a subhead, bold-faced and underlined, stopped me cold: New Evidence.

Filed with this application are two affidavits from William Z. Holmes. These affidavits establish, for the first time, what actually happened early in the early morning hours of October 11, 1997, on the corner of Ninth and Barnett.

Wait. What was that again? Wild Bill Holmes talked? A page later, the gangbanger was described as initiating this with a handwritten letter to the Alaska Innocence Project more than a year ago. The motion referred to a pair of sworn statements describing what went down.

Oberly had been sitting on this! Gobsmacked, I was hunting for Holmes's actual words, skipping over arguments about timeliness and diligence vetting the new evidence. A reference to April Monroe caught my eye; she'd found that red car! No, that wasn't it. She'd confirmed through the state DMV records that Holmes's mom *owned a red car*, a Ford Tempo, not a Monte Carlo. And Holmes identified that Tempo as the car used in assaulting Hartman. He was behind the wheel.

I was proud to see our reporting about Arlo Olson referenced, along with Gary Moore's recovery of that footprint exhibit, which an expert had apparently examined and critiqued.

Nowhere in this forty-nine-page draft document did I find the referenced sworn statements backing this up, not from Holmes, Davison, April, or anyone else. Again, I pored through the document, this time searching for the term "Holmes." He referred to Jason Wallace riding in the passenger seat with other guys in the back seat yelling at him. "I ask what happened and they all 3 simultaneously told me that upon knocking the boy to the ground, Wallace began stomping him repeatedly."

That was the only place Holmes was directly quoted verbatim. Everything else was paraphrased, supporting various legal points. Without details, *nothing here could be fact-checked!*

Okay, all Oberly requested was help proofing. Must remain private, he'd specified, though that carried no weight legally. What I was looking at was embargoed information, shared under an implicit agreement not to publish until a later time. What I chose to do with this came down to personal and professional ethics, how I conduct myself with sources. That and newsroom standards. As far as the latter, I could imagine city editor Rod Boyce's reaction: *Brian, this hasn't even been filed in court!*

Twenty-four words: That was all I had on Holmes's apparent confession. Nothing here justified breaking the embargo, but that didn't stop me from collecting perspectives for a comprehensive story down the line.

I began with a man of God with broad cultural perspective. "It's going to just underline, whatever the verb—reinforce everyone's perceptions of the situation," Reverend Scott Fisher said. "That they're out to getcha. You won't get an even break. That's already what everyone thinks."

Originally from Virginia, Father Scott found his calling in Alaska. He and his Athabascan bride settled in Beaver, a tiny village downriver from Fort Yukon. Years later, when the family moved to town, he noticed his son was treated differently.

"I remember being with him as he was being followed everywhere just walking through a grocery store." The rush to judgment coloring the Hartman verdicts echoed what he frequently heard from Native parishioners. "Everybody in the community, from prominent tribal leaders to people in the streets, has a story of similar instances with the police."

He drew parallels with the treatment Blacks experienced in the old south. "All of this," the minister said, referring to the new evidence supporting exoneration of the Fairbanks Four, "is just going to underline it."

As for the justice system itself?

"I hang around the jail enough to know you don't see any rich people in there," he quipped. "Yeah, it's too bad." Reverend Scott looked down, but only for a second. He straightened up, eyes softer, a smile spreading. "The positive of it," he declared, "is there's all those people from the families, from Shirley Demientieff on down, who have kept the faith in those kids."

"DAYLIGHT'S COMING"

RABINOWITZ COURTHOUSE, SEPTEMBER 25, 2013

Trailed by TV cameras, Bill Oberly entered the building and joined others awaiting security checks. He emptied his pockets in the cup, placed it on the conveyor belt alongside his briefcase, got the green light, picked everything back up, and proceeded toward the court clerk's station. When his turn came, the gaunt, graying defender placed a triple set of legal briefs on the counter and smiled.

The clerk collected the separate fees due for George Frese's, Kevin Pease's, and Marvin Roberts's separate motions for postconviction relief, then date-stamped the front page of each, making the submissions official. Eugene had already opened a similar case, which would soon be combined.

A crowd of more than a hundred people cheered as the Alaska Innocence

Project's director reemerged from the building alongside Tanana Chiefs Conference president Jerry Isaac and justice task force leader Shirley Lee.

Backpedaling toward the curb, I climbed a trash can and got an overhead shot of Oberly and the Native leaders basking in the moment, ringed by TV cameras, outstretched microphones, and merry supporters standing ten or more feet deep.

The crowd settled down as the gray-haired old defender prepared to speak. "What we filed," Oberly announced, "was a document claiming newly discovered evidence that established the actual innocence of our clients."

Whistles and clapping resounded off the courthouse's tall glassy walls and stone plaza frontage. Oberly stood there, hands clasped behind his back, swaying and grinning as the clamor went on and on.

Flanked by the men, Reverend Shirley Lee raised her right fist, prompting yet more cheers.

After the speeches ran their course, an aging, bewhiskered soul in a worn sweater of many colors moved to the forefront and bowed his head. "The dawn came over those northern hills," Father Scott Fisher intoned, "and the light came all the places where the darkness was and there was only light." He paused, letting that sink in. "And we give you thanks this afternoon."

"Thanks," the crowd muttered.

"This long night is ending," the reverend declared forcefully, "and its sunrise and the daylight's coming! We give you thanks," he added more softly.

"Give you thanks," observers repeated.

"Family and friends," said Father Scott, picking up rhythm, "and folks that walk through this long night carrying signs and saying prayers and saying no and refusing to give up."

Back in the newsroom, Rod Boyce and I dithered about headlines and wording right up until deadline. The result drew on recent interviews examining Wild Bill Holmes's emergence and revelations.

FORMER FAIRBANKS MAN SERVING DOUBLE-LIFE SENTENCE IN CALIFORNIA PRISON SAYS HE AND OTHERS KILLED BOY IN 1997

A 33-year-old Fairbanks man serving a double-life sentence in California claims he and a carload of Lathrop High School friends got away with killing John Hartman 16 years ago. In a sworn statement filed Wednesday in Fairbanks Superior Court by the Alaska Innocence Project, William Z. Holmes, in Lathrop's class of 1998, names convicted murderer Jason Wallace and three other school friends as accomplices in the killing...

In the handwritten letter included in Wednesday's filing, Holmes states that he and the others gathered at an apartment one Friday in October 1997, then piled into a car together and drove downtown to "have some fun" messing with "drunk natives." After chasing a pair of intoxicated men who got away, the group cruised another 20 minutes before happening upon the "white boy walking alone" on Barnette Street.

"We all got excited and say, 'We got one!'" wrote the inmate, describing the teen's fatal assault in his August 2012 letter to the Alaska Innocence Project.

The genial graying cop who'd inherited this mess pledged cooperation. "The last thing any officer wants to see," Police Chief Laren Zager said, "is an innocent person sitting in jail."

The day's breaking events left one of FPD's younger investigators feeling ill. "Ohhh," groaned Detective Chris Nolan. "This is probably what they were talking about."

Online reactions reflected long-standing community divisions:

Slcinak: Hartman was not the only victim. these men lost everything as well. nothing can every make up for the time that they lost. once they are freed. this is still going to follow them and haunt them. they are never going to be able to have a normal life. all because of the color of their skin.

Hrdharry: By not accepting responsibility, does this affect their chance of parole? If so, whose fault will it be now for them sitting in jail?

maus: The law of the land says that jurors cannot be sued if they find someone guilty, who is later found innocent. However, in many of the Innocence Project cases that result in reversal there seems to be a common thread, of jurors biased towards believing lies.

wild-alaska: Or maybe the confessions have something to do with it?

When I wasn't teaching or grading, Rod Boyce and I partnered chasing continuing developments. Neither of us collected overtime; in that respect, there really wasn't much difference between university gigs and newsrooms.

"Here's the edited version," the editor emailed me on July 11, 2014. "I did a couple small things. Added first ref on Oberly."

EUGENE VENT ATTORNEY ALLEGES "PROSECUTORIAL MISCONDUCT"

An attorney representing the youngest member of the so-called Fairbanks Four is asking a judge to toss Eugene Vent's conviction, asserting the state's delay reporting another man's confession in the case amounts to "prosecutorial misconduct."

"If I had gotten the information in 2011 when it was available to the state of Alaska," Defense Attorney Colleen Libbey said Friday, "I would have filed something immediately to get my client out of jail."

She was referring to the state's failure to notify the convicted men's defenders about a prison guard's 2011 memo reporting Holmes's description of the night Jason Wallace went crazy stomping a younger kid.

Vent, now 34, and other members of the so-called Fairbanks Four—George Frese, Kevin Pease and Marvin Roberts—all remain incarcerated.

The nickname Fairbanks Four reflected blogger April Monroe's impact. "So-called" was the editor's contribution. The truth was getting out; that was all that mattered to me.

"Benefit organizers," April posted on Fairbanks Four social media. "What's your cake walk formula? Do you start with the number of tickets sold? Or base the size of the outdoor circle on donated desserts?"

The fundraiser at Saint Raphael's Church, our family's parish, came together on the fly. Fairbanks Four supporters were still setting up when I dropped by.

I watched from behind a row of chairs as April arranged and rearranged a circle of markers on the grassy lawn. To my left, Marvin's sister worked a grill laden with hot dogs. To my right, Marvin's mom parked herself at a card table alongside the familiar old gray cash box used for making change and holding Fairbanks Four donations. I quietly counted the heads of attendees, reaching forty plus when I realized Little Marv was coming over to me, eyes shining, grinning broadly. "You want to talk to Marvin?" he said, offering me his cell phone.

OUT IN THE OPEN

A terse reference in the Alaska Innocence Project's brief provided an angle for deeper reporting on long-standing, poorly kept professional secrets about Hartman's murder.

"The nature and specifics of the next statements made by Jason Wallace is the subject of the sealed motion filed with this Application. Applicant contends these statements are no longer confidential and asks the Court to so rule and make them part of this Application."

Oberly, no surprise, refused to share or discuss the sealed motion unless a judge demanded it. I turned to legal scholars for perspective on the professional rules that justified silence, indeed concealment, of evidence about wrongful convictions. Right away, I was surprised to learn—though I should have realized this from the leak from the public defender's office that one of their clients had admitted to the murder—that privileged information is often shared within office settings. "What passes between clients and lawyers isn't as private as laymen may assume. It's a corporate secret," law professor James Moliterno told me over the phone from Washington and Lee University in Virginia. "There's a quick difference between the lawyer and a priest; the lawyer needs a lot of people to get the work done."

Anyone within a legal office tasked with handling work related to a case, from filing notes to fact-checking a client's statements, may have access to a client's secrets, confirmed Lawrence Fox of Drinker Biddle & Reath in Philadelphia, a noted legal responsibility expert. "I have to send out a memo to my law office employees," Fox said. "I get them to sign it—every year!—saying 'Don't you dare disclose any confidential information.' You who type my briefs, or you who work in the mailroom are privy to a lot of secrets. My obligation is to prevent them from disclosing anything."

That long-standing professional tenet cast a shadow over the Alaska Innocence Project's success convincing the Alaska Bar Association to amend its rules. Though Alaska lawyers now had the option of waiving client confidentiality and disclosing information "reasonably necessary" to prevent wrongful incarceration, they weren't required to come forward. That option remained theoretical.

As Bill Oberly predicted at the time, Geoff Wildridge, Jason Wallace's attorney, hadn't stepped forward.

LIKE A MANTRA

I set out to identify the original leak.

Dick Madson, now seventy-eight, had retired and was living out of state. His wife took the call and warned me that Dick's hearing wasn't so great. Though the old lawyer's voice seemed softer, he grasped who and what I was talking about right away. That leak had to have come from Wallace's defense team, he readily agreed, adding that it probably involved Investigator Thomas Bole.

GI benefits, accrued over nine years as an army infantryman, covered the costs of Bole's coursework and licensing as a private investigator. He applied those skills assisting defenders representing Marvin and the others accused of Hartman's murder. Through that work, spanning all three trials and years of appeals, Bole, perhaps better than anyone, knew Marvin's alibis and every hole in the state's case against the others. This much was clear: some five years later, Bole's new job with the Public Defender Agency thrust him into what had to be a gut-wrenching mission: assisting the defense of a man involved in a recent bloodbath, unloading privileged secrets about the Hartman case.

However it leaked, Madson applauded the results. "Whether it came from an investigator or someone else in the office," he said, "I believe it's appropriate."

Bole looked startled to find me at his doorstep one night soon after. I pointed out that he'd helped us when he was working for Madson, Bodwell, and the others. And he reminded me that we were teammates on the *News-Miner*'s co-ed softball team when I first came to Fairbanks. Indeed, we had been. Such a small town!

Bole guided me away from his house. Standing in the middle of his quiet old street, he said firmly, "I work for the public defender's office. I can't talk to you unless the head of the public defender's office or the attorney tell me to."

No matter how I phrased questions, he repeated the same line, like a mantra warding off harm.

Jennifer Hite, supervisor of the Public Defender Agency's Northern Region office, finally responded to my calls with an email: "I am unable to discuss any aspect of a client's representation."

John Skidmore, speaking for the Criminal Law Division, confirmed this much: Alaska was looking into new evidence. And he alluded to the issue under scrutiny behind closed courthouse doors: "I really can't comment on anything that's sealed."

BID MADE TO EXPOSE CLAIMS IN HARTMAN CASE
INNOCENCE PROJECT SAYS MAN'S STATEMENTS ARE NO LONGER CONFIDENTIAL

A leak breaching attorney-client privilege likely figures in a sealed court-filing and could add weight to a claimed confession by an inmate who says he and four high school friends were involved in the killing of John Hartman 16 years ago.

The client whose confidential statements will soon be weighed by a judge is Jason Wallace, who was represented by the Public Defender Agency...

What, if anything, Wallace said about the Hartman case to the public defender representing him in an unrelated 2002 murder would traditionally stay secret under attorney-client privilege. The Alaska Innocence Project is arguing a lapse in security justifies pulling back the legal curtain shielding the client's statements.

I'd run into Wildridge at a wake for a teenager whose family we'd both known for years. It wasn't the time and place; even I recognized that. Our conversation heated up, drawing stares. I didn't care and got a telling quote closing the front-page story.

Wildridge, for his part, has consistently refused to confirm or deny his client ever mentioned the Hartman case. "My position hasn't changed," he told me. "Do what you need to do."

CHAPTER 14

MESSAGE DELIVERED

Instead of interviewing delegates about issues of concern in their respective regions or corporation, as I did for many years, feeding breaking news to whatever print or TV newsroom I worked for at the time, this year's AFN self-assignment was personal. Embracing old friends, introducing myself to new delegates, I hastily outlined UAF Journalism's ongoing freedom of information fight to open court secrets about John Hartman's murder. It was a lot to take in, so I'd made flyers explaining our goals and soliciting support: "I contend public interest is served by unsealing the brief detailing Jason Wallace's statements… Whether or not the information is allowed as evidence, I believe strongly that full disclosure is vital so that society can begin to address systemic flaws that have shielded the identity of Hartman's murderers leaving four others jailed—some since their teens, for a crime they did not commit."

Governor Sean Parnell stood off to one side of the stage, awaiting his turn to address Native leaders and other delegates. His dad served in the legislature when I regularly covered legislative sessions in Juneau. Sean followed in his footsteps. He was serving in the state senate when my proposal to Kate on the floor of the house echoed through the entire capitol office speaker system. I took advantage of our long acquaintance now, cornering the governor and pressing him to look into Wallace's secret confession.

Caught off guard, seconds away from a big speech, Governor Parnell understandably had trouble processing what the hell I was talking about. He pointed to the attorney general, encouraging me to share with him whatever I thought was so important.

AG Michael Geraghty, being from Fairbanks, was all too familiar with the controversial case. He took my packet and politely said he'd get back to me.

When Parnell's turn to speak came, protesters shouted him down, conveying what I'd tried to tell him.

"Free the Fairbanks Four!"

"Free the Fairbanks Four!"

"Free the Fairbanks Four!"

Between classes, I followed up with yet another letter to the Alaska Department of Law, same topic as ever, with one big difference. "You are the first AG in a position to assess real evidence, long suppressed under attorney-client confidentiality, as to who killed John Hartman," I wrote to Geraghty. "That means you are the best hope for bringing this tragic chapter to swift closure."

"SECRECY IS THE STORY"

RABINOWITZ COURTHOUSE, MARCH 27, 2014

I brought the TV Reporting class to document Judge Paul Lyle's first hearing on a file deemed "exempt from disclosure." The judge kicked us out of the courtroom early on. Students were rattled, but I assured them it wasn't a big deal; this had become a stakeout!

Special Prosecutor Adrienne Bachman soon received the boot as well. She agreed to an interview and patiently stood by as students scrambled releveling our video camera, finding cords and headphones, the whole drill.

Grace Singh, an intense young Athabascan, had the mic for this one. "Why not fight for access to the evidence withheld under attorney-client privilege?" Grace asked the prosecutor.

Bachman, casually dressed in a soft brown blazer decorated with polka dots over her white button-down shirt, didn't bite. "A priest, a doctor, a psychotherapist, a spouse," she practically cooed. "Those are sacrosanct conversations that people need to have confidence will remain confidential. As a representative of the government, I'm not going to pry into those areas unless and until the court gives me permission."

When the doors opened next, out came local attorney Jason Gazewood, a former sportswriter and local TV anchorman I'd known for years. His eyes lit up when he saw that camera! "I can't," he said yet paused, looking dapper in a dark suit, set off by a bright-yellow-striped tie.

"Oh, come on," I said. "Bachman just talked to us. How can you not?"

"Okay," he said, grinning.

Before he opted for sharp suits and the shaved-head look, Gazewood taught our TV Reporting class at my invitation; at the time, he'd just left the prosecutor's office for private practice. He was now a bona fide newsmaker, recently appointed by Judge Lyle to represent Jason Wallace, the so-called nonparticipant party of interest.

Aaron Berner served as today's interviewer. Though thin on experience, Berner showed natural talent. "What is your witness's relationship to the man who made the confession?" the student asked with gravity and a stern demeanor that many pros would envy.

"That I can't say," responded Gazewood, smiling.

"Have you visited—" Berner began, then halted, turning toward me. "Can I say Jason Wallace?"

Gazewood and I both chuckled.

"Of course you can," I said.

"Can you?" the lawyer wondered out loud.

"Wallace is named in Lyle's order appointing you to represent him!"

"Okay," Gazewood said, grinning.

"What is your relationship," Berner asked, "with the man who made the confession?"

"That I can't say," the lawyer said thoughtfully. Every question Berner tried drew similar amused evasions, followed by the big attorney's polite exit.

"I didn't get much," Berner apologized.

"We can make this work," I assured the whole crew. "Secrecy is the story!"

———————

Smiling Sam Allen, a former *Sun Star* editor, returned to school after a hiatus. A true Alaskan raised down the highway toward Denali Park, Sam knew how to fix things, drive whatever's available, find ways to accomplish what needs to be done, or bow to the weather when it's warranted. You see that in kids raised outside urban Alaska's safety net.

That spring, I put Sam to work cracking the court's vault of secrets. "I write to request access to and a copy of any letter, or other form of correspondence referring to California prison guards or officials referring to an inmate's possible involvement in John Hartman's 1997 murder."

Sam and I filed similar requests with several other state offices. Rejections inevitably came from Criminal Division director James Skidmore.

This one was my favorite: "Your request makes clear your intent is to publish this information in the media or some other form of public communication."

Skidmore got that much right and appeared to confirm the rumor that Alaska law officials were sitting on a letter from a California prison guard regarding Hartman's murder.

Call it a Hail Mary shot at collecting supporting evidence: "To this day, many around town dismiss your confession," I wrote Wild Bill Holmes, care of Ironwood State Prison, in Blythe, California. "They figure you are screwing with the system or are trying to cash in on a reward from supporters of the Fairbanks Four. Jason's statement, which sources tell me backs up your own, remains sealed with the judge. There's a real chance it will never become public.

"Sources tell me you discussed what happened with a prison guard many years ago. That adds huge cred to your confession. I also hear that the guard might have written to the DA or police. That letter, Bill, would be the smoking gun in a legal conspiracy, because the old DA, Jeff O'Bryant, has kept silent to this day!

"So, did this happen? Is the guard still alive? Any idea where to find him?" I closed by appealing to his curiosity.

"When I get a chance," I ended that St. Patrick's Day letter, "I'll send you a not-so-serious book about another long trail."

The date, auspicious in my family, couldn't hurt.

Updating the court on the progress of the state's investigation, Special Prosecutor Bachman appeared to hedge her bets with Judge Lyle. The state's new witnesses, including one of Hartman's brothers, may support the convictions, as she put it, more than they undermined the court's confidence in the verdicts rendered fifteen years ago.

At the same time, Bachmann warned that the arguments behind closed doors needed resolution. She told the judge that the state wasn't aware of any final conclusion about the release of the confidential filing, which posed a problem for the state's response.

REWIND: ALASKA BUREAU OF INVESTIGATION, OCTOBER 3, 2013

Troopers Randy McPherron and James Gallen hadn't ever worked together, but both had years on the job and were familiar with the other's reputation within the bureau's Cold Case Investigation Unit. Word trickled down that the summons each had received involved that old Fairbanks murder, again making headlines.

The pair met with Captain Craig Allen, commander of the bureau, who confirmed their assignment vetting new evidence put forward by the Alaska Innocence Project. Three of the so-called Fairbanks Four were Alaska Natives; another was part Indian. Supporters blamed the arrests and convictions on racial bias and misconduct during the 1999 trials.

With multiple agencies involved, a scheduled introductory session was standard procedure. Gallen, a storied investigator, knew the drill: brass from various departments and divisions would take turns giving little speeches, followed by a bunch of introductions though everybody knew each other, basically spinning wheels.

As expected, ABI Commander Allen took the lead when representatives from all the agencies involved met on October 10. He recapped the case history, from the night young Hartman lay dying in the street to the emergence of the Fairbanks Four as a cause celeb.

Turning toward McPherron and Gallen, he laid out his expectations: "You guys need to look into this case," Allen said. "And if these boys committed the crimes, they need to stay in jail. But if you guys find that they are innocent? You need to make an effort to show that."

Gallen, for one, was pleased to hear such clear direction reinvestigating what everyone recognized was a sensitive case. When her turn came, however, the Department of Law's representative kicked the can in a different direction. Special Prosecutor Adrienne Bachman announced that she wasn't about to "discredit," as she put it, the decisions of judges and juries, let alone the work of a prosecutor who'd run the table landing convictions against all four charged.

Gallen and McPherron locked eyes; Bachman was leading this thing. And how was that going to work out?

The old troopers quickly sorted out roles. Conducting face-to-face interviews, one took the lead pitching questions. Usually that was McPherron, the team's designated chief investigator. The other partner listened and observed, readying follow-up questions. Afterward, both compared their write-ups.

They split up more routine tasks, such as reviewing Bill Holmes's recorded calls at Ironwood Prison. That fell on Gallen. Most of those calls involved Amina, a woman the big inmate met online and now referred to as his wife. She and Holmes had 315 conversations, paid for by the lady, with an average duration of sixteen minutes. With 78 calls still left to review, he'd only heard the couple mention the Hartman case twice.

The last week of October 2013, the cold case troopers and the prosecutor flew to Fairbanks, where the trio cruised downtown, surveying the crime scene and other key locations. About 7:00 p.m., all three visited Eagles Hall, where they got out of the car for a little walk-through weighing lighting conditions. Trooper Gallen and the prosecutor stood on the front steps as McPherron paced off five hundred feet, halting on the corner where muggers knocked down Frankie Dayton back in 1997, roughly the same time of year. From what he could see, Gallen noted car colors were black or reflected streets, and his partner had become a dark silhouette.

Checking with the school district, the troopers confirmed that Holmes, Wallace, and the other new suspects were enrolled in local schools at the time. Unfortunately, their disciplinary records and attendance sheets from that period were destroyed long ago.

The trio also dropped by the Fairbanks police station for a cursory review of boxed evidence from the old murder case. The whole visit was rushed, mainly useful for getting the lay of the land.

In mid-November, the cold case troopers returned to Fairbanks following up. This time, Gallen, McPherron, and another investigator took a detailed inventory of the case evidence, matching up each report, photo, and interview recording with FPD's itemized property forms on the case. FPD couldn't find police reports on Frankie Dayton's mugging.

Before returning home, Gallen and McPherron interviewed several parents and friends of the group identified by Holmes. They also squeezed in a quick trip to see Matt Ellsworth. No one was home at the house in North Pole; they left cards on the door.

That January, the special prosecutor and both troopers again returned to Golden Heart City. This time, Gallen and McPherron set up shop in a conference room at Fairbanks police headquarters. Chief among their priorities: collecting any physical evidence from the original investigation that might yield new insights through DNA testing. They also planned to copy interviews recorded during the 1997 murder investigation, examine the assault on Dayton earlier that same night, and review trial exhibits and such.

Flipping through FPD's folder detailing case evidence and the interview tape inventory, James Gallen came across a faxed document he didn't recall seeing during their previous visit to the station. Skimming the pages, the old trooper was certain; this document was added later.

"State of California, Memorandum," topped the upper left corner of a two-page statement by a prison guard dated December 5, 2011. It was addressed to one M. McNair, Faculty D Captain. No agency was identified, signaling this was an internal communication.

Directly below the address was a subject line in bold caps: **CONVERSATION WITH INMATE WILLIAM HOLMES.**

"On Monday, December 5, 2011," the memo stated, "inmate William Holmes implicated himself in a murder that took place in Fairbanks, Alaska, in 1997, while conversing with me."

The writer, Joseph Torquato, was a correctional officer at Calipatria, a maximum-security state prison in California known for its lethal electric fence and cow manure–scented surroundings, one hundred miles northeast of San Diego.

Inmate Holmes, according to the guard, confessed to involvement in a murder. It happened back in high school. Holmes told him that he and friends were cruising for drunk Natives to beat up and instead assaulted a white boy who later died.

A group of Native Americans had been arrested for the murder, Holmes bragged. Police got confessions out of them, and they were convicted for it. "I was able to find an article that fit the description of the crime on the internet," the guard stated in his memo. "The name of the victim was John Hartman."

Armed with that knowledge, the guard confronted him. "The following day after Inmate Holmes reported to work, I asked him if the name Hartman meant anything to him. Holmes said, 'Do you mean John Hartman?' I told Inmate Holmes to come forward, yet he refused."

Bachman was in the conference room along with Lieutenant Paul Geier, who now headed FPD's detective unit. Other officers were coming and going as Gallen passed the file to his partner. Trooper McPherron quietly scanned the prison guard's statement. He was pondering the implications when his phone rang.

His partner took the memo and handed it to the prosecutor. After a quick glance, she set the memo aside.

"Adrienne," said Gallen, "it's kind of important. You need to read that."

Watching the prosecutor scan the pages, the old investigator strongly suspected it wasn't the first time she'd seen it.

While that played out, McPherron had Matt Ellsworth on the phone. The kid had finally called at his parent's urging. He dutifully confirmed that he lived in California but declined to share his telephone number or address. Did he know Scott Davison? Yes, Ellsworth said, they used to skateboard together. How about Jason Wallace? Ellsworth said he'd need to see a photo of the guy. McPherron shared what Davison had told them, that all three were skipping school and getting stoned by the bowling alley the day Wallace suddenly confessed.

"Scott's a liar," snapped Ellsworth, quickly adding that he'd like to help but needed to go.

The call ended in time for McPherron to catch Geier explaining where police got that crazy report. Another detective good at using the internet, as the lieutenant put it, came across the memo and downloaded it. That very guy, Detective Avery Thompson, was just then approaching. Lieutenant Geier introduced him to the trooper, referring to that internet discovery.

Deer in the headlights, observed Gallen, watching Thompson's confusion. The way he read it, that lieutenant threw the poor guy under the bus.

The confirmation of Holmes's involvement attached new weight to Scott Davison, the troubled school friend whose sworn statement anchored the Alaska Innocence Project's fight. Following a round of interviews with Lathrop teachers and coaches familiar with Wild Bill's friends, the cold case troopers visited Davison's mother.

Janet Davison told the lawmen she'd followed the case, of course. It wasn't until 2011 that her son opened up, confiding he was involved. She initially cut him off, unwilling to listen, embracing denial. But Scott wouldn't let it rest. He explained that he kept quiet about Wallace's involvement for years, fearing he'd be branded as a snitch and killed by other inmates.

She was still wrestling with that, Janet Davison told the cold case

troopers, when I showed up, demanding that she read her son's sworn statement. The whole situation terrified her. Right when Scott seemed to be
getting his life together, this invited reprisals.

I was an awful person, she told Gallen and McPherron.

Following the Fairbanks visit, Special Prosecutor Bachman forwarded
the cold case troopers an email chain revealing Fairbanks police and the local
DA's office were aware of the prison guard's memo since the day it was faxed
in December 2011.

The cold case troopers swiftly made travel arrangements to interview
William Z. Holmes at Ironwood State Prison in California. Assuming the
inmate agreed, the troopers planned to give him a polygraph exam. Though
it was up to judges whether results were considered in Alaska courts, both
Gallen and McPherron viewed lie detectors as useful tools.

SMOKING GUN

"By the way," my new pen pal wrote that March, "the guards made fun of
me for the name of your book," Holmes said, referring to *My Lead Dog Was
a Lesbian*, an infamous book recounting my last-place Iditarod woes. "They
said, 'what the heck is this?' I laughed and said, 'I have no idea.'"

Wild Bill Holmes's penmanship, that was what caught my eye: the neatly
handwritten back-slanted lettering, precisely spaced from top to bottom of
that letter signaled precision I hadn't expected from the gangbanger behind
"The Stakes 'r' High."

What he had to say was every bit as surprising: "People will never understand how much of an act of God this is because that night was going to my
grave with me. God used that officer to minister to my heart and Jesus did
the rest. I'm flattered that anyone would believe I could concoct this."

He got a kick out of my comment that Torquato's letter added weight
to his own change of heart, documenting his initial refusal to come forward.

Even after the Alaska Innocence Project got involved, Holmes wrote, it never occurred to him to mention the prison guard's influence. "I deemed it not relevant." And that left him musing about it all: "Something I shared with the cold case detectives, only so the State couldn't say I held anything back," he wrote, "ends up being the smoking gun!"

Holmes sketched a happy face right below.

Sam Allen went fishing for what we now knew was waiting. "I write to request access to and a copy of any letter or email correspondence from a prison guard or official at Ironwood State Prison referring to William Z. Holmes comments about the 1997 murder."

Scott Davison's statement placed a red circle around the name Matt Ellsworth. Trooper McPherron began by leaving phone messages at his parents' house the week before Thanksgiving 2013.

Lamkje Ellsworth, Matt's mother, called to let the trooper know Matt promised to return his call Monday.

The kid did not.

On December 2, McPherron tried again. This time, Matt's mom confirmed Ellsworth was now living in California, but she refused to share his number or address. Again, she promised to pass on the trooper's request for a callback.

Two days later, McPherron's cell phone rang with no caller ID showing.

Matt Ellsworth sounded reluctant to speak and complained more than once that he didn't know anything useful. It was all so long ago. Okay, so he knew Scott Davison, mainly from skateboarding together back when both attended North Pole middle school. Maybe they attended Lathrop High afterward; Matt only attended Lathrop for maybe a year.

He flat out denied ever skipping school with Davison or Jason Wallace. Nor did he recall cruising around with them in any car.

Ellsworth insisted he had no recollection that Wallace or anyone else ever admitted they were involved in Hartman's murder. He didn't believe such a conversation even happened. That he would have remembered!

He did recall someone getting in touch with general questions about Davison and Wallace. That would have been approximately a year ago, he told McPherron, when he was still living in Alaska.

Would that be Bill Oberly? McPherron inquired.

Ellsworth didn't think so.

If innocent people were locked up, he added, he'd like to help them, then he refused the trooper's request for his phone number. Any further questions? Leave messages with his mother, Ellsworth said, and abruptly hung up.

APRIL 2014

"I got your voicemails," said Police Chief Laren Zager, returning my messages updating him about developments surrounding the secret brief, "and I very much appreciate your keeping me posted on the activity. I always get asked about things, and that helps out tremendously."

Though we'd been chatting for more than a year, I didn't know what to make of the polite, soft-spoken police chief with the southern drawl, a lawman who wore suits where others of his rank usually choose uniforms.

Unlike most of his predecessors, Chief Zager had no personal investment in the Hartman case that I could tell. News stories on his hire indicated he'd spent the latter part of his career in Anchorage and Palmer. He seemed decent and incredibly patient. That much was clear the first day we met, shortly after my return from India; the chief graciously put up with the professor ranting about secret confessions.

"Things have changed since Friday," I advised Zager, referring to our latest records request for the secret file on Wallace's confession, shot down by state Criminal Division director John Skidmore in typical bureaucratic style.

"The potential harms from disclosure—i.e., from interfering with and prematurely disclosing information regarding an ongoing conviction relief or adjudication—outweigh any potential benefit to the public at this point. As stated above this record will ultimately be available to the public, but not during the current litigation."

Skidmore basically confirmed police and perhaps state law officials buried the prison guard's revealing memo for years.

"Are you aware of this?" I asked the chief.

Cold cases inevitably draw tips, Zager said. He rambled a bit about the special prosecutor's investigation. He praised Rod Boyce's civic spirit, forwarding an unrelated tip about a potential witness for the state.

"This did arrive in our investigations unit," he finally said, returning to the memo. Someone communicated with the DA's office about it, he assured me. "But no one went on high alert. Because this is just one of dozens that come in."

"So," I said, "it turns out that this might have more significance than the standard letter, but?"

"Yeah, I can confirm that. We did receive a communication. That it was related to the case and that we contacted the DA's office with that information. And beyond that," the chief said, "my specific knowledge would be just coffee chat." Zager sounded relieved. "I'm not trying to slough off any responsibility, but it is a closed case," he said. "There's a conviction. Information comes in. The clearinghouse of that would be the prosecutors. So we forward that information to them, and then—it's kind of a shoulder shrug."

And I had my lede for a story Rod and I had quietly been sharpening.

Eight months before making the 2012 confession cited in exoneration bids for the so-called Fairbanks Four, inmate William

Z. Holmes confided to a California prison chapel officer that he and several friends got away with killing an unidentified Fairbanks boy back in high school.

By the time the press rolled, we also had Sam Allen's fresh copy of Torquato's memo to draw on, a stunning document Fairbanks police officials buried for years. Within a week, Fairbanks mayor John Eberhart issued a statement confirming local police and the district attorney were notified when it was first received three years before. The mayor closed with an appeal: "The truth is what must come out of the review, for the men incarcerated and for John Hartman."

Police Chief Laren Zager soon left on vacation and never came back.

AFTER LIFE STOPS

TANANA, MAY 1, 2014

The community's village public safety officer called Alaska state troopers requesting help with a quarrelsome local man who'd pointed a gun at him. That was the way it worked beyond the road system at that time. Though pretty much every household throughout Alaska was loaded with hunting guns and ammo, state law prohibited the indigenous ranks of village public safety officers from carrying guns of any kind.

Scott Johnson and another trooper from the Fairbanks Rural Services Unit flew out to Tanana, the storied Athabascan community near the Yukon River junction, to lend a hand restoring order.

The lawmen found the troublemaker by his house. A struggle erupted as he tried to duck inside. That was when his son, twenty-year-old Nathanial "Satch" Kangas, reached for an assault rifle, took aim at the lawmen's backs, and fired seven shots.

That weekend, heads bowed throughout the far north cities, towns, and villages, paying tribute to the fallen lawmen. In Fairbanks, many of us lined roads, bearing witness, as the bumper-to-bumper motorcade of squad cars flashing lights, fire trucks, and other official vehicles slowly passed.

"Sgt. Patrick 'Scott' Johnson and Trooper Gabriel 'Gabe' Rich made their final homecoming Saturday," the *News-Miner* reported.

> Not a voice could be heard along the crowded street as the caravan made its way. Many held their hands over their hearts, some saluted, others simply looked on solemnly. Some waved U.S. and Alaska flags, some held handmade signs. Fairbanks resident Mary Killian created her own sign to honor Johnson and Rich, though she did not know the two. "I have friends who are troopers so it sort of hits close to home," Killian said. "Alaska is big, but inside the borders we're (a) small community family..."
>
> "Today's been a very difficult day for the Alaska State Troopers," said Capt. Burke Barrick [head of the regional detachment]. "We will heal over time, but it hurts right now."

The captain's assessment proved optimistic. Revelations from a neighbor's video, along with recording devices carried by the dead troopers, revealed the father and son rearranged the troopers' bodies and weapons, attempting to mislead authorities about what happened. That stirred outrage inside and out of squad cars and courtrooms.

The case landed in Judge Lyle's lap. When it came time to pass judgment, he sentenced the son who pulled the trigger to serve 203 years in prison. He gave the father who conspired to shift blame ten years in prison, condemning them both for the dishonorable way they sought to hide what they did.

On behalf of Tanana's Tribal Council, Curtis Sommer praised Johnson's personal touch building bridges with rural residents.

CHAPTER 15

"HEAR THE MOOSE"

A pair of state troopers stood on either side of the tall double doors as a stream of lawyers and staff entered. When the time came, the troopers retreated inside, pulling the doors shut behind them.

By midmorning, groups of supporters joined the families waiting for those doors to open. One couple sat playing with a baby. Many stood in clusters, while some leaned on walls or paced alone, glued to their cell phones. A lucky few found chairs, some more or less camped on the hard-surfaced flooring, and others stood bathed in light streaming through the airy courthouse windows high above. Mainly, people debated what was happening inside.

"We're just praying and hoping that the judge does the right thing," said Sharon Roberts, Marvin's older sister. "This has gone on too long."

Julia Taylor, my sharp honors student, scooted along the hallway in her wheelchair, interviewing people about the broader message delivered by the long-disputed convictions. A woman named Safarina told her she'd raised her own boys with this case in mind. "I told them that they gotta be careful," she said. "Once you're in the law's hands, that's it. They can do anything they want."

Pete Peters, a twenty-four-year-old Alaska National Guard veteran from Venetie, a small Gwich'in village up north, angrily sounded off. "Innocent people are put behind bars when somebody confessed? That's wrong," he said. "Democracy, that's why we fought for this country and defended it."

At 1:00 p.m., the tall doors briefly opened. Out strode Tom Bole. I followed the defense investigator, making straight for the elevator. "I'm not going to answer your questions," Bole said calmly, eyes fixed on the lights marking the approaching car's progress. "Thank you for asking."

The waiting game reminded me of covering closed-door caucus meetings in Juneau and stakeouts as a young photojournalist. Not for the first time, I wished my father, the labor lawyer, were still around to hash over the maddening impasse.

Five long hours after the hearing began, the doors opened, and lawyers, staff, and witnesses spilled out. "The answer is no. I can't say anything," Bill Oberly informed TV crews camped by the door. "Even if I did have a feeling, I couldn't tell you."

Gazewood shot out of the room, head down, clutching his briefcase like a running back. I barely got a picture of him.

Down in the main lobby, I intercepted Richard Norgard, who'd flown in from Ohio for this one. It was the first time I'd seen the investigator since that day he visited my campus office. I'd since learned that he worked for the Public Defender Agency before striking out on his own. He now figured among the heroes behind the leak, though details remained unclear. "Ex parte hearing. I can't get into specifics," he said, brushing past me, continuing toward the courthouse exit.

"Richard," I pleaded, giving chase, "give me something."

Norgard kept walking but slowed down. "I'm happy to come up and do it. Anything I can do for this case."

"Hearing Opens on Secret File in John Hartman Murder Case," proclaimed the day-after headline. The lead photo conveyed more than words, showing Father Scott framed in cathedral light from high above, peering through that courtroom door crack.

ANGRY DRUMMERS

SEPTEMBER 2014

"Of course, it's very discouraging that there hasn't been more action," commented Reverend Shirley Lee in her new role as Tanana Chiefs Conference justice task force chair, alluding to the passage of a full year since that day of cheers and prayers greeting the lawyers' announcement that sworn statements from one of Hartman's killers had just been filed inside the courthouse. That moment of freedom for the Four seemed within reach.

I was putting together an advance story slugged "Unlock the Truth," framed around a planned protest over the court's extended delay reviewing the new evidence. Bill Oberly wearily walked me through continuing procedural hurdles. "It's pretty wild," the Alaska Innocence Project's director summed up, "that we're just getting a preliminary hearing in November 2014."

Responding by email, Special Prosecutor Adrienne Bachman used the term "ongoing" in describing the Department of Law's evaluation of the new evidence. "I don't think one could ever say that this investigation is over."

"I'm not surprised, but I'm pretty sickened," commented April Monroe, speaking for the Free the Fairbanks Four group. "I think it's sad and reveal-ing in terms of how little has changed in the last seventeen years."

Clamor surrounding the case offended others. "We are disgusted by the support these murderers have and get," messaged Hartman's oldest brother, Chris "Sean" Kelly. "They don't deserve it." He'd straightened out his life since the summer I visited him in jail, not that anything came easy for an ex-con tattoo artist, now raising a young daughter on his own.

When the day arrived, bitterness colored this year's rally outside the courthouse. "This is a long time that these young men have been sitting in prison when the truth is there," declared Steve Ginnis, director of Fairbanks Native Association. "What's wrong with our system? What's wrong with these people that don't seem to get it?"

Being an election year, Fairbanks's city mayor, several state lawmakers, and both of Alaska's U.S. senators joined Native leaders calling for a federal review. Reverend Shirley Lee followed, leading the crowd singing "The Battle Hymn of the Republic": "Glory, glory, hallelujah, His truth keeps marching on."

Father Scott Fisher closed the official program with a prayer for truth, invoking seasonal tradition. "The last month, people have walked through the woods," he said. "We've called, and we can hear the moose coming."

Hand drums soon surfaced from coats, bags, and fancy cases. A circle formed below the stage, where gray-haired elders and younger protesters were soon bobbing and chanting, "Hoy, hah. Who-ha hayyy! Hoy, ha. Who hahayy!"

A hefty older woman wearing a headscarf and sunglasses slowly danced, bowing low and swaying, one gloved hand cupping air, the other gripping a sign on a tall stick. ALL THESE MEN'S ALIBIS AREN'T LYING proclaimed the hand lettering. Without losing a step, the woman occasionally flipped it around. WHY DO THESE INNOCENT MEN HAVE TO SUFFER, that side read, OVER THE FPD'S SHODDY INVESTIGATION?

That drummers' circle continued to expand. A young, bearded man wearing a black jacket and backward ball cap took over setting the beat, angrily smacking his skin sound maker with a cord-wrapped stick.

"WON'T BE TRULY FREE"

NOVEMBER 2014

"Hello, my ol' friend how are you?" wrote Marvin, apologizing for his delay writing back. He described himself as calm and patient and for good reason:

"Because of my parole date. Yep. June of next year I go to the halfway house. Not overly excited yet, but I think I'm getting there. As that time draws near, time seems to slow down a little each second. So, I'm always trying to stay busy 'round here. You know what bothers me though? None of us should be in the nightmare. And I'm sad that they [Eugene, George, and Kevin] might have to spend more years in here… I won't be truly free until we are all free, you dig?"

At that point, Marvin apparently put the pen down for six days, resuming it after he caught Anchorage TV producer Steve MacDonald's latest special report.

"Wow," Marvin wrote afterward, "the story's really getting out there now, huh? I talked to Oberly, and he seemed to be in good spirits about things. I like a positive attorney."

He'd written to Geoff Wildridge, Wallace's old public defender, himself, as I suggested, but the letter was returned stamped "wrong address." He remained upset that Oberly refused to forward it.

"He said it was well written but wasn't the right time. My thing is who cares about their friendship," Marvin griped. "I'm here for crimes I did not commit, you know? If the letter is good, it should be sent. Take all the shots while we can. I might have to call him this week and see if he will ever send it. Let me know what you think on this issue."

I saw red. If the Four were lawyers' kids or simply white kids from middle-class homes, errant pleas would be forwarded special delivery.

Marvin caught my appearance in a TV interview. "A few more grays on your noggin," he couldn't help but notice. And he asked me to pass on his regards to Kate and our kids. "With any luck I'll be having, or more like starting, a family when I'm free."

HOT PURSUIT

REWIND: JULY 2014

That July, Troopers Gallen and McPherron landed in San Francisco, rented a car, and headed across the bay toward the registered address for both a 2009 Kia and 1996 Toyota. Matt Ellsworth was identified as the owner of one of those vehicles. Records indicated the other belonged to a woman named Desiree, Matt's girlfriend.

The man who answered the door identified himself as Desiree's father. The young couple lived together on a boat berthed at a marina on the south side of town, somewhere near Marina Village, the man told the troopers and offered to guide them to it. The Alaska lawmen took him up on the offer.

Presenting their credentials at the harbormaster's office, the troopers learned that Ellsworth rented a slip for a boat named *2nd Opportunity*. They located the boat easily enough, but it was padlocked, and searching the parking lot turned up no sign of either car. The troopers commenced a stakeout. Hours passed with no signs of activity, and they quit for the night.

In the morning, the duo returned and spotted the Kia right away. They found Desiree aboard the boat. She confirmed they lived together on the boat. Ellsworth was an aviation mechanic and had already left for work, she said.

From there, it got sketchy. Ellsworth hadn't ever told her the name of the company he worked for, Desiree said. And he'd never mentioned any murder back in Alaska. "She refused to provide us Ellsworth's telephone number," McPherron noted, adding "she promised to try to convince him to call."

Back at the rental car, the lawmen huddled over a map. A quick internet search turned up Sterling Aviation, a potential employer, twenty-seven miles away. They had no idea how long that might take given local traffic, and they didn't dare call ahead. Worth a shot, the troopers decided. "We observed Ellsworth's Toyota parked in the lot in front of the business," Gallen's report states. "A clerk we contacted in the front escorted us back to a hangar where we contacted Ellsworth."

Interviewed in a secluded office at the company, Ellsworth began the interview by announcing that he had "problems with authority." Yet he agreed to talk.

He and Scott Davison were close in high school, he said. The boys skipped high school together all the time. Usually, he was behind the wheel in his own car, driving Davison and other friends to the bowling alley close to school. That was where they all got stoned, he said. Sometimes kids he didn't even know piled in the car and came along. So long as they brought weed to share, Ellsworth said, he didn't care.

The name Jason Wallace was familiar, he told Gallen and McPherron. But he didn't recall that anyone he knew ever admitted being involved in a murder. In the same breath, he acknowledged that all of it might be true. "Just that Ellsworth could not remember it," the troopers noted. Ellsworth explained that he'd had a concussion sometime after high school that affected his memory. "He also claimed he had amnesia once."

Ellsworth couldn't identify Jason Wallace in a lineup photo. When McPherron pointed him out, "He claimed the person in the photograph was not familiar to him," the trooper wrote, concluding his write-up.

The lawmen returned to Alaska empty-handed; Ellsworth hadn't even given up his phone number.

DOORS OPEN

JANUARY 6, 2015

"I believe that the sealed matter is far enough along that I can confidently set a trial date," Judge Paul Lyle announced from his high bench in Rabinowitz Courtroom 401. After more than a year of closed-door arguments, he set aside two weeks in October 2015 for scheduled hearings on the Alaska Innocence Project's case. The schedule overlapped with the eighteenth anniversary of John Hartman's murder.

Unless appellate courts intervened, Lyle's temporary order preserving Jason Wallace's secrets was set to expire at 4:30 p.m.

At least one of the lawyers involved looked to be a short timer. Responding to a direct question from the judge, Gazewood agreed that his client likely wouldn't need representation in the upcoming October proceedings. Exiting the courthouse that wintery day, Gazewood mentioned he had an idea he wanted to run by me. Sitting together in a cold van, bathed by a blower hurling frigid air, he asked whether I thought the Four would go for an Alford plea.

"What's that?"

The way he described it, an Alford plea amounted to a deal for quick release by a prisoner asserting innocence without overturning or erasing the original conviction. The state, for its part, essentially acknowledges that it might lose another trial on the original charges because of new evidence or other considerations. Something to that effect.

"No way," I said after hearing him out. "Why would they agree to that?"

COOK INLET PRETRIAL FACILITY, ANCHORAGE, APRIL 2015

"Just go ahead," said the guard at the maximum-security prison, pausing to let the other visitor into the first cubicle we came across on the second floor. The cream-white corridor was tall and narrow. Unlike other sections we'd passed through, there were no doors or windows. I counted off ninety-five paces, passing only one other entrance before I reached the locked door at the end.

I'd been told downstairs that the prisoner I'd come to see, a guy I'd never met face-to-face, though we'd affected each other's lives, would be in V-17.

"Actually, that's V-18," the guard corrected when he caught up. He unlocked the door at the end of the hallway, and we continued, passing a series of double-windowed booths. V-13, V-14, and V-15 were empty. V-18 was drawing closer when I glanced at V-17 and immediately recognized the slim inmate with the ponytail waiting inside.

George Frese glanced up. Our smiles spread on both sides of the glass as the guard unlocked the last door. I slid into the chair and picked up the handset, and each of us just eyed the other with disbelief.

George, the skinny inmate with the long ponytail, light beard, and mustache, who never had the grades, according to Marvin, needed to make the Howard Luke Hawks' basketball team, soon had my head spinning, going on about Alexis de Tocqueville's mid-1800s critique of democracy. The French philosopher's point about tyranny of the majority! That particularly interested George. Time raced by; our conversation veered all over. The support for the Fairbanks Four? Amazing! George Frese seemed grateful and wary at the same time. It hurt so much when favorable rulings died on appeal.

It was the first time I'd met the high school dropout who'd never written us that I recalled. I left the massive jail delighted and surprised.

Construction delays jeopardized my planned interviews in the Mat-Su Valley, a region marked by staggering development and population sprawl since I first landed in Alaska. Visiting hours were over by the time I parked and raced inside Palmer's minimum-security jail. Staff proved cool; within minutes, a guard delivered Marvin Roberts to the interview room.

Marvin looked smaller and thinner than I remembered. He wore shades now. Though he greeted me like a brother, he too seemed wary, a familiar effect of long-term incarceration. He'd been scheduled for parole and mentioned it was tough counting down the remaining weeks until his scheduled release. I cautioned him to be careful when he got out. "A lot of people would like to see you guys fail," I told him.

One last stop. Turning left on Knik Road, I raced for Cook Inlet. Though

better paved, with more homes on either side, the road felt intensely familiar. I soon passed the turnoff for the tree-house apartment my sportswriter
pal Tim "the Mowth" Mowry and I shared after *Frontiersman* want ads lured
the dairy farm kid and this DC lawyer's son to the far north in 1986. I was
glad to see muddy ruts left by fat tires and paws running parallel with the
road, a sure sign serious mushers were already running dogs teams hitched
to four-wheelers. "Smokin' Joe" Redington, now in heaven, would approve.

I made it to the prison at Point MacKenzie before sundown, scoring a
walk-in visit with Eugene, supersize version. We joked about his expanding
belt size; working as a prison cook clearly had benefits. He seemed younger
than a man in his late thirties, more like a nervous undergrad, a vulnerable
one it seemed to me.

By the time I flew home, I'd logged 240 miles visiting the three prisons.
I justified charging the car rental to UAF through recruiting visits to several
local high schools earlier in the week. "Keep your eyes out for stories about
the Fairbanks Four's exoneration," I told classes and teachers. "It's going to
happen. Our students played a big part in that."

"You and I used to go out together," one teacher mentioned after my
presentation.

I did a double take. She did look familiar. That likely would have been
twenty years ago, when I covered the valley for the *Anchorage Daily News*.
Right before Kate and I got serious. A former boyfriend somehow figured.
"Emily?" I blurted out. "Wasn't your last name different?"

"I married the guy," she said, smiling.

HOMECOMING

LATE JUNE 2015

The surprise appearance by a family member absent roughly half his life left the tearful hostess scrambling. "He wanted to eat moose and French fries, but we didn't know he was coming so soon," said Hazel Roberts, explaining that new parolee Marvin wasn't expected to receive permission for a dinner visit until Sunday. "But we ate, and it was just so awesome. We have pictures. Pictures of everybody."

"Little Marv" Mayo chuckled, describing his adopted older brother's reaction to household upgrades. "He's nowhere with technology."

Urged to take a selfie documenting his return, Marvin initially balked, questioning why he'd want pictures of himself. He finally took one, his sister Sharon recalled, smiling. And he complained about how he looked.

That weekend, Marvin teared up speaking to the 120 people gathered at the tribal hall for a fundraiser supporting the Alaska Innocence Project's efforts. "It's very wonderful to be here right now," he began, then stopped, clasping his hands behind his back. "Pretty emotional," he said and paused again. "A lot of times in prison, I thought of what I might say in a situation like this. Now that I'm here," he said, smiling, "I can't think of nothing!"

Everybody cracked up.

Returning to his seat, the thirty-seven-year-old parolee, unaccustomed to the spotlight, was itching for escape. That was soon foiled, amid cheers and tears, as Marvin was outfitted with a traditional moose-hide vest, emblazoned with a beaded eagle so fine its eyes sparkled.

CAUGHT IN THE CROSS FIRE

Judge Lyle neatly sidestepped his Gordian dilemma. His ruling lifted the veil of attorney-client privilege, allowing consideration of what Jason Wallace told his lawyer and investigator Bole about Hartman's murder. At the same time, the judge issued a protective order, shielding Wildridge's former client from future prosecution over his own self-incriminating statements.

Like his partner William Holmes and most Alaska prisoners serving long sentences, Jason Wallace was locked up in the Lower 48, where prison beds were cheaper. That June, as Lyle geared up for a full hearing on the Alaska Innocence Project's case for exoneration of the Fairbanks Four, authorities transferred Wallace to Spring Creek Correctional Center in Seward, Alaska, a maximum-security prison complex some 450 miles due south of Fairbanks, nestled among mountains overlooking Prince William Sound.

Emails flew as lawyers and the prosecutor weighed dates for a group visit.

From the lead attorney of Dorsey, a big law firm now assisting the Alaska Innocence Project:

Subject: Wallace Deposition Unopposed motion

Jason and Adrienne, I believe we are ready to confirm Mr. Wallace's deposition for Aug. 3. We will file a motion to depose (the) incarcerated person today, and I'd like to say it's unopposed. Please confirm.

Thank you,

Jahna. M. Lindemuth

When twenty minutes passed without any direct response from Jason Gazewood, Special Prosecutor Bachman reached out, urging Wallace's lawyer to advise his client to plead the Fifth Amendment and refuse to cooperate. "Are you really not going to oppose deposition of a client whose statements will be used to incriminate him?... There is nothing the petitioners can ask that will not result in him incriminating himself. I can fill you in vis-a-vis Scott Davison and William Holmes... Unless you don't expect him to invoke," she added, "I can't see any utility to the group of us traveling down to Seward."

UAF JOURNALISM DEPARTMENT, JULY 24, 2015

A tall, balding state trooper sporting a big, holstered gun showed up at the office with a subpoena. Handing my cell phone to Amy, our admin, I posed alongside the lawman for a photo accepting service.

He fled the scene right after.

"Notice of Taking Deposition of Brian O'Donoghue" stated the prose-cutor's order, directing me to appear on July 30 at noon at the DA's office, bringing "all records, letters, emails, documents, in whatever form, received from or sent to" the Four, April, Wallace, Holmes, Davison, Stone, Oberly, a half dozen other lawyers and staff, "or any of their other family members or representatives."

Jesus, that could take weeks to collect.

I immediately called John McKay. The day of the deposition, the media lawyer flew up from Anchorage. "Don't volunteer anything," he warned me going in. Of course, I didn't listen until he literally kicked me under the table.

With the subpoena pending and what I recognized was a clear conflict of interest, I voluntarily withdrew from covering the case for the *News-Miner*. Sam Friedman, the paper's outdoors reporter, took over daily coverage. Some in the newsroom questioned that decision; it made sense to me. He had a lot of experience reporting on hunting and fishing, a highly regulated sector involving state and federal rules, enforcement agencies, and special interest groups and lawyers, lots of lawyers.

Friedman copied me on new filings; I flagged newsworthy developments and provided background.

Sipping beer, skimming Gazewood's latest appellate argument late one night, I opened an attachment. One glance, and I was gagging and cough-ing. The secret brief, all seven gray copied pages, was appended to Wallace's latest motion.

DOCUMENT CORROBORATES, CHALLENGES NEW CLAIM IN "FAIRBANKS FOUR" CASE

A sealed court document obtained by the *Daily News-Miner* corroborates some details of an alternate account of the 1997 John

Hartman murder but also clashes with key aspects of the 2012 statement that is being presented as a confession by one of the teen's true killers.

The big press downstairs wouldn't roll for hours yet. Breaking with tradition, city editor Rod Boyce posted Friedman's scoop on the paper's website. When Wallace's attorney, Jason Gazewood, caught word of the breaking story, he threatened to sue; the *News-Miner* blocked viewer access while the publisher, editors, and the company's lawyer considered the merits. McKay called in from Anchorage, sharing his expertise as well.

Too late. April's team had grabbed screenshots of Sam Friedman's scoop when the story first broke. The group trumpeted its version on the Fairbanks Four blog.

"Jason Wallace's Confession Leaked to a Reporter," proclaimed the post.

The newspaper's website revealed the specifics of the confession, apparently made in 2003 to an attorney and investigator employed with the Fairbanks Public Defender's Office. The *News-Miner* reported the details of Jason Wallace's statements were leaked 'inadvertently' by a party who was in lawful possession of the material. The article then goes on to detail the confession of Jason Wallace in the murder of John Hartman.

The post listed the key points:

Wallace confessed in 2003 while awaiting trial on an unrelated murder to public defender Geoff Wildridge.

Wildridge then sent public defender investigator Tom Boles to speak to Wallace, presumably to investigate the veracity of his claim.

Wallace, like Holmes, describes leaving a party in a car with the intention to assault people. He describes first assaulting a man on First Avenue and robbing him. Holmes also describes an assault that preceded the Hartman beating, but in less detail. Wallace's description of the assault closely matches the facts known about the Dayton assault, which figured predominantly into the case...

For over fifteen years, public employees sworn to act as agents for justice have kept the confession of Jason Wallace secret under the auspices of privilege, despite the fact that failure to reveal the information has contributed to the unlawful detainment of four citizens.

Judge Lyle swiftly scheduled a hearing on Wallace's motion to block publication.

Oddly, I was the only independent observer as Lyle weighed the legal arguments. Attorneys had been going at it for an hour when the judge fully grasped the attention Sam's story already commanded through *Free the Fairbanks Four*'s social media channels.

"You're telling me," Judge Lyle cried, "this already has eighteen thousand views?"

He swiftly tossed Gazewood's motion.

SPRING CREEK CORRECTIONAL CENTER, SEWARD, SEPTEMBER 10, 2015

"The date is September 10, 2015," the videographer stated for the record. She had the lens trained on a scruffy-haired, Black inmate seated alone wearing a buttonless, bright-yellow top that complemented his almond skin. Other than licking his lips once, the video subject stared straight ahead, listening impassively as the woman described the recording session's purpose. "This deposition is being taken on behalf of the petitioners."

After she finished, the eyes behind the subject's dark full-rim glasses soon jumped from side to side, tracking introductions by visitors seated off-screen. His own court-appointed attorney went first. "I'm Jason Gazewood. I'm here for the affected person, Jason Wallace."

Michael Grisham, from the big Anchorage firm assisting the Alaska Innocence Project, identified himself as George Frese's lawyer. Eugene Vent's public defender went next, then Bill Oberly, who explained that he represented both Marvin Roberts and Kevin Pease.

Prosecutor Adrienne Bachman introduced herself on the video, then immediately called for delay, renewing the state's pitch in favor of first deposing investigators Bole and Norgard. "And any other persons whose information was relevant to the violation of Mr. Wallace's attorney-client privilege," she said, explaining that she was "staking position lines for further argument."

The video showed Wallace seated with his hands cuffed that day, eyes riveted on the prosecutor, following her every word.

"The court denied that," conceded Bachman, referring to Judge Lyle's ruling on the issue, "but I continue to pose that objection to going forward today."

By then, Wallace had dropped his head and sucked in his lips, staring at his lap.

With formalities out of the way, Grisham asked Wallace about his life growing up. The inmate appeared game though vague. His big family relocated from Virginia to Fairbanks when he was twelve or thirteen, he said. The move had to do with his father's military transfer. He wasn't certain about the particular branch of the service but agreed it was probably the army. Wallace, then thirty-four, couldn't come up with the name of his middle school, only that it was located on a local military base.

"Do you recall what high school you went to?" Grisham asked.

"Yes, I do. Yes, I do," Wallace said, nodding. He attended Lathrop High, Fairbanks's biggest public high school. Nowhere else.

"And did you graduate?"

"No."

"When was it that you dropped out?" the lawyer gently prodded. "Or did you move away? Did you stop going to school?"

"Yeah, I just stopped going to school," reflected the inmate, addressing the off-screen voice. "I can't remember," he said, rocking backward. "I just stopped going. It was, yeah, I can't remember. I know I got my GED," he added, "but I just stopped going to school."

The prisoner and Grisham appeared to hit it off. Wallace rocked back and forward, grinning at questions about his teenage preferences in baseball caps and athletic gear associated with various teams. Likewise, he seemed amused by the lawyer's stumbling inquiries about his early smoking habits.

"I mean, I don't know," Wallace said. "Back then? Social? I was just smokin' cigarettes. You know, just being a kid."

And what about smoking pot?

"I'm going to object," Gazewood interrupted from off camera.

"You can go ahead and answer," Grisham assured Wallace.

"Did I smoke marijuana at the time?" the inmate mused out loud.

"Again," Gazewood said, "I object. I'm asserting privilege here."

"To smoking marijuana? In high school?" Grisham spluttered.

"To its relevance, I'm going to assert privilege to smoking marijuana in high school!" Gazewood said he assumed this would come back up to his client's detriment. "You're going to relate this to something you believe is relevant."

"What privilege exactly, sir?"

"The Fifth!" Gazewood countered. "You're asking this for an event."

Grisham sounded flummoxed. "You're refusing to answer questions about smoking marijuana? In the mid-'90s?" Casting for another approach, he said, "Okay. So. Who'd you hang out with when you were in high school?"

"Yeah, I'm not gonna," Wallace said. "I'm gonna plead the Fifth."

"So. Again," Grisham pressed on. "I'm just asking about the names of people. I'm not asking about what you did with specific people at this point or anything else. I'm just asking for you, for your companions in the mid-1990s during high school."

"What do you mean by companions?" challenged Gazewood.

Wallace's head whipped from side to side, following the haggling, then he signaled he'd caught the drift. "I really had no close friends in high school."

"Must have hung out with some people," Grisham offered.

His lawyer pounced. "He hung out with teachers!" barked Gazewood. "He hung out with parents! He hung out with so many other people!"

Following that outburst, the deposition video captured an abrupt shift in the inmate's tone. Wallace began listening to his court-appointed lawyer, sidestepping questions or taking the Fifth.

The special prosecutor reminded Wallace about Wild Bill Holmes's calls from his own house, in the company of his wife, pressuring him to clean up loose ends in their drug rip-off. "Essentially," Bachman said, "he insisted that you needed to carry through with your end of this plan. And that scared you?"

"Yes, ma'am."

"Did you talk to your wife during that period of time as well?"

"I don't remember," the witness mumbled.

"Have you done anything to make amends with the family of Teacka Bacote at this point?"

Wallace seemed startled by the idea. "Up until this point, no, ma'am."

"Is it your intention?" the prosecutor asked encouragingly.

"Yes, ma'am. Later. It's just I don't have any way to go about doing it. I mean. It's just, you know. The position I'm in," he added before trailing off. "There's a stigma to where certain things you do. It just…" He faltered. "It doesn't look right. To give an example," Wallace offered, "when Scott Johnson passed away, I wanted to, like, reach out to his family. But I know they wouldn't even." His voice fell. "They would look at it some type of way they wasn't supposed to look at it." A pause followed. "No," Wallace continued, "just to answer your question, I haven't figured out a way to do it—without looking some type a way." Again, his voice trailed off.

"Without it offending?" the prosecutor suggested.

"Yes, ma'am."

The prosecutor's supportive tone had Oberly fuming. On cross-examination, he circled back. "Ms. Bachman talked about the crime you're in here on."

Wallace leaned forward and rubbed his eyes, then covered his mouth, listening.

"The crime you're in here on is killing a person with the use of a hammer," Oberly said. "Right?"

The inmate looked up, nodding. "Yes, sir."

"You bludgeoned her to death with that hammer."

"Yes, sir," said Wallace, nodding again, followed by a deep breath.

"And then you left," continued his examiner.

Wallace hunched forward, sucking in his lips.

Oberly left nothing out. "You proceeded to stab someone in the neck with a screwdriver, right?"

"Yes, sir."

"And then you went back to the apartment where you had bludgeoned the woman to death with a hammer and started the apartment building on fire," he said. "Isn't that correct?"

"Yes, sir," said Wallace, eyes down, already nodding.

"And that was not a single apartment," the attorney pointed out, emphasizing the greater scope of potential harm glossed over by the prosecutor. "That was an apartment building that you started on fire, right?"

"Yes. Yes, sir," said Wallace, nodding vigorously.

"No further questions."

CHAPTER 16

THE WEIGHT OF INNOCENCE

The Alaska Innocence Project's case for exoneration of the Fairbanks Four was scheduled for hearing in October 2015. I immediately applied for a courtroom video permit, noting UAF Journalism's commitment to documenting the full proceedings, predicted to go as long as two whole weeks, a staffing commitment local TV news would never attempt. Judge Lyle granted our request, and I began recruiting students to staff this, divvying up the workload into four-hour slots and creating a Doodle poll for scheduling.

Feeling super organized, I bragged about it to colleagues. Rob, our documentary professor, scoffed. "Two weeks of taping? Man, what you need is a student project manager."

"I'll fill in if need be."

"Brian, you've really got to have a manager on this," he said wearily. "And what's your budget to pay them?"

Hadn't even considered that.

A new journalism recruit volunteered to serve as crew boss. Corey Gray didn't know much about video, but the former marine assured me he'd keep fellow students on task.

"Sounds perfect," my colleague agreed.

Julia Taylor lobbied for a spot on the video crew. Camera operators would be standing behind a tall tripod, potentially for hours on end, shooting from a designated corner of the room. That didn't seem realistic given her serious back problems. Not even midway into fall semester, Julia seemed more and more reliant on her wheelchair.

"What do you know about Twitter?" I asked Julia the Friday before the hearing opened. She didn't even have an account, but I spied a gleam in her eyes.

DAY 1: POSTCONVICTION RELIEF HEARING, MONDAY, OCTOBER 5, 2015

> In the Matter of Eugene Vent
>> In the Matter of Marvin Roberts
>> In the Matter of George Frese
>> In the Matter of Kevin Pease
> VS.
> State of Alaska

Doubling as judge and jury and being, as he put it, sole trier of facts, Superior Court Judge Paul Lyle banged that gavel, opening Alaska's first judicial proceeding weighing lawful convictions against claimed evidence of actual innocence.

> @JuliaFBXLawRpt—"Solemn, civic responsibility that the court is about to embark on." Judge Lyle telling court watchers that he needs his attention on court.

The hearing began with a dispute over security expenses. Inmates Eugene, Kevin, and George required two troopers apiece for security, costing an estimated $3,000 daily, according to Deputy AG John Skidmore. That likely meant reducing staff in other communities, he warned.

Lyle couldn't justify that, which left Eugene, George, and Kevin listening from jail on days they weren't scheduled to testify.

Parolee Marvin Roberts was free to come and go. Flanked by Oberly and the team of high-powered pro bono defenders, he sat facing the judge, proudly wearing his bead-studded tribal vest.

With attendance policy settled for the plaintiffs, Special Prosecutor Bachman invoked a rule excluding witnesses from attendance. Gallery watchers grumbled. The witness list numbered in the dozens; many were relatives of the Four, the victim's oldest brother as well. After some discussion, Bachman dropped objections to the presence of family members.

Being under state subpoena, I technically faced eviction. So I'd been mulling over my First Amendment rights as a journalist, framing an argument ensuring the judge would allow me to stay and quietly observe the proceedings from the gallery. "For the record, Your Honor," I began, rising from my seat. "I object."

"You will not speak," barked Judge Lyle, staring me down. "If you have anything to say to this court, you need a lawyer to make that argument."

The lawyers up front conferred. The state dug in. Julia relayed the outcome in her twenty-fourth morning tweet.

@JuliaFBXLawRpt—Sides could not agree. @redIntrn excluded as he stays on the State's witness list. #UAFJournalism #FairbanksFour

The hulking thirty-five-year-old inmate under escort bore scant resemblance to the smiling senior in the old yearbooks. Bill Holmes now wore thick-rimmed eyeglasses and an orange prison jumpsuit. Both of his wrists were shackled; the leg chains jangled with each step toward the witness chair.

"We were all saying let's see if we can find drunk Natives to mess with," Holmes said of that night back in high school when he and his friends went hunting after a party broke up.

@JuliaFBXLawRpt—Holmes: Left because we were bored, and the girls were not putting out. Late at night when left. Nobody on the streets. #FairbanksFour

After looping though downtown, Holmes said he was waiting at a stoplight when a lone person crossed the street behind the car. "We all got excited," he recalled, "Everybody was saying, 'We got one. We got one.'"

Wallace, Rashan Brown, and Marquis Pennington, another Fairbanks rapper, jumped out, according to Holmes. He continued on, "busted a turn" near a school, and headed back.

Bushes concealed what was going on. Holmes pulled over and was about to get out, he said, when the others came racing back and piled into the car, yelling "Go, go, go!"

Everybody was shouting about what Jason Wallace did to that kid, Holmes recalled. "They were just saying, 'Little J, he was tripping. He was tripping. He stomped him out.'"

Racing away, Jason Wallace shared the front seat, stone-faced, and never uttered a word, according to Holmes.

———————

When the judge broke away for lunch, April Monroe kicked off a rally on the courthouse steps. She began by praising such a turnout on a chilly day. Though smiling more broadly than I'd ever seen her, the Fairbanks Four leader sounded mystified. "I couldn't begin to explain why we're still here and why we need a month for the court to do the right thing." And that, she reminded supporters, is the point. "Sometimes it takes a community to come together and force them," April declared. "And you guys have done that."

The lawyers and several Native leaders had been held up inside. The gravity of events unfolding within became apparent as the tall doors opened and Victor Joseph, the Tanana Chiefs Conference's new chairman, Bill Oberly, and a somber-faced Marvin Roberts joined the swelling crowd.

"It's no longer about their innocence," declared Joseph, a tall heavy man wearing bookish glasses and the chief's moose-hide vest. "The facts are in place," he thundered. "The people who did it have stated they did it! This is about the judicial system as a whole," he said. "In the eyes of the Native people, is it going to be just?"

He wasn't waiting to find out.

"It's time now for our people!" Chief Joseph thundered. "Our young men, to be exonerated of this crime. And set free!"

Witnesses called by Oberly and Dorsey, the big law firm assisting the Fairbanks Four pro bono, dominated the opening days of the hearing. Testimony, for the most part, focused on three areas: the party that set Holmes's crew prowling for victims, Wallace's threats if anyone talked, and the authorities' ongoing failure to recognize Marvin's alibis and others they ignored. That prison guard's memo figured as well.

Special Prosecutor Bachman and the state's team counter-punched throughout, attacking the integrity of witnesses supporting the innocence claims.

EYES WERE ON THEM

DAY 4: POSTCONVICTION RELIEF HEARING, THURSDAY, OCTOBER 8, 2015

"Just how many classes Scott Davison skipped," Matt Buxton reported for the *News-Miner*, "or even how many classes he had at Lathrop High School, was a fuzzy and distant memory for the 36-year-old man who was called to testify Thursday about what he knew about the long ago killing of a Fairbanks teen."

What he'd never forget, Scott Davison swore from the witness box, was Jason Wallace's claims as they skipped school and cruised around the week after Hartman's death. "I never encountered anybody taking ownership of a murder before," he said. "It really stood out. Tattooed on my mind."

When the state's turn came, Prosecutor Bachman seized on factual errors in Davison's 2011 sworn statement for the Alaska Innocence Project. That was Holmes's car, he conceded, not Wallace's. And how about Harold? the prosecutor asked, referring to the fourth person he'd claimed heard Wallace confess.

Davison got that wrong, he agreed. He was riding with Matt Ellsworth and another guy named Phillip when Wallace unloaded. There was no Harold, he now clarified. Oberly prepared that affidavit based on visiting him in jail, where their meeting drew a lot of attention. Eyes were on them.

@JuliaFBXLawRpt—Davison: Felt like he was doing something wrong, so he was scared that he was breaking the jail code. #FairbanksFour

At the hearing, Scott Davison stood by what he'd heard: Jason Wallace told him he was directly involved in the kid's murder, describing how he burned his own shoes and clothes, covering up the crime.

Davison conceded he'd had drug problems and forgot other things. Not this. He named others he told at the time, including the mother of his children and a fellow inmate.

PI BOLE'S DILEMMA

DAY 5: POSTCONVICTION RELIEF HEARING, FRIDAY, OCTOBER 9, 2015

After he retired from the military, Thomas Bole spent thirteen years as a private investigator. From mid-October 1997 on through several years after, the investigator's billable hours were consumed by the Hartman case, assisting

Dick Madson and other defenders. Convictions against all four were on the books with appeals pending by the time Bole landed a new gig as staff investigator for the Public Defender Agency. That was where Geoff Wildridge's January 2003 request hurled Bole into an ethical quandary. The PI, who knew better than anyone that his former clients were innocent, found himself assisting the defense of John Hartman's self-proclaimed murderer.

Another twist: Wallace and his partners didn't initially realize they were responsible, Bole explained in the witness box eighteen years later. They assumed someone else came along later and "actually murdered Mr. Hartman."

"And why was that?" asked defense lawyer Bob Bundy, gazing down on the white-haired investigator.

"Because of the allegation of sexual assault," said Bole, somewhat amazed all these years at the rumors arising from Hartman's baggy borrowed pants dropping during the attack, perhaps tripping the lean teen as he ran for his life. "They knew they hadn't sexually assaulted him," the investigator said, referring to Holmes and Wallace's crew. "They discussed it. And they thought someone must have come along and did that to him."

"What was Mr. Wallace's demeanor as he was telling you this?"

"Very, very emotional," Bole recalled. "Crying at times." He paused, silently hunting words, then looked up. "Seemed very remorseful, about that and his present crimes," he said of Wallace, followed by another pause. "He talked about God a lot. He talked about his wife. He talked about a lot of things. Mostly, he was just crying."

Yet the investigator also sensed Wallace had an agenda, perhaps angling for a deal lowering his sentence for Teacka Bacote's murder.

@JuliaFBXLawRpt—Bole: Brought up the Hartman murder to get lower sentence in the circumstances. Consideration for testifying against Holmes. #FairbanksFour

That initial interview wasn't recorded, the PI told the court, explaining he seldom taped meetings with clients. "Because it was so emotionally charged, and I realized the importance of what he was saying," Bole said. "I told him I would probably be back the next day with a tape recorder, take a statement once he'd calmed down."

When he returned, Jason Wallace declined to talk about the Hartman case.

"Fair to say that over the years, somebody's memory can morph a little bit?" inquired Bachman. "Add, subtract some of the memories?"

"Yes," Bole granted.

"And you've experienced that yourself?"

"Yes," he agreed, faintly smiling.

"Have you ever heard of the notion of confirmation bias?"

"Yes."

"In fact," the prosecutor continued, "that's one of your theories about the Hartman case, isn't it?"

The investigator shook his head. "Not one of my theories, no."

She rephrased that: "A theory about the Hartman investigation?"

"Okay," he conceded.

"And so," the prosecutor offered, "there is the possibility, sir, is there not, that when you spoke with Mr. Wallace, you heard what you wanted to hear?"

Thomas Bole blinked rapidly. "No!" he said, openly grinning.

"Not possible?" she challenged.

Head bowed, eyes on his lap, the investigator repeated, "No." That smile spread, and soon he literally shook with apparent mirth. "Not at all!" Bole gasped.

The man gazing down on them sought clarification. "When you were asked, 'Did you discuss the Hartman case with others in the agency?' I need to know what understanding you had of that question," Judge Lyle said. "There's discussing the Hartman case," he emphasized, "and there's discussing what Jason Wallace told you."

Bole named three public defenders along with the agency's Fairbanks office director.

"Did you speak to them?" the judge pointedly asked.

"Yes," Bole said, meeting his eyes and nodding.

Judge Lyle appeared taken aback.

CONFLICTING ACCOUNTS

The next witness, a bookish, older man wearing a thick black-and-gray sweater, settled into the witness box, surveilling the crowd.

"When you were in the army," began Bill Oberly, "were you involved in any kind of investigative work?"

"My field was counterintelligence," said Richard Norgard. As part of that job, he developed and taught a six-week course in investigative techniques. "That would have been in 1972," he said. All told, he spent twenty years in the service before retiring with the rank of chief warrant officer 3.

Afterward, he put his skills to use as a private investigator in Anchorage, where he eventually founded the Alaska Investigators Association. Later, working for the Office of Public Advocacy, Norgard supervised Tom Bole. He never forgot the Fairbanks investigator's distress over a case he sometimes alluded to without mentioning names. "You know, they're in prison," Bole confided without getting into specifics. "I really think they might be innocent."

He was referring to the Fairbanks Four.

After the Alaska Innocence Project got off the ground, Norgard, a founding board member, recalled that conversation and pressed Bole for details about the case. This time, "very reluctantly," Norgard said, the Fairbanks PI opened up. "He says, 'I know who did it. I know who really killed the guy.'"

Skipping ahead to a later phone conversation, Oberly asked for the record, "And what were those names?"

"William Z. Holmes, Rashan Brown, and Jason Wallace," Norgard said.

Bachman, on cross-examination, demanded to know whether Bole assumed he was having a confidential conversation with a supervisor.

"I wasn't holding a gun to his head," snapped Norgard, pointing out that he'd left the agency by the time Bole opened up. "I just asked him. He was volunteering, you know?"

According to Norgard, the secret emerged during his 2010 visit to Fairbanks. The pair were driving around when Bole pointed out Eagles Hall, the site of the wedding reception that figured in the earlier attack on Dayton, and other landmarks, including the street where Hartman lay dying. "He described things that Mr. Wallace told him happened there," Norgard recalled.

The special prosecutor seemed offended; she expected more from a credentialed investigative instructor. Following several insinuations of professional misconduct, Bachman accused Norgard of taking advantage of Bole as well. "You didn't care that his career could be at risk."

"Of course I cared," he said.

"But you made the decision to do it anyway."

"I made the decision to write down what he told me."

LIVING SHADOW

"Have you ever given a deposition before?" attorney Jahna Lindemuth asked from off-screen.

"I don't remember," replied the Native man with the long, scruffy chin beard, wearing the yellow short-sleeved prison smock.

From outside the frame, Lindemuth thanked Arlo Olson for agreeing to record his statement. "It's the same as in a courtroom," she explained, advising him he had to tell the truth.

Olson glanced toward the voice, nodded, then stared straight ahead, brows raised, dark-rimmed eyes wider than I ever recalled. The sluggish, heavyset inmate filling the court's big roll-down screen had little in common with the hustler I fondly recalled.

Lindemuth prodded him about a recent incident, violating Franklene's protective order, resulting in his latest arrest. "Are you two married?" the lawyer asked him.

"Yes," replied Olson, "but we've been separated since 2009."

He blamed their breakup on his own long-standing depression. Drugs prescribed for that messed with his memory, he added. So did alcohol. Always had, Olson said, including that night he saw muggers jump Frankie Dayton that fateful night. All of it, so far away, he didn't realize that was Frankie taking the beatdown until the poor guy later made his way to Eagles Hall.

"In '97, you were twenty years old?" asked Lindemuth.

"Yeah," he said.

"Your drinking was an issue even then?"

"Well," Olson explained, "I would drink once or twice a year, but I would go to jail once or twice a year for drinking."

His troubles began, he said, after running into George that night. That was where the police got his name and began calling his family.

"So," the lawyer prompted, "you finally did contact the police and talk to them?"

Olson did. He didn't recall the exact day; the police were hounding his grandparents, urging them to pass on the word they wanted to talk to him. To get everyone off his back, Olson finally showed up at the station, he said. The police took him downstairs and got in his face, disputing his description of the car used by Dayton's assailants. "I remember, I kept saying it was a beige car, four-door. Detective Ring kept saying it was a two-door blue car."

Ring took him into the garage and showed him a blue car, Marvin's car, insisting he never let anyone else use it.

"Marvin Roberts had to have been the driver," Olson recalled being told over and over. Looking at the camera, the weary-eyed inmate added, "Once the story started shaping up, that's when he said he was going to record it, and he did."

In the courtroom that morning, no one appeared more engaged watching the video than the gaunt, gray-haired man in the black robe. At times, Judge Lyle cupped an ear to better catch Olson's remarks or rested his chin on that same hand, studying the plodding, occasionally wide-eyed character on the screen. Several times, he grabbed his blue pen, hurriedly taking notes on a small flip pad.

Prosecutor Adrienne Bachman, another off-camera voice in the deposition, pointedly asked Olson whether drugs were to blame for his poor memory, citing the high-dosage effects of a particular mood enhancer he was taking.

Olson wearily smiled. "They said they had me on enough to tranquilize a horse."

"And is that a good thing or a bad thing?" Bachman softly asked.

"Well, I don't know," Olson shot back. "If you're in jail, you can sleep all the time, but it sucks."

"The jail, the medication, or both?" the prosecutor asked.

"Both," he said.

And what about "suicidal ideation? Did you have suicidal thoughts?" inquired the prosecutor.

"I still do," said Olson, again hanging his head.

"Enhanced," Bachman suggested, "because of your incarceration?"

"Nope," Olson shot back, studying his own hands on that courtroom screen. "Even when I'm walking around on the streets, I have suicidal thoughts."

That evening, when I reviewed the clip, preparing a post for UAF's new Dissenting Opinion site, Arlo Olson's voice taking the oath seemed lower and slower than I remembered.

The way he dropped that arm right after, staring at his lap? To me, that signaled surrender.

"OH MY GOD!"

DAY 6: POSTCONVICTION RELIEF HEARING, MONDAY, OCTOBER 12, 2015

After several years of looking into the original case against the Four, the cold case troopers were cut loose in January 2015. The state's investigation of the innocence claims had run its course, they were told when they were laid off.

That summer, a lingering difference of opinion surfaced when Bill Oberly ran into recent retiree James Gallen at a restaurant. Internal disagreements over the state's investigation became a matter of record when both Gallen and his cold case unit partner testified on behalf of the Fairbanks Four.

"I want to ask you about the crime scene experiment at the Eagles Hall," said Bachman, opening her cross-examination of Gallen, a legendary former trooper investigator with dark, arching brows, a thin mustache, and a quick smile. She was referring to the state's October 2014 field test, visiting streets many UAF Journalism students would find familiar. Special Prosecutor Bachman and Gallen stood in for Arlo Olson, while the other plainclothes trooper played mugging victim Frankie Dayton. "He walked two hundred feet, and it's your testimony that you were able to recognize that it was Randy McPherron?"

"A blurry face of Randy, yes," said Gallen, observing that his partner's coat looked familiar, of course. Likewise, that slouch hat with a brim. His gait as well.

"And so that sort of recognition aided you in watching Randy McPherron walk down the street," Bachman said. "Or, if you turned away, to be able to pick him out down the street, right?"

"Depending on the distance, yes," conceded the old detective.

"You didn't write that in your report," the prosecutor snapped, circling words on a legal pad, then jabbing it. "That I recognized Detective McPherron! Did you?"

"You did not advise me of that," Gallen cheerily responded.

"You don't recall seeing the white face?"

"The white face? Yes."

"What was described as a Charlie Chaplin walk?"

Gallen had had enough. "You know we never lost contact with Investigator McPherron," he pointed out. "So we knew who he was. I'm describing [that] once he's standing out there, you could not see him. And you stated, 'Oh my God, oh my God!'" Locking eyes with the prosecutor, he added, smiling, "And I didn't know what you meant by that."

"So you don't," the prosecutor said, searching for words. "You don't remember my ability to see…"

"Your ability to see him?" Gallen finished her sentence, a big grin spreading. "I don't think you said that."

"You spent fifteen months investigating this case?" Lindemuth summarized, addressing the old trooper. "And during that time, you spent 95 percent of your working hours devoted to it?"

"Yes," confirmed Gallen, whose thirty-six-year career ended with the disbanding of the cold case unit shortly after he and McPherron took one last shot at getting Matt Ellsworth to open up.

"From the result of your investigation," Lindemuth asked, "do you have an opinion on the innocence or guilt of the petitioners?"

"Objection," cried Special Prosecutor Bachman. "What's the relevance of this? Police officers never get to say who's guilty and not guilty," she argued. "It's not relevant."

"This is not the usual case," Lindemuth smoothly countered. "This is not a police officer trying to put somebody in prison. This is a police officer testifying potentially as to the innocence of the petitioners."

Lyle cut them off. Turning away, the judge cast his eyes down, resting his chin between clenched knuckles and a raised forefinger. After a long pause, he opened a binder close at hand and studied that a while, then leaned back, took off his glasses, and addressed the lawyers, gallery watchers, and Marvin and his three codefendants, listening by teleconference.

"Whether or not the petitioners are innocent is a conclusion for this court to draw. Not for him to draw," said Lyle, using his glasses like a pointer, directed at the old trooper. "What has to be determined by the court," he continued, "is whether or not there's clear and convincing evidence of actual innocence based upon *all of the evidence in the record*. The evidence he has," the judge continued, nodding at Gallen, "may not all be in the record at the end of the day. For that reason, his opinion on an ultimate conclusion in this case is not relevant."

END-AROUND MANEUVER

Randy McPherron followed his Cold Case partner in the witness box. At issue now: Detective Ring's approach questioning Eugene Vent, following the seventeen-year-old's arrest fleeing the Alaskan Motor Inn.

"Would you have handled his interview differently?" Lindemuth asked.

"I'm going to object," interrupted Prosecutor Bachman. "Relevance." McPherron wasn't in the room that morning in October 1997, she pointed out.

"We're establishing that it wasn't done properly," countered Lindemuth.

The hefty, balding plainclothes detective watched from the witness box as the pair went at it, eyeing them like a curious watch dog.

Lyle finally stepped in, narrowing the scope of inquiry. "He can testify how he would have done it," the judge said, not whether "FPD did it right or did it wrong."

For starters, McPherron assured the court, he would have kept his ears open, listening to what the kid had to say. Ring started with accusations, he said, assuming the drunk teenager joined in attacking Hartman. "Though nothing substantiated that," he pointed out. "Given his age and the fact he was still intoxicated, this kind of technique is pretty risky," he said, inviting bad information.

"An interrogation is something you usually do at the end of an investigation," McPherron said, holding up his hand, fingers spread wide, as if cautioning someone. "Not with the first people you have contact with. You need to gather information."

Lindemuth continued. "Who provided any facts about the homicide?"

"Detective Ring," McPherron said. "He was the only one."

She closed by asking the witness for his assessment of the innocence claims.

"It's irrelevant," interrupted Lyle, reminding the lawyers and everyone else present that remained his burden to decide.

Lindemuth rephrased her question. "Had the investigation been completed in January of 2015?"

"From our perspective? No," declared McPherron.

"In the course of your investigation, did you find any evidence that Mr. Pease, Mr. Frese, Mr. Vent, and Mr. Roberts were at the corner of Ninth and Barnette when John Hartman was assaulted and murdered?"

Shaking his head side to side: "No!"

DAY 7: POSTCONVICTION RELIEF HEARING, TUESDAY, OCTOBER 13, 2015

Nearing the end of his second appearance in that front-and-center hot seat, McPherron wore his game face, hunching forward in a crisp black suit enlivened by a red striped tie, lips set, weighing every word.

The special prosecutor's cross-examination veered into a civics lesson. "I assume that you agree with the principal, Investigator McPherron, that the testimony of witnesses at a trial is evidence, right?"

"Testimony of witnesses at trials is evidence?" the trooper hesitantly repeated.

"Yes," prompted Bachman.

"Yes," he conceded.

"Sort of a basic, jurisprudence proposition, right?"

"I suppose, yes."

"And you believe in the jury system, do you not?"

"Yes."

"And there were three jury trials in this case, correct?"

"Yes," the cold case investigator acknowledged.

"And thirty-six jurors agreed, apparently, that there was evidence the four defendants were at the corner of Ninth and Barnett. Correct?"

"Yes," he confirmed.

"You," she challenged, "concluded otherwise?"

McPherron needed but a word: "Yes."

"Okay, thanks," said Bachman, retreating on an upbeat note.

CHAPTER 17

COURAGE UNDER FIRE

DAY 8: POSTCONVICTION RELIEF HEARING,
WEDNESDAY, OCTOBER 14, 2015

Late that afternoon, Arlo Olson made a live appearance. He entered the courtroom under a double trooper escort, wearing a loose orange smock, both hands cuffed to a cable encircling his waist, legs shackled to prevent sudden sprints. Lest there be any confusion regarding his status, PRISONER proclaimed three-inch lettering across the back of that orange suit.

Bringing Olson back to Fairbanks was the prosecutor's call. "We learned some things after your deposition that the rules say we have to ask you about personally," she said, followed by, "Do you recall having a telephone and correspondence relationship with Brian O'Donoghue?"

"Somewhat."

"Quite a long time ago?" she observed.

"Yes," Olson said.

"Do you recall what Mr. O'Donoghue did to get you to talk to him about your personal history?"

"Nope."

With the judge's permission, the prosecutor approached the witness box with a packet of transcribed conversations, pointing to a particular page.

"Does that refresh your recollection of what Mr. O'Donoghue said to get you talking about your personal life?"

"Not really," said Olson, and that seemed to throw her.

"Do you recall him saying, 'I'm serious about wanting you to start from the beginning, hearing what it was like growing up, jumping from village to village following your dad's work'?"

Olson didn't. "You know I was on a lot of medicines," he calmly pointed out.

Bachman dug in, reading portions of our November 27, 2002, prison call, which I'd laboriously transcribed, seeking his perspective on a changing night. "The larger story that finds you and your friends at the wedding reception and all you've gone through as a result of testifying at the Hartman trials."

Again she prodded the witness. "Do you remember that at all?"

"Nope," said Olson.

"And were you aware he was recording your conversations?"

He wasn't and didn't appear concerned.

"Did you give him permission to record you six different times?"

"No."

She requested the court's permission to play one of our longer recorded conversations. Judge Lyle seemed taken aback. "Why have all of this played for twenty minutes? When none of it's pertinent to my decision?"

"The first twelve pages provide context," she argued.

Lyle looked weary. "Why not simply read relevant portions from the transcript?"

Bachman explained that she hadn't verified that what I submitted was word-for-word accurate.

Lyle consulted a thick procedural book, nodded, then put it away. "Well, let's get started," he said. "If it can't be edited, then it just needs to be played."

"It's all contextual," Bachman said brightly as she handed out copies.

"How Mr. O'Donoghue primes the pump to get information out of Mr. Olson."

Amplified by the court's audio system, a rambling call from thirteen years ago commanded attention anew.

"It worked for once!" my recorded voice blasted from the courtroom speakers, referring to the button I'd pushed as instructed by the service provider, accepting prisoner Arlo Olson's call. That recording preserved both of us chuckling, followed by my quick update on his girlfriend. "Hey, I've got bad news about Franklene. I called her this morning, called her last night. Your clothes were in a bag, but she chucked them out."

Lyle's head was bowed, reading along, as the inmate and I debated whether Franklene would do such a thing; Olson declared she was bluffing and urged me to ask her again. I refused to even consider that.

Gallery observers were looking at one another with puzzled expressions. But that wasn't all we'd discussed that day.

"I got my pen and notebook and everything now," I told Olson. "Give me the hard details about where you grew up and when."

Olson poured his heart out, describing his sister's suicide and other personal ups and downs. After a while, I abruptly pivoted, inquiring about the tactics detectives and the DA applied coaxing his identification of Dayton's muggers.

Following Bachman's audio selections, Lindemuth loaded yet another recorded phone call for Lyle's consideration: a heated discussion after Arlo Olson admitted he'd just lied at a hearing. He blamed Detective Ring's threat he'd face perjury charges if he retracted his original trial testimony. This recording also preserved our 2003 prison call discussing how he came to embrace the police version of events. "I didn't want to testify. I told them I wasn't sure," Olson recalled. "They just kept showing me bits and pieces of testimony. To make me sure of what I was doing. And it did."

"Right, right," I'd encouraged him at the time.

That call was interrupted by a recorded notification announcing the prisoner's call was about to end.

"Why should anyone believe you now?" I pressed.

"Why should anyone believe me? Why shouldn't they believe me?" said Olson right before the tape cut off.

All these years later, on this day in Lyle's courtroom, Lindemuth asked the witness: "Mr. Olson, in this call we just heard, did you tell Mr. O'Donoghue the truth?"

Olson gazed down at the transcript. Flipping another page, he read some more, then looked up. "Yeah," he said.

"Did you tell me the truth?" Lindemuth asked.

Gazing straight, he repeated, "Yeah."

Olson soon followed the trooper out, rocking from side to side with each ponderous, shackled step. Though he'd definitely put on a lot of weight since I last visited him in jail, UAF video captured a guy who'd just unloaded something heavy.

SIGN OF THE FOUR

DAY 9: POSTCONVICTION RELIEF HEARING, THURSDAY, OCTOBER 15, 2015

The thin Native inmate with long dreadlocks slowly rocked in the witness box, awaiting his turn to testify, eyeing the room warily. Though he had Bob Bundy, a former U.S. attorney for Alaska, in his corner today, George Frese remained nervous. He'd been so drunk that night back in 1997. Eighteen years later? How was he supposed to explain anything.

"The footprint matches," George recalled an officer telling him. "Maybe you just kicked him a couple times, then did whatever. Maybe Kevin started it?"

"They mentioned Kevin Pease?" prompted Bundy, who was handling this witness for the Alaska Innocence Project.

"Repeatedly," George said. "Over and over."

"Did you tell them that you remembered anything?" the defender asked softly.

"I kept telling them I don't remember," George recalled. "That I don't know."

"Had they told you you were under arrest?"

"No, they did not."

Did detectives imply he could leave, if he chose to? Bundy asked.

"They did," George said firmly. "And I asked to leave."

"Were you able to leave?"

"No!"

He remembered telling the police he was scared. "And why was that?" the big lawyer asked.

George pitched forward in the witness box, face concealed by his knees, breathing hard for more than a minute.

When he finally raised his head, he struggled to find words. "They're telling me, ahh, I did all this shit." Voice rising, visibly distraught: "And I didn't fucking do it!" He smacked the wooden trim encircling him, shaking his head. "You motherfuckers know we're innocent," briefly bowing his head. "I'm tired of this shit," he cried, then ducked, hugged his knees.

@JuliaFBXLawRpt—Judge calls for a break. Lawyers not allowed to approach Frese. Officers trying to calm Frese down. #FairbanksFour

Openly sobbing now, George raised his head. "I didn't fucking do this shit, God damn it!"

@JuliaFBXLawRpt—Members of the audience crying at the outburst from Frese. #FairbanksFour

@JuliaFBXLawRpt—Frese lawyers not allowed to approach him. Frese being taken out of the courtroom by AST, presumably to calm down. #FairbanksFour

@JuliaFBXLawRpt—3:28 pm Most of courtroom holding up 4 fingers in solidarity. #FairbanksFour

@JuliaFBXLawRpt—Lyle: Clear to all of the people in the courtroom to tell them that no additional. Reiterated—no one can text from courtroom. #FairbanksFour

@JuliaFBXLawRpt—Lyle: Reiterated—No further demonstrations in the courtroom and anyone who did, he would kick out for the rest of the day. #Fairbanks Four

JUST NOISE

DAY 14: POSTCONVICTION RELIEF HEARING, THURSDAY, OCTOBER 22, 2015
Ninety minutes into the polygraph expert's testimony, Judge Lyle begged for mercy. "Hey, just stop," he said calmly yet firmly, gazing down at celebrated researcher David Raskin. "I don't understand any of this. This doesn't make any sense to me at all! I'm sorry."

Turning toward Bob Bundy, the Fairbanks Four attorney handling the eminent professor's direct examination, Lyle said, "I'm not trying to be obtuse, but this does not make any sense to me." He frowned and shook his head. "I am not processing what this man's telling me."

"No offense to you, sir," Lyle assured Raskin. "It's just me. I do not understand the explanation."

Again facing Bundy: "You need to start over."

Under a 1970s state supreme court decision, Alaska prosecutors weren't allowed to bring up polygraph results in Alaska courts. Ten years after Gary Cohn and I discussed the merits of vetting the innocence claims of the Fairbanks Four through polygraph testing, Judge Lyle had cracked open the door, inviting this discussion. While he hadn't made a final decision on the merits, he'd agreed to allow David Raskin to present the results of his recent examination of Marvin Roberts's truthfulness.

Lyle made it clear; he alone would determine the exam's relevance in weighing actual innocence. For that, he needed to understand the science.

Raskin, a glib, bright-eyed eighty-year-old founding father in the field, spent the morning attempting to do just that. He'd gotten as far as explaining how reactions to broad general questions differ between truthful subjects and individuals with something to hide, say, a bank robber. How do you distinguish that criminal from a truthful person who initially denies stealing anything ever yet might acknowledge, say, a small theft, which can be used to assess his candor?

He demonstrated that process, playing both sides. As the examiner: "And what was that?" As polygraph subject: "When I was a kid, I used to take change out of my parents' dresser." That last answer, Raskin declared, typifies "a truthful subject's response."

Again, playing examiner: "You never did anything else like that when you knew better, did you?"

Reading the charted waves, the expert stressed, takes nuanced analysis, discerning the difference between relevant issues and relevant questions using comparison questions. Raskin conceded it's not perfect. "It's about 90 percent accurate. And then," he continued, "there's another type of comparison question, which we developed in my laboratory. I learned about this at a Secret Service meeting from a fellow who had been developing a preliminary version. It's called the directed lie."

That was where Judge Lyle lost it.

After backtracking another hour, Raskin arrived at the crux of his testimony: his assessment of Marvin Roberts's truthfulness answering questions posed to him multiple times in various ways during his June 2014 lie detector exam.

- "Were you present at Ninth and Barnette when John Hartman was assaulted?"
- "Did you participate in any way?"
- "Was Frese, Pease, or Vent in your care at any time the night John Hartman was assaulted?"
- "Did you first learn of John Hartman's assault when police first interviewed you about it?"

Roberts's answers—no, no, no, and yes—scored plus 47, according to the well-traveled expert witness. "You only need eight to pass," Rasken assured the court. "This is way beyond the minimum."

Deputy Attorney General Leonard Linton, a tall, white-haired, former Anchorage DA, handled cross-examination. He began by handing the judge copies of several exhibits he planned to discuss, then he walked to the overhead projector brought in for the day's session.

"Doctor, I'd like you to catch us up on what happened at that test," Linton said, then positioned a bluish chart showing several waves on Courtroom 503's drop-down screen. "That is the polygraph you gave Mr. Roberts. You recognize this as a printout?"

Raskin stood in front of the screen and identified audio channels presented as waveforms, explaining how they collectively factor in a skilled analyst's interpretation.

"And how many breaths were reflected?" asked Linton, pointing to a particular waveform track. Turning his back on the witness, he chewed his lip, awaiting the answer.

"You can't determine that," the polygraph expert said. Roberts's prison clothing muffled the signal from one sensor. "So you have to rely more on the abdominal one."

Linton loaded an image of Raskin standing alongside Roberts, seated in a chair, wired for that polygraph examination. He asked the expert to point out the bum sensor.

"I can't see it," Raskin conceded, gazing up at the tall bright screen, hands clasped behind him, bald scalp showing under his combed-over hair.

"In fact, Doctor," Linton said, "there was only one respiration probe attached."

@JuliaFBXLawRpt—State: Attacking Raskin about transducer and the polygraph was broken. #FairbanksFour

Breaking for lunch, Lyle referred to "business" with Wallace's attorney and put off further cross-examination until 2:00 p.m.

When the hearing reconvened, Raskin slumped in the chair; he knew what was coming. Yes, the sensor was missing. No, it didn't matter. "It's just noise," he insisted. He'd checked his calendar, figuring this out. "I had just returned from Colombia, Bogotá," he said, eyes wide, "giving some invited lectures and exams." Somewhere along the way, he'd lost a sensor and realized that when he hooked up Marvin. None of that affected the validity of the test whatsoever, he insisted.

@JuliaFBXLawRpt—State: Moves to strike the results re: polygraph test results on the basis of the TR graph. (Knows judge will decide later.) #FairbanksFour

The state attorney leading the charge took a moment to savor this.

@JuliaFBXLawRpt—Strange Behavior: State lawyer turns his back, sits down in his chair, sits down and turns his chair & smiles at gallery. #FairbanksFour

Fairbanks Four lawyers protested!

Lyle ordered Linton to face forward. The flogging resumed until the judge called a brief recess. Bundy leaped to his feet, offering to cut the expert loose.

"All right, if you—" the judge began.

"I have no regrets," the defender cheerfully finished his sentence.

DAY 19: POSTCONVICTION RELIEF HEARING, THURSDAY, OCTOBER 29, 2015

The hearing opened with an announcement: Alaska's attorney general had granted Jason Wallace immunity. "For his important testimony," Special Prosecutor Bachman explained to the attorneys, Marvin, reporters and others present, and those listening from offices linked to the courthouse audio system.

Judge Lyle hadn't entered the room yet. The state's first witness of the day, a compact, Hispanic-looking fellow with a dark mustache and short fuzzy goatee, was already seated in the box across from the judge's high bench. The young man poured himself a cup of water and leaned back in the chair, gathering himself.

Matt Ellsworth hadn't volunteered for this, that was for sure. Today's appearance on the witness stand? That was the prosecutor's call.

Bachman began by asking the witness about his secondary-school experiences, starting with North Pole High. Ellsworth acknowledged he wasn't much of a student, resulting in a year down at a military academy in Anchorage. On his return to town, he enrolled across town at Lathrop High, which he attended for a year and a half before dropping out. Roughly a year later, he got his GED, he added with pride.

Matt Ellsworth chose his words carefully. He endured twenty minutes of prodding before he finally confirmed that Scott Davison was an old skateboarding buddy, and yes, they were convicted of a property crime with a friend named Harold.

Another twenty minutes slipped by as Ellsworth danced around who owned what car back in high school and how often he and Davison smoked pot. His own life didn't revolve around it, the coy witness insisted. On the other hand, when Davison was smoking weed in his presence, Ellsworth conceded, it was unlikely that he would not himself partake.

He acknowledged talking to troopers about the current case a couple times. Then Ellsworth took a deep breath and announced there was more to it. Aspects he'd never discussed. "There was a story that led up to a recent event," he began. It concerned a "Caucasian boy" beaten to death by Jason Wallace—the person telling the story that day skipping school. "He made statements referring to this crime," Ellsworth said. "He was involved and stated that if 'I ever find out that anybody'—and this is just paraphrasing—'If I ever find out that anybody tells anybody, I'll end their life' or something like that. 'I'll kill you and make sure that person doesn't live.'"

Ellsworth and Bachman spent the next ten minutes quibbling over his memory. She reminded him that he repeatedly denied all this when troopers questioned him.

"I can't help but not see the case," her witness shot back. "It's a tragic one if there are people that are involved that are not guilty," Ellsworth said, straightening himself. "Then it's kind of sad," he added, looking the prosecutor in the eyes.

"So," she said slowly and with emphasis, "when you read about this well-documented case, you felt 'I need to do something about it. I need to go tell someone.'"

"No," said Ellsworth. "I never felt the need to do something."

"Because?"

"I was scared for my life."

After a few more thrusts, the prosecutor gazed at her legal pad, drew a line across it, and changed course. "So when you talked about it with people, was there any suggestion in your conscience, sir, that you ought to go talk to people about this?"

"Yeah," Ellsworth said, blinking and taking a breath. "There was." He nodded to himself. "There is a little bit. I was a little reserved to keep quiet. But there was a part of me that wanted to." Looking down, he repeated, "There's a part of me that wanted to, but I just, it didn't feel like I could."

"Until today?"

"Yes."

"And the only reason that you're here today is that, ah, the state, ah, had to go to court. In your home state. And compel you to come here, right?"

He shrugged. "I felt the need to say something. I'm under oath."

The prosecutor continued, off balance. "But the only reason you're here is because the state compelled you to be here?"

"Correct," Ellsworth said, again looking up at her. "And I'm in court."

"So," Bachman said slowly, "today is the first day you feel comfortable talking about it?"

"I wouldn't say comfortable."

"Okay. Compelled?"

"Compelled," he agreed.

"You're compelled because the state brought you here?"

"Sure."

They had been at it ninety minutes, and Bachman remained off balance. "And you would not be here," she reasoned out loud, "but for the state of Alaska bringing you here?"

"Correct!" declared Ellsworth, leaning into the microphone.

Eyes down, the prosecutor hurriedly gathered her notes. "Thank you," she said and spun away.

Another lesson about liars: Trust at your own risk.

Oberly remained in his chair for a minute or two, rubbing his upper lip with a forefinger, then chewing on a pen held in the same hand, trying to conceal a spreading smile.

Bachman conferred with Linton. Oberly and Lindemuth hustled toward a conference room. Bundy stood and faced the public gallery. "Wow!" he said.

@JuliaFBXLawRpt—Overheard in the courtroom: If this was Battleship, the State just had their case torpedoed. re: Ellsworth testimony. #FairbanksFour

Though banned from directly observing what was going on, I swung by the courthouse every day, collecting video cards for transfer and delivering Julia's special-diet lunches. That was the situation as I rolled down First Avenue scanning for a parking place, when a silver-haired guy in a suit dashed into the street headed right for me, waving both arms.

"Brian!" whooped Bill Oberly. "Ellsworth gave it up! He gave it up!"

CHAPTER 18

THE DEVIL SUITS UP

DAY 19: POSTCONVICTION RELIEF HEARING, THURSDAY, OCTOBER 29, 2015

The listless, unkempt, monosyllabic inmate court observers previously viewed on video appeared reborn. His hair appeared professionally styled, the short beard and thin mustache tamed. For this scheduled appearance, the witness traded his usual prison jumpsuit for a light-purple button-down shirt and tan business jacket set off by a yellow-plaid bow tie.

Seated in the witness box, Jason Wallace quietly took it all in, eyes behind those golden oval wire-framed glasses darting all over. It wasn't until the judge entered and Wallace raised his right arm for the oath that the heavy wrist chain showed under his oversize jacket.

He'd been granted immunity by Alaska attorney general Craig Richards, a former law firm partner of Governor Bill Walker, a genial, well-intentioned fool.

Prosecutor Bachman prefaced her questions for the inmate with a reminder. "You can be prosecuted for false testimony."

Wallace nodded. "Yes, ma'am."

"And you have nothing to lose unless you provide false testimony."

He nodded again.

"Those are the rules." After a pause, she added, "I want you to think about Scott Johnson before you answer the next."

"Objection," snapped Bundy. "Not a question. That's leading."

"It's not a leading question," Bachman countered. "I haven't asked a question yet." Addressing the judge, she said, "I'm trying to impart the seriousness for the witness to consider these next questions."

"Sustained," the judge ruled. He stared off in the distance for a moment, then quietly added, "Invoking Trooper Johnson's name, the court finds, is inappropriate. Just as inappropriate as apologizing or sending condolences yesterday."

He was referring to an opening comment by Eugene's attorney, who got slapped for expressing sympathy to the fallen trooper's family.

At first, Jason Wallace said, he was the one carrying packets taped to his body, smuggling cocaine into Alaska for Hakeem Bryant. Eventually his wife did too, flying in carrying five to ten ounces of coke at a time. "She was about nineteen," he recalled. "Church going."

Wild Bill Holmes was then on the outs with Bryant's gang, according to Wallace. As Christmas approached, the big man maneuvered his way into the dealer's inner circle, plotting to kill Bryant and his associates.

On cross-examination, Bob Bundy, a former Alaska AG, assisting the expanded defense team, pressed Wallace about the letter he got from California officials praising his help prosecuting Holmes. That helped shaved twenty-nine years off Wallace's ninety-nine-year sentence for killing Teacka Bacote with a hammer and stabbing his old friend Corey Spears in the neck, not to mention endangering everybody living in the apartment complex he'd torched covering his tracks. "So," the old lawyer said, "turns out your cooperation with California authorities helped you out in this case. Your case. Didn't it?"

"Yeah, it did," Wallace agreed.

"And that's a good lesson to learn," Bundy emphasized.

"I don't know what you mean," Wallace said, "by 'that's a good lesson to learn'?"

"I'm going to object," the prosecutor said. "Argumentative."

"Sustained," Lyle agreed.

Bundy kept jabbing. "In this case, you just got immunity from the state of Alaska, right? To testify here?"

"Well, okay," the witness countered, pointing out he faced no charges in this case.

"Just a couple weeks ago," Bundy observed, "you got immunity from the attorney general of the state of Alaska for you to give testimony in this case, about the Hartman matter. Correct?"

"Correct."

"And before that, you'd refused to say anything about it to anybody. Okay?"

The prosecutor jumped in. "I'm going to object to the comment on his implications."

"Well, Your Honor," Bundy said in a merry tone, "that was played on the record in this courtroom."

"Overruled."

Bundy gripped the podium, leaning forward. "And in fact, you've been thinking about this immunity for quite a while before you actually got that letter. Hadn't you?"

"No, sir," the witness said.

"Well, do you remember when the deposition was taken in September and Ms. Bachman asked you whether you'd been thinking about immunity? Remember that?"

"I remember that clearly."

"And in fact, you said that you 'had been thinking about immunity,' didn't you?"

"I thought about it."

"Praying on it," Bundy declared. "You told her that too."

"Yes, I did."

"Now they granted you immunity and—"

"Objection," Bachman said. "Speculation. He doesn't know what the state wants."

"I object to her making speaking objections," Bundy shot back.

"Counsel," Lyle said wearily, "perhaps it's getting a little late. We're done."

"EVERYBODY HAS AN AGENDA"

DAY 20: POSTCONVICTION RELIEF HEARING, FRIDAY, OCTOBER 30, 2015

On his second day in the witness box, Jason Wallace again sported a suit. This time, he had a dark coat, white dress shirt, steel-gray bow tie, and what Julia referred to as "very expensive shoes." Gazewood hovered nearby, pouring his client tall cups of water and placing them within easy reach. He filled a third for himself before returning to his seat.

> @JuliaFBXLawRpt—Overheard in the courtroom: What makes the killer get the fancy clothes when the #FairbanksFour were in plain or in prison clothes?

Resuming cross-examination, Bundy bore down on the inmate's sworn statement that he earned his high school equivalency certificate and quit going to classes by the time of Hartman's murder. So, the lawyer asked, how do you explain 1998 Lathrop High attendance sheets noting his presence in classes?

> @JuliaFBXLawRpt—Wallace isn't sure that he would stay enrolled after getting his GED. Not sure if the GED date is wrong. #FairbanksFour

Wallace initially denied, then grudgingly acknowledged leaving the scene of a traffic accident in high school, injuring a person as he fled. Bundy questioned how anyone could forget something like that as well, particularly considering his driver's license was suspended in the aftermath.

"I can't remember what would have been a big deal as a juvenile," Wallace said. "Now that I am an adult, it would make a big impression on me. As a child, I'm not sure."

Bundy needled the witness over his deal with the state. "And the people that decide if you're going to be prosecuted for perjury are the prosecutors right here, right?"

"I don't know," said Wallace, scanning the room with a smile. "I don't know who's gonna decide. But I'm not going to be prosecuted for perjury 'cause I'm not committing perjury."

"You don't decide," thundered the big defense attorney. "The state Department of Law decides if you're going to be prosecuted for perjury."

"I'm pretty sure—" Wallace began.

Bundy cut him off. "And you know that they are taking a position that petitioners are not innocent of that crime, you know that. Don't you?"

Bachman objected. "Beyond the knowledge of this witness, the position of the government in this case."

"Overruled," Lyle said.

Bundy didn't let up. "But you know that the government, the state of Alaska, they are taking a position that these petitioners are not innocent, right?"

"What I do know," Wallace shot back, "is that everybody has an agenda. You know the state does." Turning toward Oberly and Marvin, he raised his eyebrows. "The petitioners' counsel does. And y'all agenda doesn't really concern me," he said, sitting back. "Looks like I'm really just caught in the middle. My agenda is," the witness began, then paused, "to sit here and tell the truth. Which is—I did not kill John Hartman." He had "no opinion" regarding the Four, he insisted. "I never took a stance on it. I never will. And I'm not working for the state."

"The state—" Bundy jumped in, again talking over him.

"And that is my position," the witness continued,

"—gets to decide if you are prosecuted for perjury!" shot back the lawyer, gesturing like a referee making a call. "Only the state! Isn't that right?"

"I don't know what the state does or how the state does it," Wallace countered. "Once again, I'm here not taking sides. I'm not trying to tip the scales of justice in any way. I'm clearly here to tell the truth. And truth being I did not kill John Hartman."

"Until you got that grant of immunity," Bundy continued, "you refused to say anything at all, didn't you?"

"It's easy making me look like the bad guy," Wallace calmly observed. "And you know what? I probably was a terrible person. I did terrible acts," he said, again locking eyes with the defender, his accuser. "But that doesn't mean I killed John Hartman. And whoever accused me of this is lying," Wallace added, raising his eyebrows as he stared over his glasses. "I don't care who it is. They're lying."

"All of them?" the big defender challenged.

"Yes."

"Every single one of them is lying?"

"Yes."

Bundy abruptly turned to the judge. "That's all I have, Your Honor."

————————————

The Fairbanks Four blogger declared war.

STATE OF ALASKA CONSPIRES WITH SERIAL KILLER. GROSS.

Jason Wallace is what he is. If someone sets a rabid dog loose in a playground the dog is not to blame for what comes next. The one holding the leash, the one who knows better, the one who wanted this pet—that is the State of Alaska, and they are more responsible for what comes next out of Wallace than even he is, because they have seen his nature and chose to make the deal.

An action as depraved as the one seen in Alaska courts through the immunity deal with Wallace deserves to be responded to. We will end this post with a series of promises and assure you we will keep them all.

- We will see that any elected official who has accountability in this decision does not see re-election, with special attention to Governor Bill Walker who appears to have forgotten entirely that he would not be Governor without the Native vote.

- We will fight until we prevail to see that Jason Wallace does not get any form of early release. We will do everything we can to see the illegal, disgusting immunity deal revoked and justice for John Hartman. We will see Wallace prosecuted for perjury...

- If it takes us 18 more years, and our children 18 more, and 18 more, and their children more years than we can fathom, we will correct this injustice and do what we can to stop the corruption that destroys lives, steals children, and goes unanswered. We will answer it. And we will not lose, because we raise our children to fight, and you raise yours to lie and hide.

#FairbanksFour

PERMISSION TO TREAT AS HOSTILE WITNESS

DAY 21: POSTCONVICTION RELIEF HEARING, MONDAY, NOVEMBER 2, 2015
The tall doors of Courtroom 503 remained closed as attorney John McKay and I huddled in the hallway discussing tactics. Alaska's press champion seemed shorter and more rumpled than ever; thick reading glasses balanced

on the tip of his nose as he leaned to one side, offsetting the tug of his bulging, shoulder-strap briefcase. Listen to the prosecutor's questions, McKay stressed. Weigh every word. Above all, he stressed, give Oberly and the other Fairbanks Four lawyers the chance to object before saying anything! He ducked back inside.

When the big doors reopened, Bachman emerged, studying her clipboard, then signaled my turn had come.

As soon as we entered, McKay jumped up from his seat in the gallery and followed her to the podium.

Awaiting further directions in the rear of room, I inadvertently blocked Detective Ring's exit. I smiled and shrugged as the retired detective approached. He brushed past, eyes down, stone-faced, surprisingly short. And when did his hair turn white?

"Mr. O'Donoghue," I heard the judge call. "Raise your right hand," he directed as I approached. "Remain standing, and the clerk will administer the oath."

Reversing course, I spun around and halted in front of the court clerk, raising my arm.

Lyle wearily glanced up and gestured for me to continue over to the jury box. "So we can record it, sir."

I'd barely finished spelling my name out loud when McKay spoke out. "Before we start, if I may," he addressed the judge, identifying himself as my lawyer. "I'll make just a brief statement regarding an agreement that we have concerning his testimony."

"Ms. Bachman?" Lyle prompted.

"He is here to testify about his contacts with the convicted men," the prosecutor said, "and witness Arlo Olson."

McKay again spoke up. "We have a specific—Your Honor, if I may, we have a specific—"

"You're not a party in this case," Lyle said calmly. "So what's going on?"

"Well," McKay began, "Your Honor, we—"

"You're not a party in this case," the judge interrupted again. "So what is your role here?"

"If I might," said McKay, then referred to a tentative agreement he'd reached with the state limiting the scope of my testimony.

"If there's a stipulation," the judge said patiently, "why can't Ms. Bachman just read it and put it into the record?"

"That would be fine with me," said McKay. "It's not the stipulation we entered into right before."

"Well," Lyle said wearily, "perhaps the two of you should get together and find out what your stipulation is, and then Ms. Bachman can tell me." Turning to the gallery, the judge announced, "We will take a five-minute break."

McKay approached the prosecutor, open laptop in hand. She glanced at the screen and folded her arms. He began reading out loud. Bachman shook her head.

@JuliaFBXLawRpt—4:02 pm Bachman obviously upset by the conversation with McKay. Has turned her back on McKay—is pulling out evidence books. #FairbanksFour

Gathering her papers, she walked away. McKay paused, then followed her to a side table where she was conferring with staff. As the pair returned to the podium, McKay could be heard saying, "From what I understand, there shouldn't be a problem."

"I don't think so," the prosecutor said.

———————

"Mr. O'Donoghue, did you, as a reporter, develop a relationship with Marvin Roberts?" Bachman asked me after we resumed.

"Marvin Roberts is a source," I said, gazing up at her. "He's someone I've been in touch with on an important story I've been working on for a long time."

"Are you pen pals?"

"I would never use that definition for a person I'm working with on a story."

"Do you consider him a friend?"

"To the extent that, um, things he's told me have generally checked out," I began. "And, uh, he's been informative. Ah, I would say that we've been closer than with some sources."

"So he's just a source to you?"

"This is a very serious story," I said, staring at my hands. "I have shades of familiar relationships with a lot of different parties."

"That's not a responsive answer." She handed me a copy of a letter I'd written Marvin along with a land sales brochure. "Your discussion in this is about land prices? Midway between Fairbanks and Nenana?"

Marvin had often mentioned he hoped to buy property someday. "It's the sort of thing I'd stuff in an envelope for a person I thought was interested," I explained, "as a way of keeping a conversation going."

"Did you also talk to Mr. Roberts about your efforts to investigate the story?"

Of course I had.

Why, she demanded, did I urge Marvin to take a polygraph?

"I worked very hard to try and arrange it," I said. "It's very complicated."

She cut me off before I explained Gary Cohn's advice about testing sources. She handed me a copy of a letter addressed to Marvin and asked if I'd written it. I verified my signature, nothing more. "Read the whole letter."

"I look at the calendar," I began reading out loud, "and it makes me sick to think—"

@JuliaFBXLawRpt—Lyle stops O'D and asks him to read it to himself—
not out loud. O'D reads it and says he is discussing work by his
students. #Fairbanks Four

"I'm describing how I obtained a copy of the trooper interview tape
made when he [Arlo Olson] was arrested on the kidnapping charge. He had
told the troopers that his life was ruined by testifying in the Hartman case."

She was more interested in a different passage. "Why would you tell
Marvin Roberts that Olson has been transferred to Palmer?"

"It's a place," I said after a pause, realizing she'd twist this. "He'd been in
Fairbanks. And I… It's just… I don't know what the implication is."

"Olson told you he had been harassed in jail," the prosecutor sadly
observed. "Right? His whereabouts in jail might facilitate further
harassment."

McKay stood up. "I might, sir—" he began.

Judge Lyle wasn't having it. "If you want to make objections, you can
talk to the parties."

"And I apologize," said McKay, observing that my appearance was
scheduled with little notice.

"This witness is not a party to this case," Lyle said reasonably yet firmly.
"And you're not going to interject yourself—"

"I would just say—" McKay continued.

A hard slap on the bench silenced him. The man in the black robe glared
down.

Did Olson know I was taping him, Bachman kept asking.

"Lawfully recorded calls," I insisted.

"Nonresponsive," she declared and began insinuating I'd pressured
Olson into retracting his testimony.

I got defensive, responding with snide comments before the Fairbanks
Four attorney had time to object. Yes, I'd heard Olson complain that Ricko

DeWilde stuffed him in a prison urinal. But I let Marvin know he deserved protection.

"You didn't focus on the bad treatment he received in jail. Right?"

"It came up," I said, adding that Olson's treatment of women was far worse. "He called *me* from jail," I added. "That was his choice."

@JuliaFBXLawRpt—O'D believed that Arlo was calling to spill out his life story. Both assumed prison was recording the conversation. #FairbanksFour

Bachman referred to that as a ruse.

Hearing that one, I smiled. "I have published Arlo's life story!"

Bachman had me flip to page 4 of one of my hand-transcribed prison calls, a conversation challenging my initial assessment of his motives. The prosecutor had this much right; I took it for granted the squirrely inmate benefited from testifying in the Hartman trials.

@JuliaFBXLawRpt—O'D confirming that his life ruined by the case, was wondering if Arlo was shopping for a deal during the interview. #FairbanksFour

@JuliaFBXLawRpt—O'D says that Arlo was asking for advice. Went back & forth all the time. Want to come forward, then worried about perjury. #FairbanksFour

@JuliaFBXLawRpt—O'D never found any evidence that Arlo got a deal. Arlo never alleged that he got a deal. #FairbanksFour

"The air up there is pretty rarefied," Oberly observed to Kate after the gavel sounded for the last time that day.

"Why did you sit so far back in the room?" I asked her when we caught up. "I could hardly find you."

"Babe," she said, "I was in the front row. There are just so many lawyers in between."

Media outlets called it accurately: "The state argued that O'Donoghue had coached Olson on how to recant his testimony, the man whose evidence was central to the convictions," reported the *News-Miner*.

"Combative," wrote my former editor Dermot Cole, now working as a columnist for *Alaska Dispatch News*, the upstart paper that swallowed Anchorage's big daily.

All that quibbling over sources and relationships left me brooding, feeling as if I were covering up. The prosecutor won that round, hands down, and I was due back in that box bright and early the next day.

DAY 22: POSTCONVICTION RELIEF HEARING, TUESDAY, NOVEMBER 3, 2015

Kate and I spent a long night dwelling on things the prosecutor might yet twist, misconstruing my effort.

As it played out in real time, dread gave way to astonishment. That morning, I spent hours penned in the box watching Bachman, Grisham, Lindemuth, and other lawyers quibble over old statements by Arlo Olson and others. From what I could tell, Olson's endless griping about police encounters and the prosecutor's pressure, often captured on taped calls, gained weight as prior inconsistent statements.

"Does the state have any more questions for this witness?" asked Lyle during a midmorning lull. "He's got a lawyer here," he added, nodding at McKay. "I'm sure he wants to go home."

"No," said the prosecutor.

"Well, all right," said the judge and again addressed Alaska's press defender. "I'm sorry you had to stay overnight," he told McKay.

My old friend seized the moment. "Can he be freed from the exclusionary rule?"

"I don't see any reason he can't." Turning toward me, Judge Lyle said, "Sir, you're released and can take your seat in the gallery."

In a daze, I traded that witness box for a seat alongside Steve MacDonald, the TV documentary producer from Anchorage. He and I slapped hands, then settled in watching April Monroe's turn on the stand.

Though advanced pregnancy offered an easy out, April elected to testify against her doctor's orders. Her attorney made the judge aware of that, warning the judge not to take offense if her client bolts for the bathroom.

"If you need to go, no words needed," Judge Lyle assured April, flashing a rare smile. "Just go!"

The prosecutor questioned April's financial involvement in the case, raising, what was it? $35,000? And what was she doing visiting the governor's office in Juneau? Just how close was she to the men convicted of Hartman's murder?

The young mother never blinked: April put the value of her fundraising at $50,000 or more. Yes, over the years, she'd discussed the case with plenty of lawmakers in Juneau and more than one governor. Though younger than the men convicted, she described George and Eugene as longtime friends.

"Have you worked with Brian O'Donoghue?"

"He was my professor," April said.

"Do you collaborate with Mr. O'Donoghue in efforts to bring attention to this case?"

"No, I wouldn't say so," she said, describing me as a "good source of information," someone she turned to for background on the case. "That kind of thing. But Brian's stuck, you know, really to journalism."

"It's your position that you haven't collaborated with him?"

Exchanging ideas and information, April conceded. "But we never collaborated on, like, a singular project or singular effort."

"Who is Ricko DeWilde?" the prosecutor abruptly asked.

"Friend of mine," April said. "Advocate for the four convicted men."

And what about her efforts to enlist the Spring Creek prison chaplain's help in persuading Jason Wallace to come forward?

Reverend Shirley Lee came up with the idea, said April. Encouraging a man of God to help Wallace see the light had a lot of merit. Beyond that, April said she didn't recall much, describing the conversation as a "physical blank."

"But you did acknowledge," the prosecutor pointed out, "that there was an email that tracked exactly that idea?"

April conceded that she saw an email on the general subject.

The chaplain complained about that to the authorities, the prosecutor reminded her.

"I remember you showed me an email from the chaplain saying I had called," confirmed April, stating she didn't recall the contents with "specificity."

"And that tracked exactly the idea you expressed here."

Hearing an objection, "Don't answer," the judge told April.

Marvin, seated alongside Oberly, leaned back in his chair, rocking and stroking his mustache.

April asked to see a copy of that email.

"The email you don't remember?" the prosecutor jabbed.

"I don't remember it with enough specificity to say whether or not it matches what I just told you," April coolly responded. "But I would be happy to look at it."

The prosecutor handed her a copy of a letter from Eugene, attached to the email, and directed April to "read aloud" a highlighted portion of page 4. Leaving the witness to study it, she returned to the podium. "You remember this email?"

"Oh yes," said the hazel-eyed founder of *Free the Fairbanks Four*. "'Being a member of a large group inside these walls,'" she began to read, "'people often equate a Brotherhood to another racist group, but we are not that. Not even close. I will say this, Our Brotherhood was founded with the mission to end a long cycle of other races preying on Natives for too long. We are proud to be Native.' Want me to keep going?" No one spoke up, so April kept rolling. "'It doesn't matter if you are Inupiat, Athabascan, or Apache. We're proud to be together and—'"

The prosecutor interrupted. "That's beyond the highlighted section. Correct?"

"Yeah," April coolly acknowledged.

Bachman and other lawyers argued over the relevance of Eugene's reference to the Brotherhood, a term broadly associated with an Alaska prison gang.

Judge Lyle soon stepped in. "Capital B or not," he again cautioned the prosecutor against suggesting witnesses faced reprisals for testifying against the Four.

All sides were again caught up reviewing Arlo Olson's troubled path before and after those trials. The prosecutor insisted Olson was likely pressured into retracting his trial testimony.

Lyle pointed out that the state itself abandoned that argument earlier in the proceedings. "I'm not reciting my ruling," the judge said. "I'm reciting your statement to the court that you have no evidence that any one of the four has either themselves assaulted or procured others to assault or otherwise harassed Mr. Olson. Is that still a correct statement?" Lyle demanded.

"It is a correct statement," conceded Bachman, "but the court thwarted my efforts to ask those questions of Mr. Frese and Mr. Vent."

My own reporting reflected that, she pointed out, reminding the court she'd even been blocked from putting Ricko DeWilde on the witness stand, the guy Olson told me stuffed him in a prison toilet.

Lyle didn't waver. The state hadn't proved Olson's change of heart wasn't genuine.

DAY 24: POSTCONVICTION RELIEF HEARING,
THURSDAY, NOVEMBER 5, 2015

Jeffrey O'Bryant, the prosecutor who put the Four away, faced a scary drive just getting to the courthouse in Anchorage. He'd come 350 miles, enduring "quite the storm" and "significant winds" in Healy.

Of course, that was nothing compared to managing his star witness through preliminary hearings and three on-again, off-again 1999 trial dates. It wasn't that Arlo Olson refused to testify, not at the start anyway. Initially, his stance was "I don't want to, but I will," or "I'm not comfortable, but I will," according to O'Bryant, who described the witnesses' state of mind around the time jurors convicted George in the February 1999 trial, a year and a half after Hartman's murder. The former DA sensed an attitude change afterward. "Hesitation had gone to resistance in the second and third trial," O'Bryant told the court, adding that he recognized that "but didn't know what to make of it."

Up until that point, the star witness impressed him. "He presented as a young man I thought had a lot on the ball. He had this easygoing kind of joviality. He was fun to visit. We had a lot of good talks. We had good rapport."

As delays continued, O'Bryant observed a change. "The shine in his eyes, his 'joie de vivre,' was gone."

Though the former DA's prosecution of the Four drew lasting enmity in many Native communities, few likely realized Jeffrey O'Bryant had long-standing personal and professional interests in Native culture. After earning bachelor's degrees in both Eskimo and linguistics at UAF, followed by a law degree out of state, O'Bryant returned to Alaska and worked for years in Native communities.

The witness drew on that experience assessing Olson's downward spiral. "He's not belonging," O'Bryant told the court. "Basically, what he's telling me is he doesn't feel he belongs where he comes from. He doesn't feel as if he belongs in the community here. And he's certainly not welcome at the jail, where they're spitting on his food, on his person, and whatnot."

The DA denied pressuring or rewarding the star witness for the testimony that tipped the scales of justice in all three trials.

> @JuliaFBXLawRpt: O'Br says Arlo didn't do anything to make his life easier or give him any kind of a deal. #FairbanksFour

Observing from the gallery, I felt bad that I hadn't kept in touch with Arlo Olson. At the same time, I was proud he'd found his voice, setting the record straight in this same courtroom.

Wishful thinking, perhaps, but as the hearing neared its end, the trio of lawmen who arguably did the most to lock up the Fairbanks Four and keep them there seemed to be hedging their bets concerning the Fairbanks Four's case for innocence.

Prosecutor Jeff O'Bryant had acknowledged possible errors in the original trials.

Detective Aaron Ring had defended his interrogation techniques yet seemed to waver regarding the results.

Detective Paul Geier compared the deductive process yielding Exhibit #30, the gory boot-bruise photo overlay, to a child's hidden picture game. "I shouldn't put it this way," Geier said, "but all of the sudden, there's the dolphin. That was those tread marks."

From my seat in the gallery, that last comparison rang true. Hunches and assumptions, that summed up FPD's investigation. Forensic science never even figured.

Damn sad, all of it.

WAITING GAME

TUESDAY, NOVEMBER 10, 2015

"Evidence has to be admissible," Judge Lyle said, addressing the petitioners, lawyers, and everyone else present. "So those determinations have to be made. This court is not writing on a blank slate. It's writing on the history of four cases." The record of testimony and other evidence assembled over the past weeks amounted to a starting point for considering the petitioners' request to erase the verdicts through proof of actual innocence.

Lyle explained that he now had to go back and read thousands of pages of transcripts, weigh the testimony, and apply facts properly under the law. "That's the court's goal. The court's mandate. And that is what I'm going to do my very best to do," Lyle said. "Wherever that leads, that's where I have to go."

Alaska judges have six months to decide fully briefed cases, or they face having their salary cut off. Lyle warned everyone in the room or listening from jail, he wasn't going to rush it. "I don't want you to think if I don't meet the six-month deadline that I haven't been working on it," he said, or worry how he was paying his own bills if he didn't. "The court is prepared to deal with that," Lyle said, declaring what mattered to him was getting it right, which could take seven months. Or even more.

SPECIAL GUEST

IR CLASS, DECEMBER 6, 2015

I'd promised students we'd have a special guest but hadn't let on who that might be.

True to his word, Marvin Roberts soon quietly joined us in the journalism department's conference room. Though more than twice as old as most of these students, the young man sporting a ballcap flipped backward under his hoodie blended right in.

After quick introductions, the parolee confirmed that a proposed settlement was on the table. He didn't like it, but he couldn't speak for the others, nor was he allowed to talk to them right now.

"If you could talk to them, what would you say?" asked Katie Luper, an ambitious young TV anchor pursuing her BA on the side.

"I'd say, hold fast!" Marvin declared, grinning. "In six months to a year, it's worth millions of dollars. That's what I'd probably tell them."

He looked down at his lap for a long moment. "Someone put it to me like this," he continued softly. "No guarantee Judge Lyle will make the right decision. The terms might not get us exonerated." Almost to himself, he added, "Freedom right now is worth more than money." He rolled his thumbs, eyes down. "I don't know," he said, then raised his head, locking eyes with mine. "Maybe Brian will give me a cut of his book!" Marvin declared, grinning.

"Or a cut of the movie rights," finished Heather Penn, a practical military vet and mother of five.

After the class broke up, we took a group picture in front of a hallway display featuring UAF's coverage over the years.

On the way out, Marvin privately outlined the state law department's all-or-none offer in greater detail.

Didn't sound good to me.

He agreed, but being on the outside, how could he justify holding this up?

Over the following days, what I heard about the terms sounded worse and worse: convictions erased, yet original charges remain on the books? And the state apparently wanted all four to waive damages?

SULLIVAN ARENA, ANCHORAGE, DECEMBER 13, 2015

Bill Oberly and I made plans to get together for the annual Governor's

Cup hockey game, determining bragging rights between our UAF Nanooks against his son's UAA Seawolves. On my end, the pregame festivities extended to getting my face painted blue and gold at a party organized by Kate, UAF's alumni director.

Oberly and I discussed the proposed settlement in the beer tent. Though Judge Lyle had just rejected the initial terms, the Alaska Innocence Project's director defended the deal. "Freedom is on the table," he argued. "It's their decision."

"You're their lawyer," I countered, still wearing my UAF blue and gold face paint. "Advise them!"

Oberly reminded me that Lyle warned everybody that sorting through the five weeks of testimony, evidentiary challenges, and other legal issues would take months and months with no guarantee that Marvin and the others would cheer the outcome.

"It's not going to go the distance," I countered. "Pressure is on the state to settle this. The hearing opened eyes. Terms will only get better."

Oberly shrugged. "They are ready to get out." He sounded tired.

When we got back from Anchorage, I called Kevin's aunt Billie down in Mat-Su, urging her to relay a message from me: Politics were shifting. Their cause had broad support. Terms were sure to get better as we got closer to the legislature's return in January. "You've got to let Kevin know," I emphasized. "He and the others hold the cards."

Billie sighed. While she agreed with me, those boys felt life slipping away.

I called Hazel Roberts with the same message: "Talk to Marvin. Convince him to stand his ground. The guys inside will thank him later."

"He won't do it," she said. "I wish he would, but he won't."

I urged April to use the FF blog to get the word out. "Terms will only improve. Hold tough."

"I'm worried about George," she said. "He really needs to get out."

"Put on your big girl boots," I told her. "The prosecutor roughed everyone up. So what? Truth is on the record now."

And so was the judge's warning, she pointed out. "Lyle said it could take seven months."

CHAPTER 19

JAILBREAK!

THURSDAY, DECEMBER 17, 2015

VINELink.com showed no change in the prisoners' status, but word had it that Kevin, George, and Eugene were spotted under escort at Fairbanks airport. No one answered the phone at Judge Lyle's office. A quick check of the court's online docket offered nothing relevant. On a hunch, I raced over to FCC and requested to see Kevin Pease. "He's here," confirmed the guy at the front desk. "But he's not available."

George and Eugene were also in town, April soon confirmed by text. Apparently, a settlement offer was on the table: My guess is still today or tomorrow, she predicted.

As the day unfolded, her texts got more interesting.

April: Oh, and all of their attorneys are here too.

Then came a direct order.

April: Head to the courthouse! Now!

———————

The entrance door to Courtroom 501 was locked. A dozen or more people, this professor included, stood watch in the lobby outside. Stephanie Woodward, a local TV reporter currently taking News Writing, positioned herself by the door crack, calling out updates. Judge Lyle wasn't part of the group that she could tell. Only lawyers.

Julia Taylor scooted around in her wheelchair, cutting lanes through swelling hallway traffic, hunting for tweet-worthy developments.

@JuliaFBXLawRpt—146 people in the 5th floor hallway at 1:38 pm. #FairbanksFour

Courtroom 503 had room for maybe half that many observers. And every time the elevator opened, more spilled out.

@JuliaFBXLawRpt—Overheard in the hall: If we don't get this right, we will never get justice for Alaska Natives on our own land. #FairbanksFour

Cheers resounded as top executives from the Tanana Chiefs Conference and Doyon, the regional Native corporation, delivered pizzas and cases of bottled water.

@JuliaFBXLawRpt—Judge, attorneys and petitioners are in the courtroom. Doors still locked. #FairbanksFour

Supporters prepared to celebrate. Several unpacked drums.

An older Native man leaning against the far wall looked familiar. Andy Jimmy grinned as he saw me approaching. Harley, one of the main leaders in my 1991 Iditarod team, came from the old sprint musher's kennel in Minto. After the race, I made a point of visiting the village, named for its location on a high bluff overlooking Minto Flats, and personally thanked him. Now, we reminisced about that huge hungry dog, happily snarfing up scraps left by teams ahead of mine on that one road to Nome, as the saying goes.

The diversion was welcome.

What were they doing behind those tall, locked doors? The hallway became so crowded, I felt a little dizzy, yet there stood April, rocking on her feet nearby, baby due any second.

@JuliaFBXLawRpt—Overheard in the hall: There should be nothing that is a secret in this case. Open the doors. #FairbanksFour

About 4:00 p.m., "They're removing shackles," yelled a door-crack watcher.

Those tall doors opened, and we spilled inside.

Judge Lyle returned and called for order. With lawyers on both sides taking part, a series of procedural stipulations rapidly entered the record.

@JuliaFBXLawRpt—State has stopped objects to new evidence without petitioners having to meet the higher standard. #FairbanksFour

@JuliaFBXLawRpt—After previous convictions are vacated, the petitioners will drop prosecutorial misconduct charges. #FairbanksFour

Hartman's oldest brother was listening by teleconference. Lyle asked if he wanted to speak for the family. Chris Kelly had been briefed. He'd heard the terms. He also knew what it meant to spend years behind bars as life passes you by. "If they're innocent," his voice carried over the speaker system. "If you believe that all of a sudden now, I don't see why you could even justify doing this to them." He wasn't done. "And if they're guilty," Kelly declared, clearly anguished, "I don't see how you can justify making a deal!"

Unspecified terms of release were quickly approved. Kevin Pease stood up, escorted by troopers, and marched past Lyle's bench, exiting the room amid cheers. Ponytailed George Frese exited next with bouncing steps, one hand thrust in a pocket, the other raised, displaying four fingers. Looking somewhat stunned, Eugene Vent, a huge man, squared his big shoulders and followed them.

All three, Lyle explained, technically remained Corrections Department clients. Discharge would take place at FCC. With that settled, he too left by the side door. The rest of us were stuck inside Courtroom 501 with troopers guarding the doors until the prisoners and their security detail cleared the building. Baby-faced Attorney General Craig Richards and John Skidmore were penned up in the room with everyone else. Both huddled together on the left side of the gallery, eyes on the main door, poised to bolt. Others hugged and cried.

"Tonight, at the tribal hall, 6:30," shouted Victor Joseph.

"Are you sure it's available?" someone asked.

Joseph, being the head of the Tanana Chiefs Conference, waved her off, laughing. "Bring whatever's in your freezer!" he shouted.

KTUU's Steve MacDonald approached the Department of Law officials, requesting an interview. Too crowded, the AG said. Downstairs, perhaps?

Columnist Dermot Cole made his way over and shook my hand.

The doors finally opened, and people spilled into the hallway. Packed though it was, a drumming circle formed near the elevators. Julia Taylor used her cell phone to shoot videos of Joseph, Marvin, and others filled with the spirit, crouching, leaping, and flapping their arms like wings.

"Have you seen the attorney general?" someone remarked.

Dermot and I rushed for the elevator. Down in the main lobby, there was no sign of the lawmen or MacDonald's TV crew. We dashed outside, where the interview appeared to be wrapping up over by the street corner.

"Okay," I said, busting in on the group. "So the verdicts were set aside, right?"

"Yes is the answer," said AG Richards. "They are dismissed. They can be brought again upon new evidence. Upon the discovery of new evidence."

"That would be evidence dating from now?" I asked.

AG Richards confirmed that. "There is finality on all fronts from now."

"So this is like it never happened?" asked Dermot.

"I wouldn't go so far as to say they never happened," said John Skidmore, the criminal division's hard-nosed director, referring to the convictions. "The agreement today states they were properly obtained," he said. "There was nothing improper done, either by the Fairbanks Police Department, by Detective Aaron Ring, or by any prosecutor that's worked on the case."

AG Richards backed that up, characterizing the agreement as "mainly procedural." They had been working this out since 2:30 a.m. In the end, he assured us, the terms were essentially the same; only a criminal lawyer would understand the particulars.

"What about the new suspects?" Dermot asked. "Is the Department of Law going to investigate them?"

That was up to the police, the law officials agreed.

"So no one is held accountable," I said, "for the eighteen years these guys served in a situation where their verdicts have been set aside."

"There was nothing improper in what happened originally," insisted Skidmore.

"Accountable for what?" the AG muttered.

"What this said," added Skidmore, "is there was sufficient evidence to convict them at the time they were convicted. They've agreed to that."

I had my doubts but hadn't seen the terms. What the hell did they sign?

Drained, I headed home. Robin, seventeen, and Rachel, eleven, weren't keen on attending whatever it was I was talking about. Kate was supportive, but 6:30 tonight, really? That meant leaving almost immediately, though she and I both knew that Native gatherings are rarely punctual.

"Well, I'm going," I declared. "It's going to be something to see. The Four are free. It's special."

Rachel, my little pal, agreed to come. Kate quietly got ready.

JAVA RUN

Marvin bolted the courthouse crowd and jumped in his dark-gray 2007 Chevy Silverado truck. He parked outside FCC, awaiting the completion of the discharge paperwork underway within. After George, Eugene, and Kevin were kicked loose, Marvin took them straight to a coffee hut, an entirely new experience for those old Howard Luke boys. There was so much to take in, it made them all giddy. Perhaps this more than anything: it was the first time the Fairbanks Four ever cruised together, let alone with Marvin Roberts at the wheel.

Official capacity of the new tribal hall, a deep and long massive log structure, was six hundred people. It was already close to full when Kate, Rachel, and I arrived, and more were pouring in every minute.

We hadn't been there long when a guy with a long ponytail grabbed my hand. George! Big buff Kevin, sporting a brand-new blue button-down shirt and gray pants, smiled shyly and shook my hand as well. Eugene beamed like a huge kid and hugged me.

The crowd quieted when Poldine Carlo approached the mic with a special song in mind for this special day. At ninety-five, her voice remained rich, though softer than ever, or so it seemed to me. Though I couldn't make out the words, she sounded proud.

We took it all in from a bench alongside the wall. Kate couldn't get over how quickly the feast came together, pan after pan offering everything from moose stew to spaghetti. Native leaders, esteemed elders, anyone who wanted the microphone, got their turn speaking, including the Four. George looked and sounded the most assertive, ready to seize life.

When the drums got going, so did the dancing, and the Four were soon pulled into the middle of it. They in turn yanked Bill Oberly from his chair. Before long, more and more of their white lawyers were shedding suit coats and taking the floor, cautiously at first, soon leaping and flexing those elbows.

I'd been angry at the lawyers. Naysayers were going to disparage this deal as a concession, wink, wink, affirming those original verdicts. My gloom lifted as I watched the Four dancing and hugging supporters, tasting life outside razor-wire fences and walls. The feeling in the room was euphoric. For all but Marvin, this was their first night of freedom in eighteen years. That was big.

BITTER FRUIT

When I did get my hands on it, the document George, Kevin, Eugene, and Marvin signed on December 9, 2015, proved to be a stunning bid to erase responsibility for eighteen years of wrongful imprisonment.

> By virtue of this Settlement Agreement and Mutual Release of All Claims, Marvin L. Roberts unequivocally releases and discharges the Releasees from any and all claims, known, unknown, or discovered in the future, arising out of the investigation into the death of Jonathan Hartman and the subsequent prosecution and incarceration of Marvin L. Roberts, whether based on tort, contract, the United States Constitution, the Alaska Constitution, or any other theory of liability, including but not limited to, claims for malicious prosecution, wrongful imprisonment, prosecutorial misconduct, legal malpractice, violation or deprivation of rights civil or constitutional, personal injury, and pain and suffering, loss of enjoyment of life, emotional or mental suffering, emotional distress or trauma, loss of consortium, loss of

society, negligence, internal acts or omissions, medical expenses, medical malpractice, past or future loss of wages... Roberts hereby covenants and agrees that he will not, either individually, jointly, or in concert with others...assist in the bringing of claims or actions of any kind against the Releasee for damages or losses arising out of the matters or claims references above.

For its part, the State of Alaska was dropping charges against Marvin Roberts and the others "with prejudice," according to the document, reserving the right to "file charges in the future and seek retrial, only if substantial new evidence of guilt is discovered, of which the state was not previously aware."

The agreement was loaded with reminders that Alaska's Law Department wasn't acknowledging any error on its part, much less recognizing eighteen years of injustice. Page 6, for example, under the heading "No Admission of Liability," stated, "The parties have not reached agreement as to Roberts's actual guilt or innocence."

———————

Within a year of their release, the Fairbanks Four brought a federal suit, challenging the settlement, citing the coercive pressure on Marvin to sign off, forgoing compensation, though he'd already served his full sentence. Knowing what George, Kevin, and Eugene faced every day inside prison walls, he couldn't turn his back on them.

The injustice inflicted on George Frese, Kevin Pease, Marvin Roberts, and Eugene Vent has since been recognized by the National Registry of Exonerations, a nonprofit initiative of Michigan State Law School and several others, "to prevent future false convictions by learning from past errors." Since its launch in 1989, the registry has identified over thirty-three hundred individuals exonerated in the wake of new evidence and other proof of innocence.

The case summaries for the Fairbanks Four include this text: "In 2008, following more than seven years of investigating the case, Brian O'Donoghue, a former reporter for the *Fairbanks Daily News-Miner* newspaper who was a journalism professor at the University of Alaska Fairbanks, published a series of articles in the newspaper that strongly suggested that the men, who were known as the 'Fairbanks Four,' were innocent. The series drew on years of reporting by O'Donoghue's students. Based on the articles, the Alaska Innocence Project began re-investigating the case."

SPECIAL AWARDS

At the end of this bittersweet trail, I found an insider whose disgust over the years of silence about privileged secrets rivaled mine. Bill Spiers was a public defender when a client confided that he'd falsely testified against one of the defendants in the Hartman trials. Later, working as a state prosecutor, Spiers shared what he knew about Hartman's confessed killer with Judge Lyle. "Here's what made me retire," said the lawyer who'd worked both sides.

The setting was a law conference the year following the Fairbanks Four's release. "They had this thing they called the football," he said. "So you got the football if you did something that was supposedly noble, but it was a terribly hard thing that you did, and then you failed."

The winner? Prosecutor Adrienne Bachman.

"Everybody in that goddamn room, except for me, got up and gave her the biggest standing ovation for defending this? Except for me. Gave her the biggest standing ovation," Spiers recalled. "For defending these awful convictions. And I said to myself, that's it: I can't stand this. I can't. I cannot. Why the fuck would anybody get up and applaud somebody for defending a wrongful conviction? What in God's name? What kind of an agency are we? That's always bothered me and even right to the minute I was called in to talk to the judge," he said, referring to his closed-door 2015 meeting with Lyle. "I had people from public defenders, the OPA [Office of Public Advocacy] just lobbying me right until I was going into the room not to disclose what I knew. They knew these guys were innocent, but they're fighting like bloody hell to keep them in jail, right? And the DAs—who know that they're innocent—are fighting bloody hell to keep them in jail. Something is wrong with the system," he said. "It's broken, and it's broken bad. It's broken in the worst possible way. And I don't know how to fix it."

Checking further turned this up: the Fairbanks Four litigation was named "Trial of the Year" at the state Department of Law's 2016 criminal division annual conference, according to the November-December issue of *Alaska Bar Rag*. The award meant "to recognize the litigation that had the most significant impact on a community," according to the citation, honored Assistant Attorneys General Adrienne Bachman, Leonard Linton, and Ali Rahoi.

RECLAIMED PROPERTY

The Facebook Live video opened on a dusty blue compact resting on a tilt trailer, ready for unloading. Long-legged shadows stretched across the snow, casting the silhouettes on the side door of an old Dodge Shadow hatchback.

"How you feeling, Marv? You finally getting your ride back?" called Ricko DeWilde, doubling as videographer and director of this production for Fairbanks Four social media followers.

"A big shout-out to Interior Towing," an unseen observer yelled over the sound of a throbbing truck engine, "for bringing my car back for free."

The camera view swung to a solid, compact, mustached Athabascan man giving a thumbs-up and grinning.

"It's about nineteen years since I seen this car," Marvin Roberts announced. "It's done more time than me," he added, a wistful catch in his voice. Turning, he watched that old blue car rolling off the tilt trailer. "Still looks intact," he said. "Kind of a bittersweet moment."

From off camera: "They ever find evidence in that thing?"

The owner of that dusty Dodge Shadow hatchback spun around. "There was no evidence in this car," Marvin declared, facing the camera. "There was no evidence in this case," he added. "I'm innocent. The Fairbanks Four was innocent."

Voice lifting, Marvin Roberts issued this final opinion: "My car was innocent!"

ACKNOWLEDGMENTS

Dedicated to the dozens of undergraduate student investigators who chased leads on campus, downtown, in bush villages, and in prisons near and far. I'm humbled by the courage and faith of the families who opened their doors, sharing stories about their sons and daughters. Credit Kelly Bostian, then *News-Miner* managing editor, for ignoring naysayers and letting that big press roll, reopening the case. Special recognition goes to the late Shirley Demientieff, first among many Native and non-Native Alaskans demanding justice for John Hartman *and* the Fairbanks Four. I'm forever grateful to book agent Jane Dystel, who shared the long road, keeping faith with her least productive client.

NOTES

CHAPTER 1: "LOOK, LOOK, THERE'S A LITTLE BOY!"

northern lights cold: Brian O'Donoghue, "Decade of Doubt," pt. 2, "A Cry in the Night: A Horrifying Discovery Is Made on the Streets of Fairbanks," *Fairbanks Daily News-Miner*, July 7, 2008, https://drive.google.com/file/d/18znCw 93WpIC8TrwcE3EdLLgEIzDvumz6/view?usp=drive_link.

Melanie couldn't make out the words: Melanie Durham, interview by Investigator Peggy Sullivan, October 11, 1997, Fairbanks Police Department, supplemental report.

the $720 million distribution: "Permanent Fund Dividend," State of Alaska, Department of Revenue, accessed September 23, 2023, https://pfd.alaska.gov/Division-Info/summary -of-dividend-applications-payments.

"Rollers call it the dividend season": Brian O'Donoghue and Nate Raymond, "Decade of Doubt," pt. 3, "A Wild Night: Motel Party Sets the Stage for Murder Investigation," *Fairbanks Daily News-Miner*, July 7, 2008, https://drive.google.com/file/d /18znCw93WpIC8TrwcE3EdLLgEIzDvumz6/view?usp=drive_link.

"Now the neighbor": Brian O'Donoghue, "Wild Night Downtown," October 11, 1997, originally hosted on UAF Extreme Alaska podcast (no longer available), https://drive.google.com/file/d/1HYQfwLSDEPH1Aul5feRTncsrapfHTkzM/view ?usp=sharing.

"Look right there": Louise Lambert, interview by Investigator Paul Geier, November

13, 1997, Fairbanks Police Department, supplemental report; Brian O'Donoghue, "Decade of Doubt: John Hartman's 1997 Murder Remains Divisive for the Interior," pt. 1, *Fairbanks Daily News-Miner*, July 6, 2008, https://drive.google.com/file/d /18znCw93WpIC8TrwcE3EdLLgEIzDvumz6/view?usp=drive_link.

"some kind of trauma": O'Donoghue, "Cry in the Night."

"I need someone to come": Carol Pease, recorded 911 call, 2:58 a.m., October 11, 1997.

"Kevin Pease, nineteen years of age": Dispatch Center recording, October 11, 1997.

"And they're all minors": Alaskan Motor Inn night manager Mike Baca, Chief Detective Keller, Fairbanks Dispatch Center recordings, and motel's office surveillance camera video, October 11, 1997.

"Foot pain": Outpatient record, Fairbanks Memorial Hospital, 3:50 p.m., October 11, 1997.

"If you were there": Brian O'Donoghue, "Decade of Doubt," pt. 4, "Case Solved? Confessions to Police Remain at Center of Trial's Debate," *Fairbanks Daily News-Miner*, July 9, 2008, https://drive.google.com/file/d/18znCw93WpIC8TrwcE3EdLLgEIzDvumz6/view?usp =drive_link.

"Teen Dies in Hospital": Erin Lillie, "Teen Dies in Hospital after Downtown Attack, Police Arrest 4 Suspects," *Fairbanks Daily News-Miner*, October 13, 1997.

"He came out with his gun": Al Slavin, Jolie Lewis, and Douglas Fischer, "Attack Called Random Violence; 4 Suspects Charged with 1st Degree Murder," *Fairbanks Daily News-Miner*, October 14, 1997.

"It should be a total embarrassment": Brian O'Donoghue, "Troopers: Snaring Incident Bungled; No Charges Expected," *Fairbanks Daily News-Miner*, October 14, 1997.

"Anyone of us": Bob Fischer, letter to the editor, *Fairbanks Daily News-Miner*, October 21, 1997.

"Fairbanks needs to take": Karen Kreiser, "Set Example," letter to the editor, *Fairbanks Daily News-Miner*, October 27, 1997, https://drive.google.com/file/d /18Mm6IdNAqVIFONnXrneaURPZGTtHBrbD/view?usp=drive_link.

"The answer is Christ": Dot Keith, "Godless," letter to the editor, *Fairbanks Daily News-Miner*, October 28, 1997, https://drive.google.com/file/d/18Mm6IdNAq VIFONnXrneaURPZGTtHBrbD/view?usp=sharing.

"What happened to innocent": Carla Bonney, "More to It," letter to the editor, *Fairbanks Daily News-Miner*, October 27, 1997, https://drive.google.com/file/d /18Mm6IdNAqVIFONnXrneaURPZGTtHBrbD/view?usp=sharing.

civic leaders convened: Jolie Lewis, "Killing Prompts Calls for Action," *Fairbanks Daily News-Miner*, October 17, 1997.

"This ground is holy": Patricia Jones, "Community Rallies against Violence," *Fairbanks Daily News-Miner*, November 9, 1997, https://drive.google.com/file/d /1gA3AcWaYBYDoTG3Zng8PLaJN6m7h3wTS/view?usp=drive_link.

CHAPTER 2: HOWLS AND CONVICTIONS

"Well, Fairbanks, Alaska": Mary Carter, "Justice?," letter to the editor, *Fairbanks Daily News-Miner*, February 20, 1998, reprinted in Donoghue, "Case Solved?"

"We aren't some Third World country": Adrienne Grimes, "Judgmental," letter to the editor, *Fairbanks Daily News-Miner*, February 25, 1998.

"How can you wish death": Lena McCarthy, letter to the editor, *Fairbanks Daily News-Miner*, November 2, 1997, https://drive.google.com/file/d/18Mm6 IdNAqVIFONnXrneaURPZGTtHBrbD/view?usp=sharing.

"I haven't left the house": Al Slavin, "Murder Suspect Back in Jail for Violation," *Fairbanks Daily News-Miner*, January 27, 1999, https://drive.google.com/file/d/1b -c68euehY3Q6g4KihQTlW0WYhVL2joo/view?usp=drive_link.

"He called the Coast Guard": Brian O'Donoghue, "Judge Rejects Hazelwood's Immunity Bid," *Fairbanks Daily News-Miner*, November 3, 1989.

"It was in part": "Venue Change Unnecessary," editorial, *Fairbanks Daily News-Miner*, November 25, 1998.

"muttering obscenities": Larry Campbell, "Frese Guilty in Hartman Beating Death," *Fairbanks Daily News-Miner*, February 17, 1999.

"I'm very mad at the judge": Melissa Moore, "Victim's Mother Not Told Verdict Coming," *Fairbanks Daily News-Miner*, February 17, 1999.

"Hopefully, under the circumstances": Campbell, "Frese Guilty."

"They had to ignore": Margaret Bauman, "Jury Convicts 2 in Hartman Murder Case,"

Fairbanks Daily News-Miner, August 20, 1999, https://drive.google.com/file/d
/1vxkceu6EWCPBK81t7rlAh64CPea6LEgQ/view?usp=drive_link.

Take a Stand for Justice: Tanana Tribal Council, Resolution 99–33, March 10, 1999,
https://drive.google.com/file/d/1FHQAAKgGpiFR1VcbzaWQJt0urHZ-burA/view
?usp=sharing.

"Your act was so sick": Sean Cockerham, "Both Families Testify at Frese Sentencing,"
Fairbanks Daily News-Miner, January 29, 2000.

Nearly a year to the day: Amanda Bowman, "Frese Gets 97 Years in Hartman Killing,"
Fairbanks Daily News-Miner, February 1, 2000.

"I'm a scapegoat": Al Slavin, "Three Get Long Terms for Murder," *Fairbanks Daily News-
Miner*, February 5, 2000.

"This letter is about": Curtis Sommer, letter to the editor, *Fairbanks Daily News-Miner*, June 7,
2000, https://drive.google.com/file/d/181UQ75EbwFy4m6J7KpkwY89MetoMvMWH
/view?usp=sharing.

"Is there equal justice": Gary Moore, "Racial Split in Alaska Justice?," *Fairbanks Daily News-
Miner*, October 11, 2000, https://drive.google.com/file/d/1Z_z06HTuwlFtbdSr2
PA23pvrXGvunw8b/view?usp=drive_link.

"penny-pinching officials": R. E. Stratton, letter to the editor, *Fairbanks Daily News-Miner*,
October 30, 1997.

"We were supposed to hire": Al Slavin, "Police Push to Solidify Case in Hartman Killing,"
Fairbanks Daily News-Miner, November 12, 1997.

"There's not much": Sean Cockerham, "Bail Cut for Murder Defendants," *Fairbanks Daily
News-Miner*, February 6, 1998.

"Marvin Roberts plans": Wendy Hower, "Student Achiever of the Week: Marvin
Roberts," *Fairbanks Daily News-Miner*, May 7, 1996, https://drive.google.com
/file/d/0B_t4yemq94uBR214VXFQcFE2ZGc/view?usp=sharing&resourcekey=0-igLe
-3V7TXDeggEZBwwAXQ.

Marvin Roberts, nineteen: Marvin Roberts, interview by Investigator Paul Geier and
Detective Aaron Ring, October 11, 1997, Fairbanks Police Department.

Though Marvin had smoked pot: O'Donoghue, "Case Solved?"

"Every choice we make": "Class Salutatorian Marvin Roberts Gives Howard Luke Academy 1996 Graduation Speech," ExtremeAlaskaUAF, February 29, 2024, YouTube video, 3:10, https://www.youtube.com/watch?v=53xetqrk9SM.

"We were joking": Brian O'Donoghue, "Decade of Doubt," pt. 6, "'110 Percent Certain': Arlo Olson: 'Half Shot' Yet Positive in His Testimony about What He Saw," *Fairbanks Daily News-Miner*, July 11, 2008, https://drive.google.com/file/d/18znCw93WpIC8TrwcE3EdLLgEIzDvumz6/view.

"I just got this Wednesday": Brian O'Donoghue, "Auditors Examine Police," *Fairbanks Daily News-Miner*, February 25, 1996, https://drive.google.com/file/d/1eDXOfnz8YKMLXfBmhkBYGEFzuHTuHIy2/view?usp=sharing.

CHAPTER 3: "YOU CAUGHT THAT!"

"Naturally, I was kind of": "FCC inmate Marvin Roberts interview Nov. 2001," ExtremeAlaskaUAF, February 29, 2024, YouTube video, 44:00, https://www.youtube.com/watch?v=lvCekxnrAac.

Anyone participating in a phone conversation: "Alaska Reporter's Recording Guide," Reporters Committee for Freedom of the Press, last updated September 2019, https://www.rcfp.org/reporters-recording-guide/alaska/.

"DAYTON said that he fell": Franklin Dayton mugging supplemental report, Fairbanks Police Department, October 20, 1997, https://drive.google.com/file/d/1DEusZpGxd-_Z13ai8JJMz-6nYUufTT6p.

"Simply put": District Attorney Jeff O'Bryant, closing arguments, trial of Marvin Roberts and Kevin Pease, August 1999.

World Plus: Wikipedia, s.v. "World Plus," last modified January 27, 2024, 10:26, https://en.wikipedia.org/wiki/World_Plus.

"To date I have never": Brian O'Donoghue, "State Stymied in World Plus Investigation," *Fairbanks Daily News-Miner*, February 6, 1996, https://drive.google.com/file/d/1w02hfXeESJdRE-PO5WtldhqRFKd6A7CQ/view?usp=drive_link, https://drive.google.com/file/d/1D0mpZMvL3RTmPqdSZ2Q3AnhE065bzYZv/view?usp=drive_link.

"Prior to investing": Detective Paul Keller, World Plus testimonial letter, October 13, 1992, https://drive.google.com/file/d/19uY0A8e6PovuEQD9WUQLwGQK3tSt8H9v/view.

CHAPTER 4: QUESTIONS STACK UP

There wasn't enough DNA: Aaron Ring, interview by Laurel Ford, October–November 2002 story memos, https://drive.google.com/file/d/1ENbRCoJJvchFD6BADlccS3q5HokWnAaJ/view?usp=sharing.

"Let me draw you a picture": Eugene Vent, interview by Detective Aaron Ring, October 11, 1997, Fairbanks Police Department.

"The city reportedly isn't happy": Brian O'Donoghue, "Tours Spotlight Cramped Police Station," *Fairbanks Daily News-Miner*, October 3, 1996, https://drive.google.com/file/d/1pKvJ47yFaJxWf-cFjedqCAMOz4wiyddp/view?usp=sharing.

"Arlo Olson, 25, broke into": Diana Campbell, "Ex-Boyfriend Faces Charges in Kidnapping," *Fairbanks Daily-News-Miner*, November 11, 2002.

"Hey," I said: Arlo Olson, in discussion with the author, November 27, 2002, transcript, https://drive.google.com/file/d/1gkVyufn1V13y8lnJSoBaw0ToukMy04FB/view?usp=sharing.

"I told Jeff": O'Donoghue, "'110 Percent Certain.'"

"Every single person": Jamie Smykalski, interview by Tom Delaune, December 12, 2002.

"The key thing was the eyewitness": Gary Montini, interview by Sharice Walker, December 2, 2002.

"We got permission": Edmund Habza, interview by Tom Delaune, January 28, 2003.

"More than half the people": Gary Montini, interview by Sharice Walker, December 3, 2002.

CHAPTER 5: BREAKING NEWS

"Jurors Erred in Murder Case": Brian O'Donoghue, Gary Moore, Sharice Walker, Laurel Ford, and Tom Delaune, "Experts: Jurors Erred in Murder Case," *Fairbanks Daily News-Miner*, March 2, 2003; Bill O'Neil and Tom Delaune, "UAF Journalism Students Uncover Critical Error in 1999 Murder Trial," *Sun Star* (Fairbanks, AK), March 11, 2003.

"Ring is investigating": Curtis Sommer, letter to the editor, *Fairbanks Daily News-Miner*, April 5, 2003.

"It's my understanding": Mark Evans reflects on April 2004 prison interviews, in discussion with the author, January 11, 2021, https://drive.google.com/file/d/1 _1yRVBBpy5Gs1eabq7nKQ7mHxOXzdbYb/view?usp=drive_link.

"Get the fuck out": Kevin Pease, interview by Mark Evans, April 3, 2004, Spring Creek Correctional Center, transcript, https://drive.google.com/file/d/1msLDL4QX6ek UUXPkkQqkp4pxbYcmY5E7.

"I even heard": Dale Depue, interview by Mark Evans, April 3, 2004, Spring Creek Correctional Center, transcript, https://drive.google.com/file/d/1EgQl60HB -2oa6eIT5JxgOPVRJ2b1jc_l/.

CHAPTER 6: BACKSTORIES

"Dude, like, you're going to give": Casey Grove, "Last Day," Hartman Murder Files, Extreme Alaska, UAF Journalism, 2003–04 project, https://drive.google.com/file/d /11w_rAapaLpGaxJIjzWDwx6AMTWqiHBsc/view?usp=drive_link.

"The *Sun Star* not only": "Police Release Local Official's Arrest Records to Alaska University Paper," Student Press Law Center, November 3, 2004, https://splc.org/2004/11/police -release-local-officials-arrest-records-to-alaska-university-paper/.

"Is there a recorded statement": Lori Bodwell, faxed note from Bill Murphree, May 24, 1999.

"I said a beige car": Arlo Olson, phone call to the author, January 7, 2003.

IR Class Handout: Both names changed to protect privacy and reputation.

"I anticipate Frank will": Brian O'Donoghue to prison warden, Florence Correctional Center, Arizona, March 2004.

She got 'em: George Frese, interview by Jade Frank, March 22, 2004, Florence Correctional Center, Arizona, transcript, https://drive.google.com/file/d/1lJJ5X7 _DVwwzElfXp2Y9gIxBEAxlx3kf/view?usp=drive_link; Eugene Vent, interview by Jade Frank, March 22, 2004, Florence Correctional Center, Arizona, transcript, https:// drive.google.com/file/d/1pA5Ek8ky6yTRIRZkp73YBSeviQ8_u3DB/; Kevin Roberts, interview by Jade Frank, March 22, 2004, Florence Correctional Center, Arizona, transcript, https://drive.google.com/file/d/1AjGOPvosluB7eB15DIfP4–03klbHhAVz/.

"Frese has a 90-plus year sentence": Jade Frank, "Arizona Prison Interviews," Hartman Murder Files, Extreme Alaska website, UAF Journalism, fall 2004 (site discontinued).

"You ever been scared": Brian O'Donoghue, "Decade of Doubt," pt. 7, "Unopened Doors: Police Tipped Early On to Look into Chris Stone's Possible Involvement," *Fairbanks Daily News-Miner*, July 12, 2008, https://drive.google.com/file/d/18znCw93 WpIC8TrwcE3EdLLgEIzDvumz6/view.

CHAPTER 7: VILLAGE DETECTIVES

"This is the seventh year": O'Donoghue, "Unopened Doors."

"Mr. Roberts has got some problems": O'Donoghue, "'110 Percent Certain.'"

"It's basically saying": O'Donoghue, "'110 Percent Certain.'"

That matched Frankie Dayton's description: Franklin Dayton and Calvin Moses, interviews by Investigator Paul Geier, October 12, 1997, Fairbanks Police Department.

"I think maybe the Lord": Chris Stone, letter to the author, October 2005.

"I doubt things": Chris Stone, in discussion with the author, March 6, 2006, Monroe Correctional Complex, Washington.

"I told you all I know": Chris Stone, letter to the author, following March 6, 2006, interview.

"My son also happened": Evalyn Thomas, "Thomas Rebuttal," letter to the editor, *Fairbanks Daily News-Miner*, February 10, 2002, https://drive.google.com/file/d/1iTprZ6xSWCl9MTBR25oR-3boVx0sc4hl/view?usp=drive_link.

As noon approached: "Flowers for the Missing and Other Lost Souls," ExtremeAlaskaUAF, April 26, 2006, YouTube video, 1:23, https://youtu.be/INRmXJIIvI8.

CHAPTER 8: "WHO SAID THAT?"

"Police: Tacoma Man Confesses": Beth Ibsen, "Police: Tacoma Man Confesses, Suspect Charged in Ester Killing," *Fairbanks Daily News-Miner*, January 2, 2003.

"Who said that?": Brian O'Donoghue, "Bid Made to Expose Claims in Hartman Case,"

Fairbanks Daily News-Miner, October 5, 2013, https://www.newsminer.com/news/local_news/bid-made-to-expose-claims-in-hartman-case/article_02af32fa-2d91–11e3-ad13–001a4bcf6878.html.

"He was my best guy friend": O'Donoghue, "Decade of Doubt," pt. 1.

"We call forth and challenge": O'Donoghue, "Decade of Doubt," pt. 1.

"I believe there was an inquiry": O'Donoghue, "Decade of Doubt," pt. 1.

"Unopened Doors ": O'Donoghue, "Unopened Doors."

CHAPTER 9: "DECADE" ROLLS

"This seven-part series": Brian O'Donoghue, "A Murder Revisited," *Fairbanks Daily News-Miner*, July 5, 2008, https://drive.google.com/file/d/177-UiXHVmIwpZXiicripYikPRdHlRFEK/.

"I cannot speak": Deputy Attorney General Richard Svobodny to Alaska state Senator Al Kookesh, August 12, 2008.

"Sorry," said Jenny Canfield: Supreme Court Hearing, UAF Journalism video of proceedings, February 17, 2009.

"Anyone I bring": Brian O'Donoghue, application for media coverage permit of Alaska Supreme Court's February 17, 2009, hearing.

"The Supreme Court": Jennifer Canfield, Supreme Court hearing report, KUAC nightly news, Alaska Public Radio, February 17, 2009.

"'97 murder hounds journalist": Lisa Demer, "'97 Murder Hounds Journalist Who Followed It," *Alaska Dispatch News* (now *Anchorage Daily News*), February 23, 2009, https://drive.google.com/file/d/1obJ7qDCCkdiE4za8YsLzLrJ1tkQ0MQSb/view?usp=sharing.

CHAPTER 10: OF WAR AND WAITING GAMES

"The air is hot and thick": Colonel Burt Thompson, interview by Tom Hewitt, July 2009, Diyala Province, Iraq.

"The first couple times": Thompson, interview by Hewitt. For more about UAF Journalism's Iraq Embed, see *Short Timers* (blog), https://shorttimers.blogspot.com/.

"Their stomachs will pitter-pat": Richard Mauer, "UAF Quartet Joins Fort Wainwright Soldiers in Iraq," *Alaska Dispatch News* (now *Anchorage Daily News*), August 2, 2009, https://drive.google.com/file/d/104MvvUnA93U1mES-SNkEdWox2phTYKr6/view ?usp=drive_link.

"The petition for hearing": Alaska Supreme Court rejects Kevin Pease appeal, Alaska appellate slip opinions week ending August 14, 2009.

First came a terrific "whoosh": Beth Ibsen, "Investigators Probe Fatal Ester Apartment Fire," *Fairbanks Daily News-Miner*, December 28, 2002.

The paperwork didn't reference: Beth Ibsen, "Confessions Helped Police Piece Events Together," *Fairbanks Daily News-Miner*, November 24, 2004.

"Justin, how are you doing?": Jason Wallace, interviews by Alaska State Troopers Scott Johnson and Lantz Dahlke, late December 2002 and January 2003.

"Now, Scott and I came": Alaska State Troopers Lantz Dahlke and Scott Johnson, pretrial testimony, Fairbanks Superior Court, November 23, 2004.

Johnson caught a jet to Seattle: Ibsen, "Police: Tacoma Man Confesses."

"I got back first thing": Wallace, interviews by Johnson and Dahlke, trial and hearing transcripts spanning Christmas 2002 through Dahlke's testimony at 2015 postconviction relief hearing.

The attempted drug-ring takeover: Dan Rice, "Linking Complex Chain of Events," *Fairbanks Daily News-Miner*, January 3, 2003.

CHAPTER 11: THE AFFIDAVIT

"Hi Bill, it's Brian": Bill Oberly, in discussion with the author, April 11, 2011, https://drive .google.com/file/d/1UjIAthb3KDyVYtSjlRXTTgW1hcGp8NHZ/view?usp=sharing.

"I read the material": April Monroe Frick, email to the author, May 27, 2011.

CHAPTER 12: THE POWER OF STORIES

Free the Fairbanks Four: "The Beginning of Our Story," *Free the Fairbanks Four* (blog), November 2011, https://the-fairbanks-four.com/under-construction/.

updates on the Fairbanks Four: Free the Fairbanks Four, Facebook page, https://www .facebook.com/freethefairbanksfour/info/.

"Several hours into the interrogation": *The 49th Report*, "The Fairbanks Four," written and produced by Steve MacDonald, aired November 18, 2012, on KTUU-TV, Anchorage, AK.

"A fifty-to-sixty-page brief": Casey Grove, "Marchers Aim to Free Fairbanks Four," *Anchorage Daily News*, June 29, 2013, https://www.adn.com/crime-justice/article /marchers-aim-free-fairbanks-four/2013/06/30/.

CHAPTER 13: BYLINES AND HALLWAY SECRETS

"Do Students Think Gangs": Ahisha Stokes, "Do Students Thing Gangs Are Cool?," *Paystreak*, September 1997.

"No matter what form": Ahisha Stokes, "Alaska Students May Have to Take an Exit Exam," *Paystreak*, December 1997.

"The Lathrop Malemute Track": Bill Holmes, "1997 Lathrop Track Season Underway," *Paystreak*, May 1997.

"Former Fairbanks Man": Brian O'Donoghue, "Former Fairbanks Man Claims He, Others Involved in 1997 Hartman Murder," *Fairbanks Daily News-Miner*, September 25, 2013, https://www.newsminer.com/news/local_news/former-fairbanks-man-claims -he-others-involved-in-1997-hartman-murder/article_644aa318–262b-11e3-b553– 001a4bcf6878.html.

"This is probably what": Brian O'Donoghue, "Prison Memo about Hartman Killing Went Unchecked," *Fairbanks Daily News-Miner*, May 14, 2014, https://www.newsminer .com/fairbanks_four/prison-memo-about-hartman-killing-went-unchecked/article _71ec3780-dbc4–11e3–8d95–001a4bcf6878.html.

"If I had gotten": Brian O'Donoghue, "Eugene Vent Attorney Alleges 'Prosecutorial Misconduct,'" *Fairbanks Daily News-Miner*, July 12, 2014, https://www.newsminer .com/news/local_news/eugene-vent-attorney-alleges-prosecutorial-misconduct/article _f3a851ea-0992–11e4-b779–001a4bcf6878.html.

"Bid Made to Expose Claims": O'Donoghue, "Bid Made."

CHAPTER 14: MESSAGE DELIVERED

"What is your witness's relationship": "Doors Closed on Hartman Murder Arguments: 'Can I Say Jason Wallace?'," UAF Extreme, July 2, 2014, YouTube video, 2:34, https://youtu.be/BJnoGKgsEeo?si=afuxo4HRJ-Q-8kBX.

"Your request makes clear": Alaska Criminal Division director John Skidmore, letter denying UAF Journalism records request, April 4, 2014.

"You guys need to look": James Gallen and Randy McPherron, describing new assignment reviewing William Holmes claims, meeting with Captain Allen, commander of Alaska Bureau of Investigation, and Special Prosecutor Adrienne Bachman, October 3, 2013, supplementary report.

Special Prosecutor Adrienne Bachman: James Gallen and Randy McPherron, based on 2015 postconviction relief hearing testimony and follow-up interviews by the author.

The last week of October 2013: James Gallen, describing field test of Arlo Olson's testimony, October 29, 2013, supplementary report.

Before returning home: James Gallen, describing failed attempt to confirm Scott Davison's sworn statement, hunt for Matt Ellsworth, November 12, 2013, supplementary report.

Flipping through FPD's folder: James Gallen, describing Torquato memo, January 14, 2014, supplementary report.

"On Monday, December 5": Joseph Torquato, California prison guard, memo on William Holmes's claims of involvement in Alaska murder, December 5, 2011, Ironwood State Prison.

Trooper McPherron quietly scanned: Randy McPherron, describing discovery of the guard's memo and follow-up steps, supplementary report.

"Scott's a liar": Matt Ellsworth, interview by Randy McPherron, December 14, 2013, supplementary report.

Janet Davison told the lawmen: Janet Davison, interview by Randy McPherron, January 16, 2014, supplementary report.

"By the way": William Z. Holmes, letter to the author, April 7, 2014.

"I write to request": Sam Allen, UAF freedom of information request for copy of prison guard's memo to Fairbanks Police Department, March 2014.

Trooper McPherron began: Randy McPherron memo, Cold Case Unit, Alaska Department of Public Safety, Incident Report #AK13075586.

"The potential harms from disclosure": John Skidmore, freedom of information request denial, April 4, 2014.

"Eight months before making": Brian O'Donoghue, "Memo Documents Inmate's 2011 Confession in Hartman Case," *Fairbanks Daily News-Miner*, May 8, 2014, https://www .newsminer.com/news/local_news/memo-documents-inmate-s-2011-confession-in -hartman-case/article_6de14e70-d68b-11e3–99c3–001a4bcf6878.html.

"The truth is what": O'Donoghue, "Memo Documents Inmate's 2011 Confession."

"Sgt. Patrick 'Scott' Johnson": Weston Morrow, "Thousands Pay Respects as Bodies of Slain Alaska State Troopers Returned to Fairbanks," *Fairbanks Daily News-Miner*, May 3, 2014, https://www.newsminer.com/thousands-pay-respects-as-bodies-of-slain -alaska-state-troopers-returned-to-fairbanks/article_cf3db166-d345–11e3–9a46– 0017a43b2370.html.

CHAPTER 15: "HEAR THE MOOSE"

"We're just praying": Hallway interviews by Brian O'Donoghue and Julia Taylor, January 17, 2014, Rabinowitz Courthouse, Fairbanks, AK.

"Hearing Opens on Secret File": Brian O'Donoghue, "Hearing Opens on Secret File in John Hartman Murder Case," *Fairbanks Daily News-Miner*, November 10, 2014, https://www.newsminer.com/fairbanks_four/hearing-opens-on-secret-file-in-john -hartman-murder-case/article_00538486–692f-11e4-b775-db35eafa7519.html.

"Of course, it's very discouraging": Brian O'Donoghue, "The Fairbanks Four: Elusive Hunt for Truth," *Fairbanks Daily News-Miner*, September 28, 2014, https://www.newsminer .com/news/local_news/the-fairbanks-four-elusive-hunt-for-truth/article_5b68ab32– 46e1–11e4-a43e-0017a43b2370.html.

"She refused to provide": Randy McPherron, describing interviews with Matt Ellsworth and girlfriend Desiree, July 2014, supplementary report.

"He wanted to eat moose": Brian O'Donoghue, "Marvin Roberts, Convicted in Hartman Murder but Maintaining Innocence, Tastes Freedom," *Fairbanks Daily News-Miner*, June

20, 2015, https://www.newsminer.com/news/local_news/marvin-roberts-convicted -in-hartman-murder-but-maintaining-innocence-tastes-freedom/article_1bb896b6– 17e0–11e5-b6a5-b3b5f2937e60.html.

"Document Corroborates, Challenges": Sam Friedman, "Document Corroborates, Challenges New Claim in 'Fairbanks Four' Case," *Fairbanks Daily News-Miner*, August 21, 2015, https://www.newsminer.com/news/local_news/document-corroborates-challenges-new -claim-in-fairbanks-four-case/article_454ef902-4792-11e5-abef-1b7725d19e89.html.

"Jason Wallace's Confession Leaked": April Monroe, "Jason Wallace's Confession Leaked to a Reporter," *Free the Fairbanks Four* (blog), August 21, 2015, https://the-fairbanks -four.com/2015/08/21/jason-wallaces-confession-leaked-to-a-reporter.

"You're telling me": "Attorney Can't Erase What's Published," UAF Extreme, August 21, 2015, YouTube video, 0:39, https://youtu.be/BcvHH8Gt2DE?si=MQNUszQEDqtuvCtr.

CHAPTER 16: THE WEIGHT OF INNOCENCE

"Solemn, civic responsibility": Julia Taylor (@JuliaFBXLawRpt), "'Solemn, civic responsibility that the court is about to embark on,'" Twitter, October 5, 2015, 12:49 p.m., https://x.com/JuliaFBXLawRpt/status/651076699048665089.

dispute over security expenses: Sam Friedman, "Judge Denies Request to Bring 3 of the 'Fairbanks Four' to Hearing," *Fairbanks Daily News-Miner*, October 6, 2015, https://www.newsminer.com/fairbanks_four/judge-denies-request-to-bring-3-of-the -fairbanks-four-to-hearing/article_e264c220–6c87–11e5–8510-af1d4a0f5272.html.

"Sides could not agree": Julia Taylor (@JuliaFBXLawRpt), "Sides could not agree. @redlntrn excluded," Twitter, October 5, 2015, 1:24 p.m., https://x.com/JuliaFBXLawRpt/status /651085585705119744.

"We were all saying": "Fairbanks Four Hearing Day 1: Killer Witness," UAF Extreme, October 13, 2015, YouTube video, 4:58, https://youtu.be/R6NO9fN3RaY?si= czEBUZyU4pk7fMr.

"Holmes: Left because": Julia Taylor (@JuliaFBXLawRpt), "Holmes: Left because we were bored, and the girls were not putting out", Twitter, October 5, 2015, 3:32 p.m., https:// x.com/JuliaFBXLawRpt/status/651117753386991616.

"We all got excited": "Fairbanks Four Hearing Day 1."

"I couldn't begin to explain": "Courthouse Prayers: Day 1 PCR Hearing, Noon Rally Outside Rabinowitz Courthouse. Oct. 5, 2015," ExtremeAlaskaUAF, November 21, 2023, YouTube video, 2:56, https://youtu.be/-qFYsqisJcU?si=fifUzSdRkMzd0c0I.

"I never encountered": Matt Buxton, "Testimony about Alleged Confession Fills 'Fairbanks Four' Hearing," *Fairbanks Daily News-Miner*, October 8, 2015, https://www.newsminer .com/fairbanks_four/testimony-about-alleged-confession-fills-fairbanks-four-hearing /article_ab2ee32a-6e45–11e5-a84b-d3a902fd0836.html.

"Davison: Felt like he was doing": Julia Taylor (@JuliaFBXLawRpt), "Davison: Felt like he was doing something wrong," Twitter, October 8, 2015, 4:33 p.m., https://x.com /JuliaFBXLawRpt/status/652220294816362496.

They assumed someone else: "Day 5: Fairbanks Four Trial," Stephanie Woodward, October 9, 2015, YouTube video, 2:33, https://www.youtube.com/watch?v=3ZDS9EcVuIw.

"Bole: Brought up the Hartman murder": Julia Taylor (@JuliaFBXLawRpt), "Bole: Brought up the Hartman murder to get lower sentence," Twitter, October 9, 2015, 3:24 p.m., https://x.com/JuliaFBXLawRpt/status/652565211522592769.

"My field was counterintelligence": Richard Norgard, Bill Oberly, and Adrienne Bachman, direct quotes, Day 5 of PCR hearing, UAF Journalism video, October 9, 2015.

"Have you ever given a deposition": "DAY 5—PCR Heaing [sic]: Arlo Olson's suicidal thoughts, but came forward," Brian Patrick O'Donoghue, November 20, 2023, YouTube video, 0:23, https://youtu.be/CDH2e53CRII?si=CGNbS-9dtIs15Iiw.

"I want to ask you about": Sam Friedman, "Troopers Refute Prosecution Claims in Fairbanks Four Investigation," *Fairbanks Daily News-Miner*, October 12, 2015, https://www.newsminer.com/fairbanks_four/troopers-refute-prosecution-claims-in -fairbanks-four-investigation/article_a33d1bee-7153–11e5–9aa1–371a2d4d5ef8.html; additional quotes and details, UAF Journalism video, October 12, 2015.

"Would you have": "Day 6: What the Cold Case Cold [sic] troopers did not find," ExtremeAlaskaUAF, February 14, 2024, YouTube video, 7:12, https://www.youtube .com/watch?v=hl8Etxfchr4.

The special prosecutor's cross-examination: "GAME FACE: DAY 7 Trooper McPherron,"

ExtremeAlaskaUAF, March 7, 2024, YouTube video, 27:04, https://www.youtube.com
/watch?v=og6NtnENBEQ.

CHAPTER 17: COURAGE UNDER FIRE

"We learned some things": "PCR Hearing DAY 8 Arlo Olson STANDS TALL,"
ExtremeAlaskaUAF, March 9, 2024, YouTube video, 1:07:37, https://www.youtube
.com/watch?v=Ef_ZHBXtQ20.

"It worked for once": Olson, discussion.

"The footprint matches": Matt Buxton, "George Frese Gives Emotional Claim of
Innocence in Fairbanks Four Case," *Fairbanks Daily News-Miner*, October 15,
2015, https://www.newsminer.com/fairbanks_four/george-frese-gives-emotional
-claim-of-innocence-in-fairbanks-four-case/article_5cc04d6c-739c-11e5-b0ce
-333d7f6cfc57.html; "DAY 9 George Frese under fire," ExtremeAlaskaUAF,
February 20, 2024, YouTube video, 14:01, https://www.youtube.com/watch?v=
yumc2pljBD0.

"Judge calls for a break": Julia Taylor (@JuliaFBXLawRpt), "Judge calls for a break. Lawyers
not allowed to approach Frese," Twitter, October 15, 2015, 8:47 p.m., https://x.com
/JuliaFBXLawRpt/status/654820894611603456.

"Members of the audience crying": Julia Taylor (@JuliaFBXLawRpt), "Members of the
audience crying at the outburst from Frese," Twitter, October 15, 2015, 8:47 p.m.,
https://x.com/JuliaFBXLawRpt/status/654820966204178432.

"Frese lawyers not allowed": Julia Taylor (@JuliaFBXLawRpt), "Frese lawyers not allowed to
approach him," Twitter, October 15, 2015, 8:48 p.m., https://x.com/JuliaFBXLawRpt
/status/654821098320588800.

"3:28 pm Most of courtroom": Julia Taylor (@JuliaFBXLawRpt), "3:28 pm Most of
courtroom holding up 4 fingers in solidarity," Twitter, October 15, 2015, 8:48 p.m.,
https://x.com/JuliaFBXLawRpt/status/654821139152179200.

"Lyle: Clear to all of the people": Julia Taylor (@JuliaFBXLawRpt), "Lyle: Clear to all
of the people in the courtroom," Twitter, October 15, 2015, 8:49 p.m., https://x.com
/JuliaFBXLawRpt/status/654821314448850944.

"Lyle: Reiterated—No further demonstrations": Julia Taylor (@JuliaFBXLawRpt), "Lyle: Reiterated—No further demonstrations in the courtroom," Twitter, October 15, 2015, 8:49 p.m., https://x.com/JuliaFBXLawRpt/status/654821415258992640.

"Hey, just stop": Matt Buxton, "Polygraphs at Issue in Fairbanks Four Hearing," *Fairbanks Daily News-Miner*, October 22, 2015, https://www.newsminer.com/fairbanks _four/polygraphs-at-issue-in-fairbanks-four-hearing/article_7e4d190c-793b-11e5 -9370-67d5189fb20a.html; additional quotes and descriptive details, UAF Journalism video, October 22, 2015.

"State: Attacking Raskin about transducer": Julia Taylor (@JuliaFBXLawRpt), "State: Attacking Raskin about transducer," Twitter, October 22, 2015, 5:14 p.m., https://x .com/JuliaFBXLawRpt/status/657303921552027648.

"State: Moves to strike": Julia Taylor (@JuliaFBXLawRpt), "State: Moves to strike the test results," Twitter, October 23, 2015, 3:19 a.m., https://x.com/JuliaFBXLawRpt/status /657456266206298112.

"Strange Behavior: State lawyer turns": Julia Taylor (@JuliaFBXLawRpt), "Strange Behavior: State lawyer turns his back," Twitter, October 23, 2015, 3:27 a.m., https://x .com/JuliaFBXLawRpt/status/657458391120351232.

"For his important testimony": Adrienne Bachman, courtroom announcement, UAF Journalism video, October 30, 2015.

"There was a story": Matt Buxton, "Wallace Denies Involvement in 1997 Killing of Fairbanks Teen," *Fairbanks Daily News-Miner*, October 30, 2015, https://www .newsminer.com/fairbanks_four/wallace-denies-involvement-in-1997-killing-of -fairbanks-teen/article_aec98d86–7f76–11e5–8e0d-8763d56a4893.html; additional quotes and descriptive details, UAF Journalism video, October 30, 2015.

"Overheard in the courtroom": Julia Taylor (@JuliaFBXLawRpt), "Overheard in the courtroom: If this was Battleship," Twitter, October 30, 2015, 4:20 p.m., https://x.com /JuliaFBXLawRpt/status/660189674829275136.

CHAPTER 18: THE DEVIL SUITS UP

"You can be prosecuted": Matt Buxton, "Wallace Denies Involvement"; additional quotes from Adrienne Bachman, Jason Wallace, Judge Lyle, and defense attorney Bob Bundy and descriptive details, UAF Journalism video, October 30, 2015.

"Overheard in the courtroom": Julia Taylor (@JuliaFBXLawRpt), "Overheard in the courtroom: What makes the killer get the fancy clothes," Twitter, November 2, 2015, 2:16 p.m., https://x.com/JuliaFBXLawRpt/status/661260498034253824.

Resuming cross-examination: "PCR DAY-20 JW 'Everybody has an agenda,'" ExtremeAlaskaUAF, March 11, 2024, YouTube video, 27:53, https://www.youtube.com/watch?v=h_gj3siJk8k.

"Wallace isn't sure": Julia Taylor (@JuliaFBXLawRpt), "Wallace isn't sure that he would stay enrolled," Twitter, November 2, 2015, 2:20 p.m., https://x.com/JuliaFBXLawRpt/status/661261545486192640.

"State of Alaska conspires": April Monroe, "State of Alaska Conspires With a Serial Killer. Gross," *Free the Fairbanks Four* (blog), November 5, 2015, https://the-fairbanks-four.com/2015/11/05/state-of-alaska-conspires-with-serial-killer-gross/.

"Mr. O'Donoghue": "PCR DAY 21 HOSTILE WITNESS, Professor OD's turn," ExtremeAlaksaUAF, March 10, 2024, YouTube video, 1:01:39, https://www.youtube.com/watch?v=_hnsYspHfrQ.

"4:02 pm Bachman obviously upset": Julia Taylor (@JuliaFBXLawRpt), "4:02 pm Bachman obviously upset by the conversation," Twitter, November 4, 2015, 9:56 a.m., https://x.com/JuliaFBXLawRpt/status/661919917449412609.

"Lyle stops O'D": Julia Taylor (@JuliaFBXLaw), "Lyle stops O'D and asks him to read it to himself," Twitter, November 4, 2015, 10:01 a.m., https://x.com/JuliaFBXLawRpt/status/661921213791363072.

"O'D believed that Arlo": Julia Taylor (@JuliaFBXLawRpt), "O'D believed that Arlo was calling to spill out his life story," Twitter, November 4, 2015, 10:06 a.m., https://x.com/JuliaFBXLawRpt/status/661922465744949248.

"O'D confirming that his life": Julia Taylor (@JuliaFBXLawRpt), "O'D confirming that his life ruined by the case," Twitter, November 4, 10:02 a.m., https://x.com/JuliaFBXLawRpt/status/661921357223989249.

"O'D says that Arlo": Julia Taylor (@JuliaFBXLawRpt), "O'D says that Arlo was asking for advice," Twitter, November 4, 2015, 10:20 a.m., https://x.com/JuliaFBXLawRpt/status /661926022552514561.

"Combative": Dermot Cole, "Journalism Professor Spars with State Attorney in Fairbanks Four Case," *Anchorage Daily News*, November 5, 2015, https://www.adn.com /commentary/article/journalism-professor-spars-state-attorney-fairbanks-four-case /2015/11/05/.

"If you need to go": "PCR DAY 22, BRING IT ON: April Monroe," ExtremeAlaskaUAF, March 9, 2024, YouTube video, 26:34, https://www.youtube.com/watch?v= CzqaaavVCqg.

"O'Br says Arlo": Julia Taylor (@JuliaFBXLawRpt), "O'Br says Arlo didn't do anything to make his life easier," Twitter, November 6, 2015, 3:46 p.m., https://x.com /JuliaFBXLawRpt/status/662732824265420800.

"I shouldn't put it this way": "PCR DAY 23- Extreme Alaska version—'EXHIBIT PASSED EYEBALL TEST,' Courtroom video, Nov. 4, 2015," ExtremeAlaskaUAF, February 16, 2024, YouTube video, 3:31, https://www.youtube.com/watch?v= _9PQq1cdBvw; Matt Buxton, "State Defends Initial Investigation of Hartman Murder at Evidentiary Hearing," *Fairbanks Daily News-Miner*, November 6, 2015, https://www .newsminer.com/fairbanks_four/state-defends-initial-investigation-of-hartman-murder -at-evidentiary-hearing/article_3fd99646–845d-11e5-a8a4-c7858af89808.html; "Day 23: Fairbanks Four Trial," Stephanie Woodward, November 7, 2015, YouTube video, 2:37, https://youtu.be/T4Vrd4GbrGI?si=6zPct1SKBnIX37Zl.

"Evidence has to be admissible": Judge Paul Lyle, direct quotes, UAF Journalism video, November 10, 2015; Matt Buxton, "'Fairbanks Four' Judge: No Rush on Decision as Case Ends," *Fairbanks Daily News-Miner*, November 10, 2015, https://www.newsminer .com/fairbanks_four/fairbanks-four-judge-no-rush-on-decision-as-case-ends/article _80422f1e-8826–11e5–934b-d354cbdefb39.html.

CHAPTER 19: JAILBREAK!

"146 people in the 5th floor hallway": Julia Taylor (@JuliaFBXLawRpt), "146 people in the 5th floor hallway," Twitter, December 17, 2015, 5:41 p.m., https://twitter.com /JuliaFBXLawRpt/status/677619683458195456.

"Overheard in the hall": Julia Taylor (@JuliaFBXLawRpt), "Overheard in the hall: If we don't get this right, we will never get justice," Twitter, December 17, 2015, 5:01 p.m., https://x.com/JuliaFBXLawRpt/status/677609648963227648.

"Judge, attorneys and petitioners": Julia Taylor (@JuliaFBXLawRpt), "Judge, attorneys and petitioners are in the courtroom," Twitter, December 17, 2015, 5:23 p.m., https:// twitter.com/JuliaFBXLawRpt/status/677615032394375168.

"Overheard in the hall": Julia Taylor (@JuliaFBXLawRpt), "Overheard in the hall: There should be nothing that is a secret in this case," Twitter, December 17, 2015, 5:06 p.m., https://twitter.com/JuliaFBXLawRpt/status/677610767705751552.

"State has stopped objects": Julia Taylor (@JuliaFBXLawRpt), "State has stopped objects to new evidence," Twitter, December 17, 2015, 8:16 p.m., https://twitter.com /JuliaFBXLawRpt/status/677658632985681920.

"After previous convictions": Julia Taylor (@JuliaFBXLawRpt), "After previous convictions are vacated," Twitter, December 17, 2015, 8:19 p.m., https://twitter.com /JuliaFBXLawRpt/status/677659296604254210.

"Tonight, at the tribal hall": Victor Joseph, audio recording by author, December 17, 2015; Sam Friedman, "Fairbanks Four Freed as Judge Accepts Deal to Throw Out Indictments, Convictions," *Fairbanks Daily News-Miner*, December 17, 2015, https:// www.newsminer.com/news/fairbanks-four-freed-as-judge-accepts-deal-to-throw-out -indictments-convictions/article_452d29e8-a512–11e5–86e5-dfd51ae41d35.html.

"By virtue of this Settlement Agreement": State of Alaska settlement with Marvin Roberts, document signed December 9, 2015, https://drive.google.com/file/d /1KUYwZDhjWH0EUlThHmp9gGfvH_tWkmZN/view?usp=drive_link.

National Registry of Exonerations: Maurice Possley, case summaries for Eugene Vent, Kevin Pease, Marvin Roberts, and George Frese, National Registry of Exonerations, last updated November 8, 2023, https://www.law.umich.edu/special/exoneration/Pages /casedetail.aspx?caseid=4816, https://www.law.umich.edu/special/exoneration/Pages /casedetail.aspx?caseid=4817, https://www.law.umich.edu/special/exoneration/Pages

/casedetail.aspx?caseid=4818, https://www.law.umich.edu/special/exoneration/Pages /casedetail.aspx?caseid=4819.

"Here's what made me retire": William "Bill" Spiers, in discussion with the author, August 20, 2021; Dorothy Chomicz, "Retiring ADA Made a Life Outside of Law before Serving Alaska," *Fairbanks Daily News-Miner*, January 8, 2017, https://www.newsminer .com/news/local_news/retiring-ada-made-a-life-outside-of-law-before-serving-alaska /article_f1c1dbea-d644–11e6–88d2-dbee2ccf4b3f.html.

"Trial of the Year": Clint Campion, "Lindemuth Leads Her First District Attorney Conference," *Alaska Bar Rag* newsletter, November–December 2016, https://drive .google.com/file/d/13uDCqrdazl_mheA6iCKGg3oBJQSteEdr/view?usp=sharing.

"How you feeling, Marv?": "My car is innocent," Ricko De Wilde, YouTube video, 2016 (deleted).

ABOUT THE AUTHOR

———

Brian Patrick O'Donoghue, sixty-eight, is past president of the Alaska Press Club and a longtime member of Investigative Reporters and Editors. The Washington, D.C., union lawyer's son spent formative summers carrying tools in varied trades, most notably chipping bilge rust from Baltimore to Calcutta as a Seafarers International Union wiper. He holds a journalism MA from NYU, where he juggled school, alongside reporting for the *Villager*, pulling night shifts in Yellow Cab 4H43. In 1986, a want ad for the twice-weekly *Frontiersman*, in Wasilla, Alaska, lured him north. His appreciation for the forty-ninth state's beauty and diverse cultures broadened working for the *Fairbanks Daily News-Miner*, *Anchorage Daily News*, and KTVF-KTVA television, followed by a second career teaching journalism at the University of Alaska Fairbanks.

O'Donoghue and his wife, former reporter Kate Ripley, bonded covering politics and sled dog races. Rory, Robin, and Rachel O'D may testify to the result.